From Pine Forest
to
Market City

The History of Clare Michigan's Downtown

Kenneth Lingaur

Lingaur Preservation LLC
Clare, Michigan
2020

From Pine Forest to Market City
The History of Clare Michigan's Downtown

Lingaur Preservation L.L.C.
Clare, Michigan
www.lingaurpreservation.com
Printed in the U.S.A.

ISBN-13: 978-1-7322263-4-0

Cover design by Jeanne Rouston.

Cover image: 1884 Bird's-eye view of Clare, Michigan, printed by O. H. Bailey & Company, Boston, Massachusetts.

Table of Contents

Acknowledgements 4

Introduction 6

Map...8

Descriptive Section..11
    102 West Fifth...15
    104 West Fifth...17
    110 West Fifth...18
    114 West Fifth...20
    202 West Fifth...23
    109 West Fifth...25
    111 West Fifth...27
    120 East Fifth..30
    112 West Fourth..33
    114 West Fourth..35
    118 West Fourth..38
    120 West Fourth..40
    112 East Fourth 42
    402 North McEwan...44
    406 North McEwan...45
    412 North McEwan...48
    418 North McEwan...50
    420 North McEwan...52
    426 North McEwan...54
    502 North McEwan...55
    506 North McEwan...60
    518 North McEwan...63
    520 North McEwan...65
    522 North McEwan...68
    524 North McEwan...70
    532 North McEwan...73

604 North McEwan...76
Dr. Hammerberg Monument.............................79
307 North McEwan...81
Railroad Crossing at McEwan 82
321 North McEwan...84
405 North McEwan...87
407 North McEwan...89
409 North McEwan...91
415 North McEwan...92
417 North McEwan...93
425 North McEwan...95
427 North McEwan...97
429, 431 North McEwan.....................................100
501 North McEwan...105
505, 509 North McEwan.....................................107
511 North McEwan...111
513 North McEwan...113
515 North McEwan...115
517 North McEwan...117
521 North McEwan...120
523 North McEwan...122
525 North McEwan...125
601, 603, 605 North McEwan............................126
607, 609 North McEwan.....................................129
611 North McEwan...132
613 North McEwan...135

Significance Section **137**
The Founding of Clare.......................................139
The Clare Business District 141
Commerce...153
  Banks...158
  Offices..160
  Hotels 161
  Car Dealerships/Garages.............................167
Newspapers..168

2

Agriculture 170
    Early Mills and Elevators 171
    The Survivor: The Chatterton-Johnston Elevator .174
    Agriculture-related Stores 175
Oil Industry 176
Social History/Entertainment and Recreation............178
Churches 181
Architecture..182

Bibliography..**193**

Appendix – Michigan Gazetteer Listings........................**197**

Index..**223**

Acknowledgements

In 2004, Clare was designated as a Main Street community. The Main Street program is a program administered by the State Historic Preservation Office (SHPO), and features a four-step plan to encourage historic preservation in a community's downtown. From the beginning of Clare being designated a Main Street community, the SHPO encouraged Clare's leaders to have the downtown listed on the National Register of Historic Places.

The process of getting a downtown district listed on the National Register is a daunting task. Research needs to not only be conducted on the general history of the downtown, but also the history of each building. Also, a knowledge of how to complete the application and present it in the correct format is needed. At the time there was no one who had the time or willingness to move forward with the nomination.

In 2007, I started a Master's Degree program in Historic Preservation at Eastern Michigan University. In 2009, I offered to start the process of writing the nomination. This was completed in two steps. From 2009 to 2011 I worked for the City of Clare as an intern conducting the research which was later used for the nomination. The nomination was actually my final project to complete my Master's Degree. It was mostly finished when I graduated in 2014, but the final version was not submitted to the SHPO until 2015. This book is an edited version of the nomination. The Clare Downtown Historic District was listed on the National Register of Historic Places in 2016.

I appreciate the confidence the City of Clare had in me, even though I had never pursued a project this large before. Special thanks go to the Lori Schuh, who was the Main Street Manager at the time, and Ken Hibl, the Clare City Manager.

Since I was not a native of Clare I was not familiar with the history of Clare. I needed to rely on the work of others to provide the historic background I needed. Much of the research into the history of Clare's downtown was obtained through the prior work of Forrest Meek. Beginning in the 1970s, Meek had done extensive research on Clare's history. Had it not been for Meek, much of the information in the nomination would have been more difficult to acquire. Robert Knapp

4

was also a great source of information, especially in writing the Significance portion of the nomination.

Bob Christensen, former National Register coordinator for the Michigan State Historic Preservation Office, played a large role in the editing of the final nomination. He also provided additional historic information that added to the historic context of the nomination.

Finally I would like to thank my wife Sherrie. She was very supportive through the seven years it took to research and write the nomination, plus the time it took to write this book.

Early Street View in Downtown Clare
Photograph from the Forrest Meek Collection

Introduction

As mentioned before, this book is an edited version of the Clare Downtown Historic District, National Register of Historic Places nomination. A National Register nomination basically consists of two parts, a Descriptive Section and a Significance Section.

The Descriptive Section is a narrative of the current physical characteristics of each building, and how those characteristics have changed through its history. Also it tells the history of who owned each building, and in the case of a downtown district, which businesses used the buildings. Since the current architectural description of a building can be pretty dry reading, those narratives have been edited out of this book. In place of those descriptions a current photograph of each building is provided.

The final version of the nomination was submitted to the State Historic Preservation Office in November 2015. Since then there have been some changes to the downtown area. The physical changes to the district have been few. Most of the changes have consisted of new businesses occupying buildings, or businesses moving from one building to another. This book has added those changes. Other historic information was also added to this book that was not in the nomination. When researching this book most of the information was found by reading historic newspapers page by page. Most of this was done using microfilm. Since then all the historic Clare newspapers are available online and are searchable. This made acquiring new information much easier. In addition, as I was editing the nomination for the book I found a few errors that have now been corrected.

As far as the order in which the buildings are listed in the Descriptive Section, the buildings on streets running east to west are listed first. These are listed starting from north to south, and all the buildings on the same side of the street are ordered from east to west. Next are buildings listed on streets running north and south, with buildings ordered on the same side of the street from south to north.

The entries in the Descriptive Section are followed by a list of abbreviated sources specific to each building. The abbreviations for the sources are defined as follows: *CPress. = Clare Press, CCP. = Clare*

County Press, CHSY. = Clare High School Yearbook (Advertisements), *Cour. = Clare Courier, Dem. = Clare Democrat, DPress. = Clare Democrat and Press, Sent. = Clare Sentinel, Farwell = Farwell News.* For all buildings, property ownership information was obtained through deeds located at the Clare County Register of Deeds Office, Harrison, Michigan. Further information was obtained from the 1893-1934 Sanborn Maps, and tax assessment data at the Clare County Treasurer's Office, Harrison, Michigan.

The Significance Section presented in this book is unchanged from that in the nomination. There are four different criteria that a nomination can be eligible to qualify for. Those criteria are A) Association with the events that have made a significant contribution to the broad patterns of our history, B) Association with the lives of persons significant in our past, C) Properties that embody distinctive characteristics of a type, period, or method of construction or represent the work of a master, or possesses high artistic values or represent a significant and distinguished entity whose components lack individual distinction, D) Properties that yield or are likely to yield, information important in prehistory or history. Of those criteria the only one the Clare Downtown Historic District did not qualify for was Criteria D.

In writing the Significance Section the National Park Service (which administers the National Register of Historic Places) lists a number of categories for areas of significance. The areas of historic significance featured in the nomination and this book are taken from that list.

When submitting a National Register nomination, the only photographs included with the nomination are the street views showing the current appearance of the downtown district. This book however includes as many historic photographs as could practically be added.

The Period of Significance for the district is 1873 to 1965. 1873 marks the year the oldest existing buildings within the district were constructed, and 1965 represents the fifty-year cutoff required under National Register criteria. Other dates of importance as listed in the nomination are: 1887 Construction of first Italianate building, 1904 Construction of first Classical Revival buildings, 1924 Completion of Doherty Hotel construction, 1934 First Modern building constructed (City Hall), 1937 Post Office construction completed, 1961 US-27 bypass constructed around Clare.

Clare Downtown

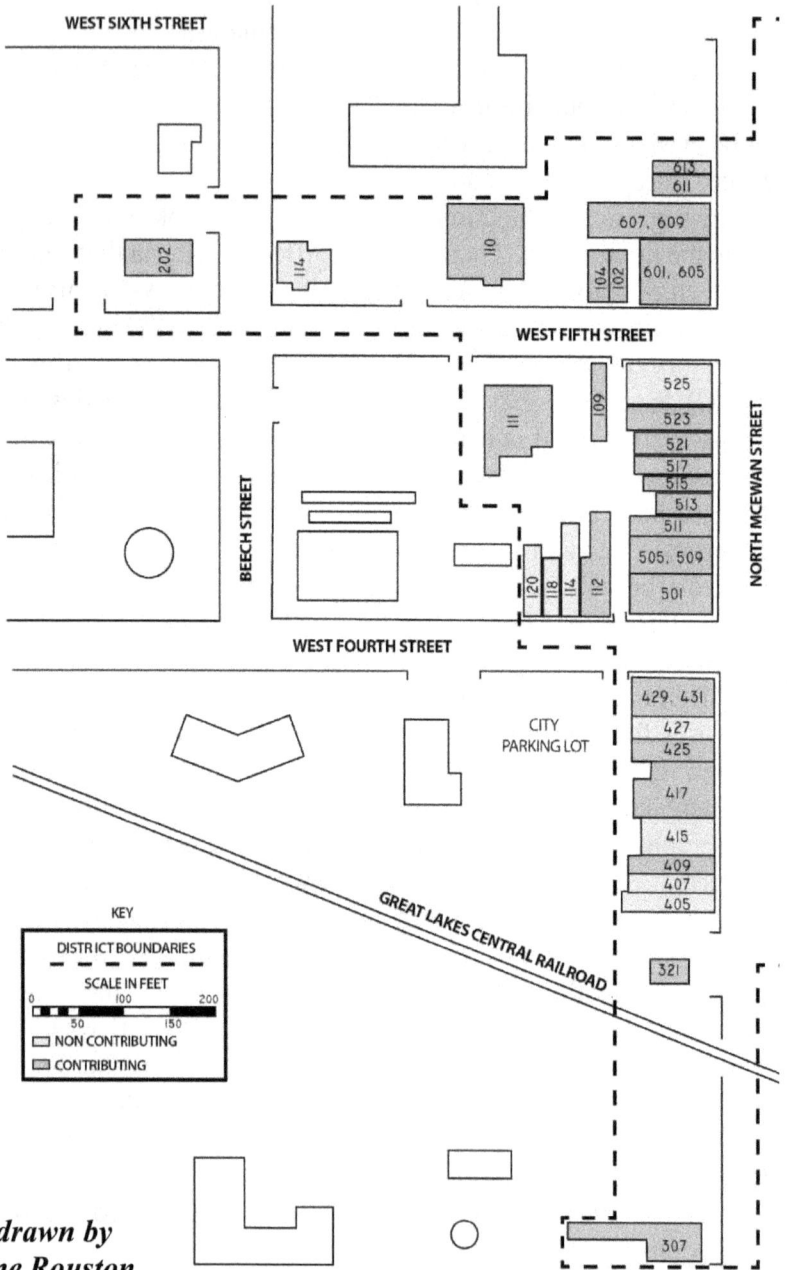

WEST SIXTH STREET

202

114

110

613
611

607, 609

104 102 601, 605

WEST FIFTH STREET

109

111

525
523
521
517
515
513
511
505, 509
501

BEECH STREET

NORTH MCEWAN STREET

120 118 114 112

WEST FOURTH STREET

CITY PARKING LOT

429, 431
427
425
417
415
409
407
405

GREAT LAKES CENTRAL RAILROAD

321

307

KEY

DISTRICT BOUNDARIES

SCALE IN FEET

0   100   200
   50   150

NON CONTRIBUTING

CONTRIBUTING

Map drawn by
Jeanne Rouston

8

Historic District Map

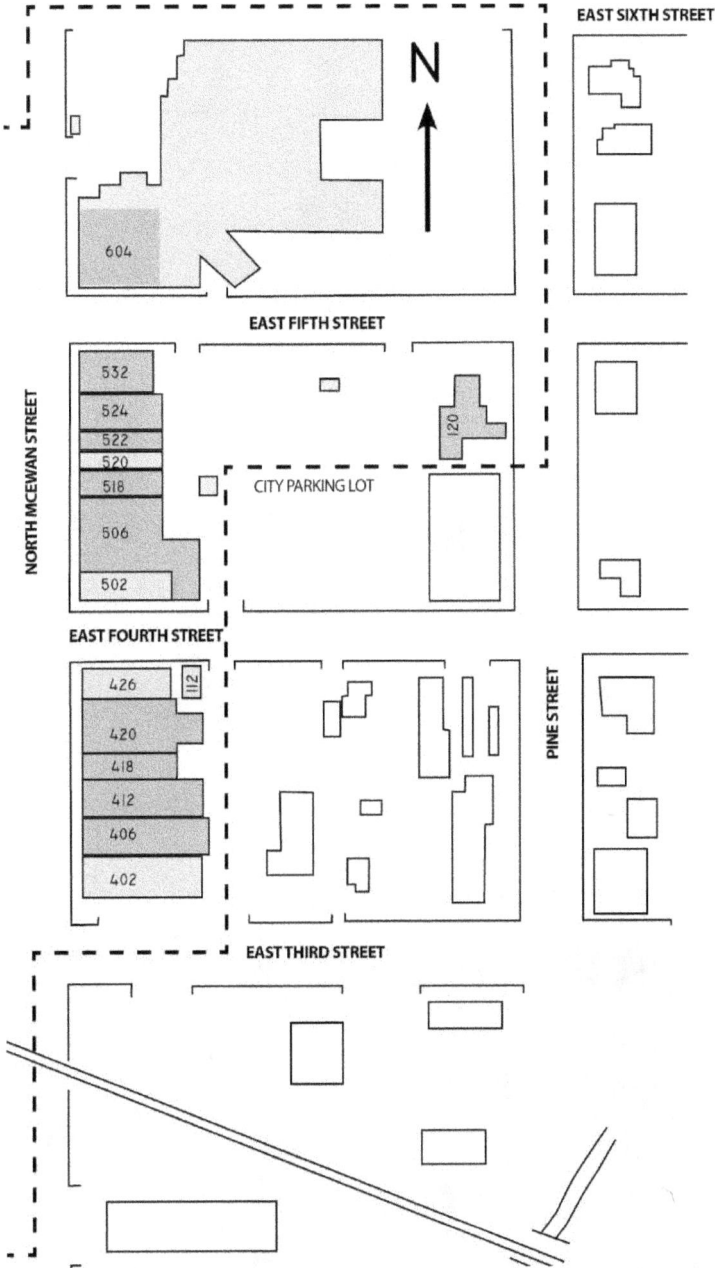

EAST SIXTH STREET

N

604

EAST FIFTH STREET

NORTH MCEWAN STREET

532
524
522
520
518
506
502

120

CITY PARKING LOT

EAST FOURTH STREET

426
112
420
418
412
406
402

PINE STREET

EAST THIRD STREET

Descriptive Section

The Clare Downtown Historic District measures approximately sixteen and one-quarter acres, and is located in the south central section of the City of Clare. It is just to the north of the Little Tobacco Drain, which meets up with the Tobacco River on the east side of the city, that river eventually merging with the Tittabawassee and Saginaw Rivers before emptying into Saginaw Bay of Lake Huron. McEwan Street, also known as Business Route US-127, running through the district, is the city's main north and south-running street. Third, Fourth and Fifth Streets intersect McEwan in an east and west direction with Fifth Street also serving as Business Route US-10. Third Street intersects McEwan only on the east side, while Fourth and Fifth Streets travel through east and west of McEwan. Also intersecting McEwan, just to the south of Third Street, is the Great Lakes Central Railroad line, which runs in a southeast to northwest direction.

McEwan Street is a busy four-lane structure north of Third Street, with room for parallel parking on both sides of the street. South of Third Street McEwan is two lanes wide with an additional center turn lane. Third, Fourth and Fifth Streets are two-lane roadways, with parallel parking located along the north side of Fourth Street. Third Street has diagonal parking on the north side of the street. Fifth Street contains no parking spaces. Since 1989 the downtown has seen changes to the streetscape in the form of brick paver areas located within the concrete sidewalks, electric lampposts, park benches, tree plantings, decorative trash cans, and bicycle racks.

The district is located entirely within the original plat of the City of Clare. The lots were platted to measure 66 feet by 132 feet, with almost ninety percent of the lots positioned in a north-south direction. All the lots located along McEwan Street were platted in an east-west direction, with narrow ends fronting on the street. The district at its greatest east and west width measures approximately 1,270 feet, and the approximate length north and south measures 3,830 feet. The topography is fairly level, with a slight increase in elevation of ten feet from the south limit of the district to the north limit along McEwan Street.

11

The district's three primary blocks of old commercial buildings extend north from the railroad line that crosses McEwan, the city's main street, at an angle. On McEwan's west side, the district's south boundary extends south of the tracks a short distance to include a large gable-roof early twentieth-century elevator building, the last remnant of agriculture-related commercial buildings that clustered around the tracks. Just north of the tracks, Third Street forms the south edge of the three blocks to the north along McEwan that contains the district's primary commercial buildings. The buildings stand side by side in the two blocks between Third and Fifth and in the south half of the block between Fifth and Sixth. The primarily one- and two-story buildings stand directly on the sidewalk line. The 1924 four-story Doherty Hotel, the district's tallest (and only four-story) building, stands at the northeast corner of McEwan and Fifth Streets. The building fronts on the two streets, with large motor inn/conference center additions of modern design but in red brick complementing the original hotel, project out behind to the east and northeast and, with their associated parking lots, occupy the entire block between Fifth and Sixth and east to Pine Street. The Doherty, as will be shown in the inventory and significance sections, is a – if not the – key landmark building in downtown Clare, and including in the district the original hotel building but not its large and functionally important extensions seems to make no sense. On the west side of the 600 block between Fifth and Sixth streets, the district's north boundary marks the south edge of a large modern hospital complex that, with its parking areas, occupies the entire rest of the block to the north and extends west to Beech Street.

East of the buildings fronting on McEwan's east side, the district includes the north half of the block between East Fourth and Fifth streets to include the 1882 upright-and-wing house at 120 E. Fifth. The house, which serves commercial uses while retaining its landscaped yard and much of its historic character, stands to the east of part of a city parking lot behind (east of) the buildings fronting on McEwan. The otherwise typical paved parking lot contains a highly atypical feature: an open shed-roof wooded shelter for the horses of horse-drawn carriages that bring members of the local Amish community from outside of the city in to shop. The south part of the block's east section, which contains the city's large new public library and more parking, is

12

excluded from the district. On the west side of the district, the area west of the post office (111 W. Fifth) is a large parking lot, while to the south, along W. Fourth east of Beech, a four-story senior citizens' apartment building, with its property, extends east to 120 W. Fourth.

The district extends west along the north side of W. Fourth and along W. Fifth to include a cluster of commercial buildings along Fourth's north side and a few commercial buildings near McEwan and historic public buildings – post office, Congregational church, and city hall – located farther west.

The district's oldest buildings date to the 1870s, and are of wood frame construction. Two of these buildings, 114 West Fifth and 611 North McEwan, were originally residences that have been since converted to commercial use. The oldest concentration of commercial buildings is located along the east and west sides of the 500 block of North McEwan, the east side of the 400 block of North McEwan, and the two buildings located at the northwest corner of Fourth and McEwan. All the buildings within the district, except for eight, were constructed with solid brick or brick veneer walls. These commercial buildings range in dates of construction from the 1880s to the 2000s, with Neoclassical and Commercial Brick buildings predominating. Two of the oldest and most distinguished buildings are the Late Victorian buildings located at 524 and 532 North McEwan, constructed in the later part of the nineteenth century.

Neoclassical elements were popular as part of the design elements of buildings within the first two decades of the twentieth century. 518 North McEwan features Ionic piers, jack arch lintels, bracketed cornice and dentils on the building's second story. 523 North McEwan displays Ionic piers, prism glass transom windows, decorative brickwork, bracketed cornice and scrollwork frieze board. Buildings exemplifying Commercial Brick design are 112 West Fourth Street and 418 and 420, 513, and 609 North McEwan. Also of note are the decorative terra cotta elements – lintels, capitals, and rosettes – in 431 North McEwan. Other buildings still retain their cornices and other classical details.

The district is surrounded by a mixture of commercial and residential buildings. The majority of the commercial buildings just outside the district are less than fifty years old, and are located to the southeast, southwest and west of the district, with residential areas located beyond

13

them. The residential areas to the north and east are located closer to the district than those formerly mentioned. The residences surrounding the district are in the oldest part of the city. Most are of a vernacular design with very few of the higher style residences still in existence. McEwan Street north and south of the district, along with Fifth Street east and west of the district, continue to be devoted primarily to commercial use.

East side of 500 block of North McEwan looking east, Circa 1970
Photograph from the Forrest Meek Collection

14

102 West Fifth
Norwood Building (1939)
Frank Roberts, contractor

This building was constructed by James Norwood in 1939. It may have actually been a remodel of an open structure that was located here prior to James Norwood owning the property. It is unknown when that structure was built or what it looked like, but it was owned by Fred Busche for Busche Motor Sales. The lot was still vacant as of October 1937. Peter Creguer and Fred Busche were the owners of the property from September 1937 to 1939.

James Norwood used the building for his "Fix-it Shop," and owned it until Fred Busche bought the building in January 1946. Genevieve Pearson opened her Pearson Dress Shop here in July 1946. The building was damaged by fire in April 1948. Later that month Mrs. Pearson was arrested on arson charges. By August of the same year the building was remodeled and The Children's Center apparel store was leasing it. Fred Busche sold the building to Harmon Ballard in September 1949. Mr.

and Mrs. Joe W. Weible sold The Children's Center store in March 1950 to Leslie Karr, who owned and operated The New Yorker children's clothing store in Mount Pleasant. Harmon Ballard sold the building to Arthur Skeets in January 1952. The Clare Office Supply Co. was the occupant in 1953. Arthur Skeets sold the building to George Scheer in April 1962. In 1963 the Clare Business Service was occupying the building. Leo Stevins bought the building from Scheer in February 1966, but sold it back to him in 1974. The Clare Factory Outlet was using the building in the late 1980s. Carolyn Murphy bought the building from Patricia Jones in March 1994. It is unknown when Patricia Jones purchased the building. In the early 2000s the building was being used by the Image Quest Active Wear business. After that the building was known as the Meeting Place. The Desired Skin tattoo shop opened here in 2009.

Sent., 4/21/1939; 6/28/1946; 4/49, 4/23 and 8/20/1948; 3/30/1950; *CHSY.*, 1953; 1963.

Children's Center Store Advertisement
Clare Sentinel August 20, 1948

Pearson Dress Shop Advertisement
Clare Sentinel April 18, 1947

104 West Fifth
Creguer Building (1937)

This building was constructed by Peter Creguer in 1937 in order to house his harness shop and shoe repair business, which was moved from another location. By the end of the 1940s and until the end of the 1950s Creguer had converted his business to selling shoes and leather goods. By 1962 the Clare Loan Company was using the building. Peter Creguer sold the building to Robert Campbell in December 1964. The Tower Finance Company opened their office here in April 1967. The Aardvark Art and Craft Supply Store opened here in February 1978. Diane Sadler-Demo purchased the building in April 1990 for her Apple Tree Lane business, and sold it to Roger and Emily Chase in March 1992 for Roger's Photographic Reverie business. The Chases sold the building in November 1998 to Michael and Michele Rengert. The Rengerts sold to Mid-Michigan Big Brothers/Big Sisters in September 2000.

Sent., 10/29 and 12/24/1937; 9/10/1948; 6/25/1959; 1/25/1962; 4/6/1967; 2/8/1978; 11/20/1990; 6/2/1992

17

110 West Fifth
Clare Congregational Church (1909)
W. T. Cooper, Saginaw, architect; House, Oles and Bailey, Marion, builders; 1958 addition by William Harper, Clare, architect; Sanford Mott, builder

This building is constructed with limestone-trimmed red brick walls in a cross-gabled Greek cross form with an octagonal dome. The church's four facades except for the side with the 1958 addition are virtually identical. The windows contain stained glass saved from the earlier, frame church building, and date to the year 1900. The auditorium occupies the building's entire main floor. It has a Greek cross form with the central dome springing from broad arches that span the openings into the cross's four arms. The arches are supported by square-plan piers with gold-leaf.

The main portion of the building remains substantially intact since its completion in 1909. The top of the dome originally contained a balustrade, which was removed circa 1950. In 1958 a major addition was made to the building's east side, providing space for classrooms, office and minister's study, kitchen and dining area, and restrooms, and the originally tiny narthex at the church's southeast corner expanded. The addition has concrete block walls except for the brick-faced south, street-facing front, and a flat roof so as to not interfere with the auditorium's windows. The designer of this addition was William Harper, principal of Clare High School. The addition's north or rear side facing the parking lot also contains a later open, gabled porte cochere. A handicap entrance constructed of red brick with a hipped roof was added to the southwest corner of the building in 1994. Also in 1994 an extensive restoration of the building's sanctuary was accomplished.

This building is significant for its architect, W. T. Cooper, and as an example of a central-plan auditorium style church of the early twentieth century. It has been listed on the National Register of Historic Places since 1995.

Sent., 9/10/1900, 8/21/1908; National Register Nomination, Clare Congregational Church 1994; Christensen.

Clare Congregational Church, circa 1930s
Photograph from the Author's Collection
19

114 West Fifth
Holridge House (1873)

The house was originally constructed as an upright-and-wing dwelling that faced south on Fifth. The original two-story upright is the present gabled section facing Fifth at the southwest corner, while the one-story wing was the present east ell also fronting on Fifth. An open porch with a shed roof extended over the south side of the east wing. By 1899 a one-story addition was built on the north end of the house in the angle between the back of the upright and wing. Between 1906 and 1910 a one-story structure was added to the northwest corner of the building. By 1923 an addition was made to the northeast corner of the building. This addition was even with the east end of the east wing and the north end of the 1899 addition. At the same time the east wing porch on the south side of the house was enclosed and its front brought flush with the south end of the upright to its west. In 1926 Charles Thurston converted the house to a funeral home. The west end of the house was used for the business while the east wing was his residence. It was at this time that he built a porch on the west elevation to serve as the entrance to his business and one on the east elevation for his residence. He also extended the second story over the 1923 addition on the northwest corner of the building in 1931.

Since 1934 two other additions have been made, both of unknown dates. One of these additions was the projecting south entryway, the other the one-story addition to the existing porch on the southwest corner of the building. A driveway exit was constructed on the Beech Street side of the building in 1948 to eliminate the inconvenience and danger of entering directly onto Fifth, then US-10. Another remodeling to the building's front was started in April 1949. At different periods of time, sheds, barns and/or automobile garages have been located at the north end of the lot.

This building was built by Henry Holridge in 1873, for use as his primary residence. In 1884 William Ross was using the building as a boarding house. Amanda Ross purchased the building in September 1886 and continued operating the boarding house. Albert Thurston purchased the house from Amanda Ross in February 1895 and Jennie Fall bought it from Thurston in March 1903. She sold it to Charles Thurston in December 1911. Charles Thurston used the house exclusively as his primary residence until 1926 when he moved his funeral business into the building. This was the first funeral home in Clare. The west end of the building was used for the funeral home, while the east wing was used for his residence. Charles Thurston's passed away in 1936, his wife Nellie died in 1944. The building was then deeded to their two sons Albert and Russell. Russell Thurston, who continued the family funeral home business, purchased Albert's interest in the building in 1945. An explosion of unknown origin created extensive damage to the building in February 1951. The damage was so extensive that the Thurstons relocated their business and place of residence. In February 1952 Russell Thurston had already moved his business and residence and sold this building to Ralph and Helen Heather (not married). By August of the same year the building had been repaired and Dr. E. J. Gushon opened an eight-room medical clinic. In 1953 Dr. C. B. Neff began using the building for his dental office. Helen Heather sold the building in June 1972 to Dr. Thomas and Gail Neff, who continued his father's dental practice. Gail Neff sold the building to Dr. James Haines in October 1998. Dr. Haines continued to use the building as a dental office.

CCP., /12/1884; *Sent.*, 2/22/1895; 7/26 and 10/8/1926; 8/20/1948; 4/23/1949; 2/2 and 2/23/1951; 3/20/1953.

114 West Fifth, Circa 1907
Photograph from the Robert Knapp Collection

202 West Fifth
Clare City Hall and Memorial Building (1934)
R. V. Gay, St. Johns, architect; Herb Randall and
D. W. Osborn, supervisors, Civil Works Administration

This building was constructed in 1934 to replace the wood framed city hall building which had been occupied for about forty years on the same site. That building was constructed in 1872 and served as the Clare Public School prior to being converted to the City Hall. The present brick building was constructed to be used not only as the city hall, but also as a meeting hall for the American Legion. The construction was performed by local labor provided through the Civil Works Administration. The Civil Works Administration was a New Deal Era program designed to temporarily put people to work from 1933-1934. The construction was first supervised by Herb Randall. Mr. Randall resigned on May 22, 1934, and was replaced by D. W. Osborn. The building was dedicated to the veterans of World War I and the

American Legion. It has always been owned by the City of Clare and used as its city hall.

A major remodeling of the building took place in 1964. The main entryway to the building was moved to its present location on the east elevation, and was enclosed in aluminum framed glass. The colored panels and louvered sections on the building's south elevation were added in 1971.

Sent., 12/15/1933; 3/23, 12/9 and 11/16/1934; 2/20/1964; 1/6/1971.

CITY HALL, CLARE, MICH.—5

Clare City Hall, circa 1940s
Post Card Image from the Robert Knapp Collection

109 West Fifth
Holbrook/Mair Building (1941)
David Mair, builder

This building was constructed jointly by Donald Holbrook Sr. and Robert Mair in 1941. The street-level retail space was originally occupied by Robert Mair's Band Box Cleaners business. Donald Holbrook Sr., who at the time was Clare County's prosecuting attorney, had his law offices on the second floor and practiced there until at least the end of the 1940s. In addition the Freeman Oil Company and Higelmire & Associates both had offices on the second floor. In 1947 the Gibraltar Insulation Company from Pontiac opened an office in the space formerly occupied by Freeman Oil. Donald Holbrook Jr.'s law office was here from the mid-1960s to early 1970s. Walter Kleiner's office of the Modern Woodman of America insurance company was using an office in the buildings second floor in the early to mid-1970s. In 1972 Donald Holbrook Jr. purchased Robert Mair's interest in the building. The Band Box Cleaners business closed in 1973 and was replaced by Norell and Barbara Mahon's American Cleaners. Donald Holbrook Jr. sold the building to the Mahons in 1984. Jon Ringelberg Attorney had an office here in the mid-1980s. The Mahons owned it until 1998 when Barabara sold it to The Seven R's Company. The American Cleaners business was located here into the mid-2010s. The building originally abutted the Dunlop building to the east which burned in the 1970s. Cops and Doughnuts purchased the building in 2016.

Sent., 7/11/1941; 6/27/1947; 7/2/1948; 2/18/1965; 3/19/1971; 10/19/1972; 2/28/1973; 4/3/1975; 10/23/1985., *CSHY.,* 1976.

Donald Holbrook Sr.
Photograph from the Forrest Meek Collection

111 West Fifth
United States Post Office (1936-37)
Office of Louis A. Simon, Washington D.C.,
Supervising Architect of the Treasury; Neal Melick,
Washington D.C., Supervising Engineer;
Spence Brothers, Saginaw, builders

This building is a simplified version of the Neoclassicism style similar to many post office buildings built across the nation during the 1930s. The flag pole located at the northeast corner of the property is not the 1937 original one, but stands in the original location. Two trees located in the grassy areas north of the building were planted in 1962.

The building's basic form has changed little since its construction in 1937. The concrete handicap ramp was constructed on the west end of the building's façade in 1989, adjoining the main steps and stoop. At the same time the front double doors and the present lamp posts, with spherical globes on the east and west sides of the steps, were added. The

27

original lampposts were shorter than the present lampposts and had semi-spherical globes. The original six over six double hung windows were replaced in 1988, and the current aluminum-framed windows were added in 2005 or 2006. The west wall of the loading dock on the southwest corner of the building was constructed in 1998.

The front door opens to a small enclosed wood-trimmed vestibule, with a low ceiling with exposed beams. The vestibule leads to the post office lobby through two wood-framed glass doors on its east and west ends. The original brass mailboxes and service windows are located along the south end of the lobby. The east wall contains mailboxes which were added in 1998. The west wall contains the original wood door to the Postmaster's office centered between two wood-framed glass-enclosed bulletin boards. Also of note in the lobby are the original cast iron radiators, and two original waist high wood tables.

Above the door and the bulletin boards is a mural by Allan Thomas, entitled "The Mail Arrives in Clare – 1871," depicting a postal worker delivering mail to a lumber camp in the late nineteenth-century. Between 1934 and 1943, murals and sometimes sculptures were produced for post offices under the direction of the Treasury Department's Section of Painting and Sculpture, and later called the Section of Fine Arts. This program was different than the Works Progress Administration/Federal Arts Project which was directed to provide economic relief to artists. The Treasury Department's Section of Painting and Sculpture was directed to place art in post offices for the purpose of boosting the morale of people suffering the effects of the Great Depression.

The work area, located behind the south wall of the lobby, contains a hardwood floor, plaster walls, and wood wainscot. The ceiling contains a skylight which is still located on the roof but has been covered over both on the interior and exterior. The fluorescent ceiling lights in the work area were added in the 1970s, and the duct work for the air conditioning in the work area's ceiling was added in 1973.

The construction of the building began in 1936 and was completed in May 1937. The postal operations moved from a building which was located just to the east of 502 North McEwan, but no longer exists. The present building has always been owned by the United States government and used for a post office.

Sent., 8/7/1936; 5/21, 10/8 and 10/15/1937.

United States Post Office 1937
Photograph from the Forrest Meek Collection

Allan Thomas Mural
Photograph from the Author's Collection

120 East Fifth
Goodman House (1882)

The main portion of the building has changed little since it was first constructed. The west-side bay window was added in 1894. Throughout the house's history changes have been made. Between 1899 and 1906 a small one-story addition was made to the building's south/rear side. In 1918 Grant Terwilliger did some remodeling on the building: most likely this was to add a one-story attached garage on the south side of the building that shows on the 1923 Sanborn map. By 1983 an older front porch had been removed and a modest entryway with an A-frame roof had replaced it. The current porch was constructed sometime between 1995 and 2004, replacing the A-frame entryway. In 1988 part of the south end of the building was removed to make room for the present large south end addition. A deck located on the south end of the building was constructed in 2006, and converted to an enclosed space in 2012. The current vinyl siding was added in 2012; prior to that some sections of the building still had their original clapboard siding. A new deck at the northwest corner of the building was constructed in 2013. The windows now have vinyl-clad trim that, added in 2012, retain the historic forms with gabled caps, but cover the original caps, with their incised detail, except in the bay window.

This building was constructed as a house for William Goodman in the spring of 1882. The property was deeded to William Goodman's wife Kittie in November 1898. She sold it in July 1901 to Charles O'Donald, who deeded it to his wife Ann in April 1905. William and Mary Cole bought the property from Ann O'Donald Kidder in December 1907. Grant and Loretta Terwilliger purchased the property from the Coles in March 1912. It was deeded to Loretta in January 1919, and sold by her to Lewis and Frances Thompson in August 1925. Hazel Oden, who bought the building from the Thompsons, owned it until November 1983. She was the last person to use the building as a residence. In 1983 she sold the house to John and Delphine Gibson, who opened the "Grandma's House" gift shop. The Gibsons sold in November 1995 to Glen and Stephanie Mogg, who continued the gift shop business. Dr. Elmer and Mary Ann Shurlow, purchased the building in May 2004 and opened the Herrick House gift shop, In 2007, Mulberry Café began operation in the south portion of the building.

CCP., 8/27/1881; 1930 Photograph, Robert Knapp Collection; 1985 Photograph, Mary Ann Shurlow Collection; Mary Ann Shurlow Interview, 5/5/2010.

Lewis and Frances Thompson Residence, Circa 1930
Photograph from the Robert Knapp Collection

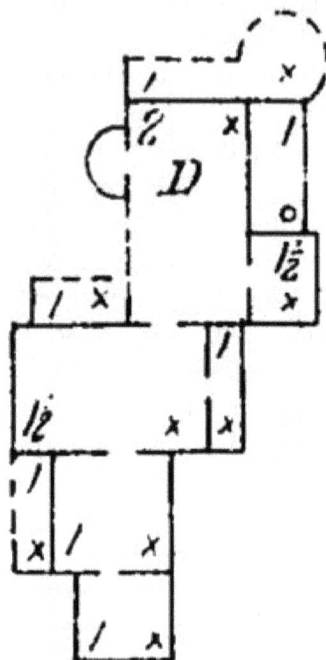

1894 Sanborn Map   *1906 Sanborn Map*

Grandma's House Gift Shop, circa 1985
Photograph from the Mary Ann Shurlow Collection

112 West Fourth
McCambly Building (1911)
E. E. Buckner, builder

Except for the panels and framing around the windows of the façade, which were added recently, this building has seen very little change. The only other notable change was a metal-sided addition to the north end of the building which was originally constructed sometime after 1934, but was also recently remodeled.

This building was constructed by John McCambly in 1911 for his harness shop. Grant Terwilliger purchased the building in January 1912 and continued the harness shop business. George Easler became the new owner in April 1920, but only owned it for four months before selling it to George Dawson in July 1920. Upon the death of George Dawson in 1922, ownership went to his two sons, Ora and Theron. Ora immediately sold his interest in the building to his brother Theron, who used the building for a cigar factory. In January 1923 Ora purchased the business from his brother and moved it to the building on the southeast corner of McEwan and Fifth Streets. Theron retained ownership of the building until May 1925 when he sold it to Sheral M. Callihan, who used the building for a lunchroom. Roy Joslin leased the building from Callihan in December 1925 for the same use. Sheral Callihan retained ownership of the building until 1930 when he sold it to Malcom D. Feighner and Florence Parish, who also owned the building immediately to the west where they printed the Clare Sentinel newspaper. That building proved to be too small for their printing needs so they moved the newspaper and printing operations to this building in April 1938. The newspaper continued to be printed here until 2003. Feighner and Parish published the paper from this building until July 1950 when William Elden became the new publisher. Feighner and Parish sold the building to William Elden in September 1960. Elden placed the ownership of the building in the name of the Clare Sentinel Inc. in January 1961. Northern Communications purchased the Clare Sentinel business and the building in August 1967. William Elden continued as publisher until his retirement in May 1969. Alfred Bransdorfer took over the publishing duties October 1969, and purchased the building in 1976. He sold the Sentinel to Clare Publishers in 2005, and sold the building to G & G Investments, in 2006. Patty Ann's Quilts was a recent occupant of the building. It then sat vacant for a while until P.T. Billings Services began using the building. Harrison & Newman Certified Public Accounts began using the building in October 2019.

Sent., 5/26/1911; 1/19/1912; 4/22/1920; 1/5/1923; 6/5 and 12/4/1925; 4/22/1938; 7/28/1950; 8/30/1967; 5/14 and 10/22/1969.

Clare Sentinel, circa 1950s
Photograph from the Forrest Meek Collection

114 West Fourth
Clare Sentinel Building (1907)
H. W. Pierce and Sons, builders

The facade was originally constructed of rock-faced concrete block. The street level contained large plate glass windows, with transoms, flanking two doors in a recessed center entry. The façade was capped by a bracketed cornice. The building originally contained two store spaces. The larger unit occupied the entire building except a separate southwest space occupying one-quarter of the footprint. It is unknown when the present façade was constructed, but it most likely happened after 1971 when Warren Keiser united the two spaces into one. When the present brick façade was built, the door was located where the east window is now and there was one window to its left. The vinyl siding on the upper facade was not added until later. The interior retains its pressed metal ceiling, and has evidence of openings in the west wall to the adjacent building made in 1950 when the store spaces in the two buildings were combined and can still be seen although now bricked up.

The cooler with its original wood door which dates from Manuel Sutton's ownership, beginning in 1959, is still present.

This building originally housed the newspaper office and press room for the Clare Sentinel, and the jewelry store of Edward White. The newspaper occupied the larger portion of the building. Edgar G. Welch and Philip A. Bennett built the building in 1907 after a fire swept through this part of the city earlier in the year. This portion of the building was sold to Erastus Palmer and Enoch Andrus in June of 1910. Erastus Palmer sold his interest in November 1911. John Paul Jones and Malcolm Feighner purchased the building in July 1921. Jones sold his interest back to Enoch Andrus in September 1922. In February 1923 Enoch Andrus sold to Benjamin Parish. The newspaper operated out of this location until 1938, when it relocated to the building immediately to the east. In September 1945 Malcolm Feighner and Florence Parish sold the building to James McKinnon (by this time Benjamin Parish was deceased). In 1949 James McKinnon was leasing the building to Feller's Cut Rate Store. The following year an archway was constructed in the west wall and Feller's expanded into the building to the west. In 1957 Drs. Keyes and Ballard, D.O., were using the building for their medical practice.

James McKinnon owned the building until September 1959, when he sold to Manuel Sutton. Manuel Sutton operated a bar in this building under the name "Manny's." Warren Keiser bought the building in July 1962 and continued the bar under the "Manny's Bar" name. He sold to Robert Ruby in August 1990, who opened Bob's Lounge. The Evening Post Bar and Grill began using the building in July 2013.

The smaller of the two units of this building was originally owned by Edward White, and was used for a jewelry store. In March 1912 Mrs. A. Beemer began renting the unit from Edward White for an unknown use. White sold to Adelpha Kump in April 1912, who operated a barber shop out of the building. Homer Douglas began renting the corner space for his barber shop in 1932 and bought it in April 1935. Vere Kinsey began leasing the barber shop from Homer Douglas in 1957. Douglas sold the unit to Warren Keiser in May 1971.

A "BAR/LIQUOR" neon sign projecting over the sidewalk from the right side of the upper façade dates from sometime shortly after the present use as a bar began about 1959, though with the name revised for different proprietors. A shallow rear extension, with concrete block lower walls, was added in 2000. "Big Chicken," a large plastic chicken rooster that stands on the sidewalk in front, an advertisement for the place's featured broasted chicken, has been a highly visible downtown fixture for about twenty-five years.

Sent., 10/25, 11/22 and 12/27/1907; 4/22/1910; 3/29, 4/29 and 5/8/1912; 7/22/1932; 5/13/1938; 9/25/1953; 1/27/1957; 8/30/1962; Photograph c.1980.

Edward White's Jewelry Store
Photograph courtesy of Clare Sentinel
December 24, 1907

118 West Fourth
M. E. Whitney Building (1907)
Walter Petit, builder

The building has concrete block walls, but its original appearance is unknown. However, it is known that the façade is of brick behind the siding below the windows. The interior retains a pressed metal ceiling.

The original owner was Melanthon E. Whitney. He built this building in 1907 after a fire swept through this part of the city earlier in the year. The original use was for Whitney's five-cent movie theater, the Palace Theatre. In May 1912 Wallace Weir, who owned the building to the west, rented this building for his new and second hand goods store. Whitney rented the building in February 1913 to George Valley, who operated the Valley Restaurant. Thomas Groves bought the restaurant in July 1915. A Mr. Broderick was using the building in 1918. In August 1920 Whitney rented the building to the Ohio Dairy Company for their cream station. The Ohio Dairy Company was managed by J. T. Brown. Brown eventually replaced the Ohio Dairy Company with his own business which lasted here to March 1922. M. E. Whitney sold the building in November 1921 to Harry Hubel. Hubel started his own produce business here in April 1922. Hubel sold the building to Everett Samborn in November 1929 and continued using it for a produce store. Clarence Tucker bought the building from Samborn in May 1945 for his produce store. In late 1949 Feller's Cut Rate Store, located in the building to the east, expanded into this building by constructing an archway connecting the two buildings. The Helping Hand Shop was leasing the building in 1959. Clarence Tucker owned the building until December 1965 when he sold it to Manuel Sutton. After the death of her husband, Violet Sutton sold the building to Warren Keiser in November 1970. The Bargain Shop was using the building in 1971, followed by the Pisces Beauty Salon from 1973 to at least 1977. Bread of Life Coffee Shop was open here in 1983. Beginning in 1984 Warren Kaiser's wife Sherry opened Sherry's Gift World, and operated it into the mid-1990s. Keiser retained ownership of the building until April 1996 when he sold it to Edward, Ramona, and Linda Prichkaitis. The Prichkaitises sold the building to Stephanie Mercer, in May 2000, to open her Stitches for Britches embroidery business. The appearance of the building, as shown on the previous page, was changed in 2018.

Sent., 7/5/1907; 5/10/1912; 2/28/1913; 7/23/1915; 12/5/1918; 8/26, 10/14//1920; 11/13/1925; 8/2/1929; 6/17/1939; 12/24/1948; 11/4/1949; 11/3/1950; 7/7/1959; 12/1/1960; 12/2/1970; 6/29/1971; 4/11/1973; 2/23/1977; 6/15/1983; 3/14/1984; 4/5/1994; *Cour.,* 4/17/1922; *Farwell,* 12/2/1970.

Feller's Cut Rate Advertisement Clare Sentinel January 12, 1951

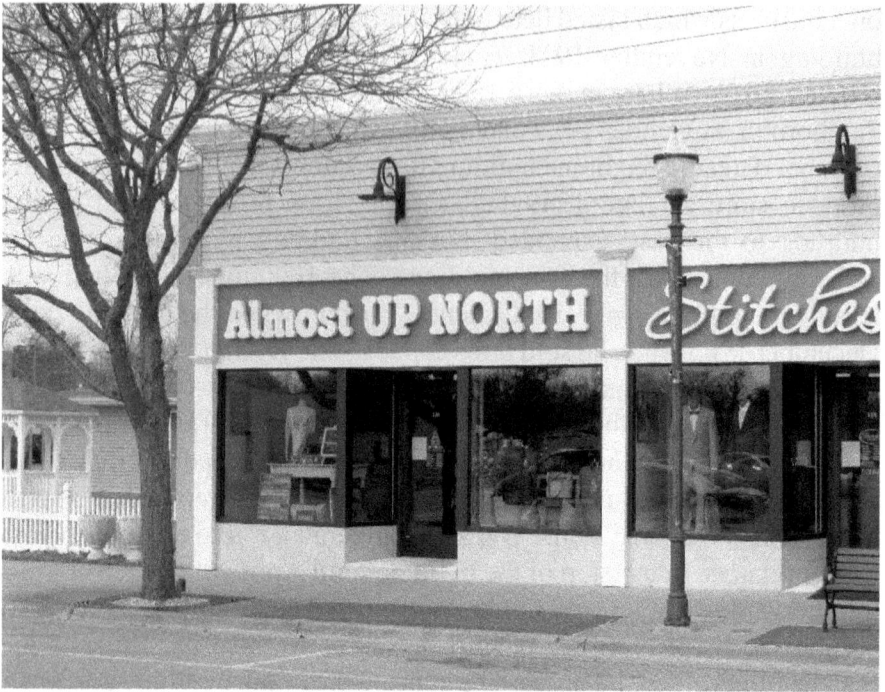

120 West Fourth
Wallace T. Weir Building (1907)

The original appearance of the building is unknown. The façade was altered in 1946 when Corky's Diner began operations. The new front was then described as a "new green and white front with French type windows and yellow columns" (*Sentinel* 6/14/1946). The façade was again altered in 1953 when Feller's Cut Rate Store opened, but it is unknown how the appearance was changed other than it was painted red. Vinyl siding was added in 1985. The building's exposed concrete block west side wall was surfaced in stucco in 2009 after the adjacent building was torn down. The façade was altered in 2018 to its appearance as shown in the above photograph.

This building was originally owned by Wallace Weir, who built it in 1907 after a fire. Weir purchased the pool room business of Jay Smith and moved it to this building, originally running a second-hand store from the basement and the pool and billiard hall on the first floor. Elmer Ford leased the basement of the building beginning in November 1912 and continued the second hand store. The pool hall was leased in May 1915 to Charles Adams, and then in late 1916 to W. J. Stephenson. Wallace Weir sold the building to George

Dawson for his cigar factory in March 1917. The George Dawson & Sons business opened in 1919, and the Dawson Brothers business was operating here in 1922. Dawson sold the building in September 1922 to Iva Holcomb. She sold the building in May 1924 to Lewis H. Thompson, who owned a farm implement store in the building to the west. Grinnell Brothers Music Store was located here in 1924. Merrell Auto Electric Service operated out of this building in the late 1920s and early 1930s. Cadillac Produce Company was opened in 1931, and eventually changed to the Cadillac Cream Station. The cream station was managed by G. O. Whiteside, but by the mid-1930s the business was operated under his name. The building was a produce store in the early 1940s. McCready's Produce was first followed by Davis Poultry and Produce in 1942, and then Brown's Produce in 1943. Everett Samborn bought the building from Lewis Thompson in June 1944, and owned it until May 1945 when Clarence Tucker purchased it. William Dunlop owned the building from February 1946 until August 1973. In June 1946 the Dunlops opened Corky's Diner here. In April 1947 Guy Mercer and Nick Kreiner purchased the diner business from the Dunlops. Mr. and Mrs. Oakley Sirrine purchased Corky's Diner in May 1950, and Harold Pugaley purchased it in November 1951. In October of the following year Corky's Diner relocated to a building on the opposite side of Fourth Street. Feller's Cut Rate Store expanded for the second time, into this building, in early 1953, along with the two buildings immediately to the east which it already occupied. The Helping Hands Shop was operating in the building in 1958, and by 1960 had changed its name to the Clare-Trading Post. Bud's Furniture was using the building in 1961 and by 1965 had changed its name to Bud's Second Hand Store. In the late 1960s and early 1970s the Family Grill was using the building. Warren Keiser purchased the building from William Dunlop in August 1973. Freida Prichkaitis moved her Drapery Boutique business here in 1979. Freida passed away in September 1994 and the same month her husband and children, Edward, Ramona and Linda Prichkaitis, purchased the building from Dianne R. (Flinn) McCarthy, and continued the Drapery Boutique business. Stephanie Badour, formerly Mercer, purchased the building in 2017. She opened her Almost Up North business in 2018 which was an expansion of her Stitches for Britches business located immediately to the east.

Sent., 8/2 and 3/6/1907; 11/15/1912; 5/21/1915; 12/7/1916; 3/1/1917; 1/30/1919; 11/3/1922; 9/26/1924; 6/7/1929; 1/30/1930; 2/6/1931; 9/16/1932; 12/18/1936; 7/3 and 10/23/1942; 4/16 and 9/24/1943; 6/14/1946; 4/15/1949; 5/5/1950; 11/2/1951; 10/31/1952; 1/14/1953; 10/23/1958; 11/10/1960; 1/19/1961; 12/2/1965; 8/8/1968; 11/8/1972.

112 East Fourth
McKinnon Blacksmith Shop (1904)
O. M. Sutherland, architect
1946 remodel, John Robert Mester, builder

The original appearance of the building is unknown. The interior was remodeled in 1946, but it is unclear how much work was then done on the exterior. The present appearance of the building is due to the remodeling work that took place in 1980. Prior to that the building was finished in red brick. The façade had two eight light, fixed sash windows with a recessed entry between. To the east and west of the door within the recess were two four-paned fixed sash windows.

The building was built in 1904 by Archie J. McKinnon for his blacksmith shop. He owned it until December 1923 when his son Roy McKinnon purchased the building. Roy McKinnon operated an automotive repair shop in the building and at one point also had a gas pump. For a short time in 1945 and 1946 the Smith's Appliance Shop used this building. In May 1946 Roy McKinnon sold the property to

Ethel Allen and Estelle Artibee. They leased the building to H. Rexford Allen in July 1946 for his insurance business. Estelle Artibee sold her interest in the building to H. Rexford Allen in November 1952, and Ethel Allen sold her interest to him in April 1959. James Allen purchased the building in October 1979. In October 1980 Robert Allen purchased the building; he continued the insurance business that his father H. Rexford Allen started. Since 2012 the building has housed Elaine's Hair & Nail Expressions.

Two Reasons
Why we Sell so Many
Kelly Springfield Tires and Tubes

1. It costs no more] to buy a Kelly;
2. The mileage plus|our service

Kelly 30x3½ Fabric $10.00
Kelly 30x3½ oversize cord $12.50
30x3½ Fabric $7.50
30x3½ Cord $8.50
30x3½ Tube $1.80

Roy McKinnon
112 East 4th Street.

Roy McKinnon Advertisement
Clare Sentinel April 10, 1925

Sent., 6/16 and 12/2/1904; 12/7/1945; 7/5/1946; Robert Allen Interview, 8/19/2009.

Allen Agency Insurance 1979
Photograph from the Robert Allen Collection

402 North McEwan
Subway Building (2000)

This building was constructed in 2000 by T. S. R. Development for use as a retail mini-mall. The building contains four tenant spaces, a northwest front corner one leased by the Schumacher Insurance Agency (prior to them it was occupied by IBT Title-Clare County). The southwest corner part contains the Subway restaurant. To the east is the unit formerly occupied by the Russell Winter Insurance Agency, and on the east end of the building is Shear Envy Hair and Tanning Salon. Shear Envy began operating out of this building in March 2019. Prior to that it was used by Brenda's Hair and Tanning Salon.

Sent., 5/16/2000.

406 North McEwan
O'Callaghan Building (1907)
H. W. Pierce and Sons, builders; 1924 renovation

The building's façade was initially constructed of rock-face concrete block and contained a large door in the center with small windows located to either side on the ground story and four windows on the second. The south elevation contained small windows at the top of the first story, and larger windows more widely spaced in the second story. In 1924 the façade was rebuilt in brick and designed to match the building to the north except for the brick color. The façade had a large garage door opening in the center. Brick piers on the north and south sides of the door extended to the bottom of the second story. Beyond the pier to either side was a large plate glass window. The windows and door all had prism glass transoms. Above the transom windows was a recessed area of dentil brickwork. At one time a gasoline pump was located at the edge of the street. The second story, intended for use as a

45

O'Callaghan Feed Barn
Photograph from the Clare Courier, 1907

406 (right) and 412 (left) North McEwan, circa 1930
Photograph from the Tom Seller's Collection

lodge room or dance hall following the renovation, instead was used for auto storage, reached by a utility elevator at the rear of the building. It is unknown when the street level of the present façade was altered, but it most likely happened in the 1970s. The steel siding on the south side of the building was added in 1982.

This building was constructed in 1907 by John O'Callaghan for use as his livery and feed barn. The building adjoined another livery to the east which was constructed in 1903 and fronted on Third Street. In March 1923 Isaac Hampton purchased the building from the O'Callaghan Estate. Isaac Hampton already owned the building immediately to the north, and wanted the extra building to expand his Ford automobile and tractor dealership. In February 1946 the Hampton Estate sold the building to Floyd and Clarence McGuire and Eugene Campbell, who the next month opened the McGuire & Campbell Firestone Home and Auto Supply store. In January 1947 Warren McGuire purchased the interest of Eugene Campbell in the building and business. The business then became McGuire Brothers Firestone Store. Woodcock and Walters were operating an auto repair garage in the rear of the building prior to the sale and continued their business after the building's sale. Floyd McGuire sold his interest in the building in April 1950. Arthur Ulrich began leasing the building in mid-1955 and opened a Pontiac car dealership. Ulrich purchased the building in May 1958. In the late 1950s or early 1960s Feller's Shoe Store was leasing the building. Larry Campbell purchased it from Mr. Ulrich in January 1976, and opened Campbell Printing. Linda Lou Campbell was deeded the property in September 1992. Riverview Leasing, purchased the property in 1998, and continued the Campbell Printing business. The building became vacant after Campbell Printing merged with a Saginaw printer in 2014, and moved their operations there.

Isaac Hampton
Photograph from the
Forrest Meek
Collection

Cour., 10/4/1907; *Sent.*, 4/12/1907; 3/16/1923; 4/11/1924; 3/15/1946; 1/10/1947; 1/20/1955.

412 North McEwan
Davis Block (1915)
1941 interior renovation, Harold Moline, contractor

The street-level front originally had a garage door located in the center. A brick pier each on the north and south sides of the door extended to the bottom of the second floor. On the outer side of each pier was a large plate glass window. The door and windows all had transoms. The street-level front was aligned with the upper facade. Above the transom windows was a recessed area of dentil brickwork. In 1916 Isaac Hampton built a thirty-two foot addition on the east end of the building. The interior of the building was renovated in 1941 to accommodate the A & P Grocery Store. The street-level façade was remodeled to its present form in 1946 with the columns supporting the second story covered in stainless steel.

This building was constructed by J. M. Davis for his automobile repair garage. Mr. Davis owned his building for less than a year before selling to Isaac Hampton. Hampton relocated his automobile repair garage here and eventually opened a Ford automobile dealership in the building. The building was used as an automobile garage and showroom until at least 1934. Band Box Odorless Dry Cleaners was using the building in 1937. The A & P grocery store moved into the building in August 1941. Lewis Siegel purchased the building from Isaac Hampton's wife Nellie in January 1946 with the intention of partnering with Elmer J. Atkinson in a hardware store here. The A & P store, which grew too large for this building, closed in the summer of 1946, and by November of the same year the Northland Hardware Store opened. Lewis Siegel sold the hardware business in May 1952 to Ivan F. Belknap of Detroit and Roy A. Warner of Saginaw. Northland Hardware operated until 1970. After Northland Hardware, the building housed the Western Auto store which continued to 1984. Lewis Siegel owned the building until January 1973 when he sold it to Richard Redick. Donald Applegreen acquired it in January 1979 and sold it to Larry Campbell in January 1985. The Clare Mini Mall opened in 1985 and housed a number of stores. The All In One Store opened in 1985, Lighthouse Book & Gift Shoppe was open in 1986, Lee's Carpet operated from 1987 to 1991, The Beach Tanning & Toning Salon opened in 1989 and Rainbow Video II in 1991. The building was deeded to Linda Lou Campbell in September 1992. Riverview Leasing, purchased the building in September 1998. Clare Family Fitness used the building from 1993 to 2011. The building was then used by Image Quest Active Wear, and was vacant for a short time after that. Four Leaf Brewing began using the building in 2015.

Sent., 8/27/1915; 4/27 and 6/15/1916; 12/31/1937; 8/1/1941; 7/19, 8/30 and 11/1/1946; 5/2/1952; 11/18/1970; 2/21/1973; 8/18/1984; 11/27/1985; 6/17/1986; 11/17/1987; 9/19/1989; 10/22/1991; Don Jones Interview, 2/20/2012.

418 North McEwan
Bicknell's Dry Goods Store (1898); 1923 renovation

The building's present appearance was the result of a 1923 renovation that made its façade match the building to the north. The building originally had a two-story front with three second-story front windows and smaller recessed panels in the brickwork between them and the façade was topped by a two-tiered ornate cornice. The building's facade was of brown brick, but the upper façade had a polychromatic look because the square recessed panels there were of a lighter colored brick. The now covered transoms contain prism glass.

The building was constructed by Nathan Bicknell in 1898 for his dry goods store. It served as his main retail location until the construction of his large store immediately to the north in 1907. When that building was constructed Bicknell moved his stock to the new location and leased 418 to the J. A. Allen & Company grocery. J. A. Allen vacated the building in 1923, and William Bicknell, who had acquired it in 1915 after the death of his father Nathan, remodeled it to expand his Bicknell

Department Store into this building. The remodeled building, now with a front identical to the existing Bicknell Department Store immediately to the north at 420, housed the store's men's and boys' ware lines. William retained ownership of the building and ran the Bicknell Department Store until his death in 1966. Nick and Norma Allen purchased the building the next year and opened Allen and Bell's Department Store there in 1968. John Bicknell purchased the building in January 1976, later selling to John and Jane Seibt. Allen and Bell's Department Store operated in the building until John and Jane Seibt sold the building to John and Lynn Bliek in August 2003. Black Bear and Broadcloth Department Store opened here in 2003. This building sat vacant for a time, until Fantastic Finds Antique Store moved here in 2011. Fantastic Finds moved to 518 N. McEwan in 2012 and the building was then used by the Central Michigan Music store. Vintage Type Antique Store used the building from 2017 to 2019.

Sent., 9/16/1898; 11/18/1989; 4/9/1915; 10/26/1923; 12/29/1966; 8/1/1968.

418 North McEwan, tall building in center, circa 1920
Photograph from the Robert Knapp Collection

51

420 North McEwan
Bicknell's Department Store (1907)
"Bogart," Saginaw, reported as "architect."

Nathan Bicknell owned and operated a dry goods and clothing store where the building to the south (418) is located. In 1907 he built this larger building and moved his business into it. Nathan's son William took over the operation of the store in 1913. William Bicknell added Bert Greer and Clyde M. Hays as partners in April 1915. In November 1915 William and James Bicknell, Nathan's sons, were deeded the property after the death of their father. In 1923, when the J. A. Allen & Company grocery vacated 418, the Bicknells expanded the store back into 418, connecting the two buildings' interiors and remodeling the front of 418 to match 420. In December 1932 Dr. C. A. Withey, a chiropodist (foot specialist), leased a portion of the building for an unknown period of time. It is unknown when James sold his interest in the building, but William retained ownership of the building and ran the Bicknell Department Store until his death in 1966.

Nick and Norma Allen then purchased the building and opened Allen and Bell's Department Store in 1968. John Bicknell bought the building in January 1976, and later sold it to John and Jane Seibt. Allen and Bell's Department Store operated in the building until John and Jane Seibt sold the building to John and Lynn Bliek in August 2003. Black Bear and Broadcloth Department Store opened here in 2003. The Willow Classic Women's Apparel Store opened for business here in 2016.

Nathan Bicknell
Photograph from the
Forrest Meek Collection

Sent., 7/19/1907; 1/10/1913; 4/9/1915; 10/26/1923; 12/29/1966; 8/1/1968.

Bicknell Department Store, circa 1930
Photograph from the Forrest Meek Collection

426 North McEwan
McEwan Professional Building (1997)

The building was constructed in 1997 by Mark Koch, owner of G.L.S. Investments, for use as an office building. The original tenant of the unit fronting on McEwan Street was New Horizon Travel, the middle unit was occupied by Russell L. Winter Insurance agency, the east unit by White Law office. Caroline Murphy purchased the building in 2004. The Edward Jones Office of Mark Smith took over the McEwan Street unit in December 1999. Subsequent tenants of the other units include; Travis Harrison CPA, which later changed to Harrison & Newman CPA, Solutions Psychotherapy, Renew Health Family Chiropractic, and GISS USA East Corp.

Sent., 6/3 and 7/29/1997; 9/29/1998; 12/14/1999.

502 North McEwan
Clare Hardware Company (1902)
Haug & Scheurman, Saginaw, architects
Citizens State Bank 1929 renovation: Bond, Hubbard
Company, Chicago, architects and contractors
Garfield Memorial Library 1988 renovation:
Marchiando and Rau, Mount Pleasant, contractors

This building has changed twice since its original construction in 1902. The building in its original form, designed by Haug & Scheurman, had a Neoclassical/Renaissance-inspired appearance, with classical piers supporting a tall entablature with modillioned cornice and a large central upstairs triple window of palladian window form. The piers and entablature continued one bay onto the south side elevation. A stringcourse of light colored stone on the façade's second story was an added feature. The first-story façade contained a large fixed sash window with a five light transom window above, and flanked

55

by two arched openings. In 1929 the building was remodeled and given an Art Deco appearance. A 1929 article in the *Clare Sentinel* describes the remodeled bank as follows: "The exterior of the building will be veneered in white cast stone with sills of natural stone, and it will present a most imposing and beautiful appearance. The interior walls are to be finished in ornamental plaster and all the woodwork will be of mahogany. The large steel posts in the present lobby are to give way to an eye-beam that will support the ceiling. A larger lobby with cages of marble and bronze will be placed along the south wall, and the center entrance to the bank will provide more room for the customers and bank officials. The floor will be of terrazzo with brass strips inserted and the present vault door will be replaced with a six-inch burglar proof, time lock door that weighs three tons. A sound-proof machine room for the bookkeeping department, ladies waiting room, private office for the cashier and a coupon booth for the convenience of safety deposit customers, are just a few features which will make this bank one of the most modern in this section of the state." During this renovation more windows were added to the building's first floor south elevation and the present arrangement of windows and doors on the building's façade was created. The work was performed by the Bond and Hubbard Company of Chicago, which specialized in bank construction and remodeling. The current brick exterior finish resulted from further remodeling performed in 1988. The vinyl windows along with the EIFS details were added in 2007. The building retains its Eureka Heating and Ventilation Company coal burning boiler which was forged in Saginaw in 1905. Also in the basement of the building are three bank vaults. Two of the vaults have doors. One of the vault doors is from the Mosler Safe Co. of Hamilton, Ohio. Also of note is a bricked over opening to the building to the north at the bottom of the stairway at the building's northwest corner.

Haug & Scheurman (Charles H. Haug and Fred T. Scheurman) of Saginaw designed the 1902 building with its long ago lost highly ornamental original façade. The same architects did the 1897-1902 Pollasky Block, 101-09 W. Superior, Alma; 1899 half of the Schlieder Building, 212-14 W. Main, Owosso; and 1902-03 old City Hall in Alma (now Liberty Professional Building) – all fine jobs. This building was constructed in 1902 by William Callam for the Clare Hardware Company. The hardware store was located on the first floor facing

McEwan Street, a harness store was located at the east end of the first floor. The second floor consisted of two private offices, a telephone office, and a tin shop on the east end. After the fire of 1904, which burned all the wood framed buildings between here and the Doherty Opera House, William Callam along with James Tatman, constructed the brick building to the north. The Clare Hardware Company expanded to include the south unit of that building, with the interior of the two buildings open to one another. In 1907 the hardware store moved completely to the building to the north and the first floor of this building was used for the Citizens Bank. The first floor east unit housed the S. H. Morse & Son harness shop, and George Benner housed his insurance business on the east end of the first floor. In late 1907 the second story of the building, which to this point was unfinished, was being converted into apartments for two families. In 1908 Catherine Callam was deeded the building after the death of William Callam. By 1910 the first floor was shared by the bank, Paul Greiser's tailor shop in a middle unit, and a restaurant in the east unit.

George Benner opened a real estate agency in the building in December 1911. In June 1912 the Greiser tailor shop was replaced with a cigar and tobacco store operated by Herschel Halsted. The Citizens State Bank took over ownership of the building from Catherine Callam in January 1917. In 1923 Joseph Bowler opened his law office in this building in the unit formerly occupied by Jones & Ross, on the building's first floor. Also on the first floor, Grant Terwilliger had a harness shop that he operated until March 1923. In 1926 the Vogue Shoppe was operating in one of the units of the building. December 1926 saw the A. L.

The Founders of the Citizens Bank, clockwise from upper left George Benner, John Goodman, Charles O'Donald, Fred Lister
Clare Courier, August 28, 1903

Rogers and Forest Shumway barber and beauty shop opening in the first floor's middle unit. In February 1930 William S. Teeter opened his real estate and oil lease exchange business in the building. The Mammoth Producing and Refining Company leased the entire second floor from April 1937 until spring of 1942. Mr. and Mrs. Gordon Mowbray opened the Mowbray Insurance Agency in October 1941. Dr. A. E. Mulder moved his dental practice to the second floor of this building in October 1942. Dr. Richard Siberneck opened an optometry office in late 1950 in the office which Dr. Mulder vacated with his retirement. Maurice Studios located to the second floor of the building in April 1953. The building was purchased by the Mammoth Oil Company from the Citizens State Bank in 1961. At the same time Mammoth Oil allowed the Clare City Library to relocate to the building's first floor. The library was allowed to occupy the space rent free in return for renaming itself the Garfield Memorial Library, in honor of the wife of Sam Garfield, Mammoth Oil's local representative. Mammoth Producing Corporation moved out of the state in 1979 and sold the building to the City of Clare. The library then occupied both floors of the building. The city sold the building to North Ten LLC in July 2007 after relocating the library to 185 East Fourth Street. North Ten LLC offices located to the second floor of the building. For a short time Curves Women's Fitness Center was leasing the first floor, before Reclaimed Wood business began using the first floor. Sarah's Law Firm began using the first floor in June 2018.

Clare Hardware Store
Drawing from the Clare Courier, March 20, 1903

Cour., 3/20/1903; 8/9/1907; Sent., 7/17/1902; 1/11, 2/1 and 2/8/1907; 12/8/1911; 6/21/1912; 4/13/1923; 4/3/1925; 4/23 and 12/24/1926; 6/12/1929; 4/16/1937; 10/3/1941; 11/3/1944; 9/15/1950; 4/17/1953; 8/31/1961; 5/16/1979; 7/5/1988.

Citizens State Bank, late 1930s
Photograph from the Forrest Meek Collection

506 North McEwan
Tatman Building (1904)
O. M. Sutherland, Clare, architect; W. H. Pierce, builder

The building was originally divided into two sections, with the entry for the south part at the building's southwest corner and for the north part in the center of that end. By 1957 the south unit's first story was clad with un-coursed stone to the second-story window sills. The present display windows were installed in 1985. The shutters on the second story windows were added at the same time. The awning which extends across the building's façade was also added in 1985 but has since been updated. The building retains its metal ceiling in the north portion of the building, and its Warner freight elevator in the south part. The second-story retains apartments that have long since been vacant.

This building was constructed in 1904 for James Tatman and William Callam. Tatman had the north half built for his grocery and shoe business, while Callam built the south half to house an expansion of his Clare Hardware Company, then located in the corner building to the south. In April of the following year John and Mary Calkins purchased the south half of the building. The south half's second story was used as a roller skating rink in 1906 but by 1910 was incorporated into the hardware store. In early 1907 the Clare Hardware Company vacated the corner building to the south (then being occupied by the Citizens Bank), and only occupied the south half of this building. A new firm, W. B. Webb and Mortimer Gallagher's Clare Hardware and Implement Company, leased the south half in March 1914. Webb and Mortimer purchased the south half in January 1916. By 1923 the second story of the south half was used for a tin shop. The name of the hardware business was changed in 1928 to the Clare Hardware and Furniture Company. W. B. Webb sold his interest in the business and by 1935 Ben Mercer was co-owner with Mortimer Gallagher, who were at the time beginning to sell Dodge and Plymouth vehicles. Stanley Burdo purchased the south half and business in February 1936 and retained the Clare Hardware and Furniture Company name. The south half was combined with the north half in 1943 when Stanley Burdo purchased it from the James Tatman Estate.

The north half of the building was owned by James Tatman and housed his grocery and shoe business. In mid-1905 James Tatman sold a half interest in his business and building to George McKeever. Joseph Bowler started his law practice here in 1908 by leasing a portion of the Tatman & McKeever building. In December 1914 James Tatman divided the first floor of the north unit into two units, leasing the north unit to L. G. Fox, jeweler and optometrist, while running his grocery business out of the south unit. In January 1919 D. E. Mater leased the north unit for his furniture business. In January 1930 the National Grocer Company opened the R. Chain grocery store in the south unit. This business was managed by E. W. Brown, who purchased the business in September 1930 and began to run it under his name after that. E. W. Brown ran the grocery store for an unknown period of time. In 1938 one of the units in the building's north half was leased to the Clare Restaurant.

The north half's second story initially contained three suites of offices and a lodge room. One the offices served the Secretary of Michigan's Republican Party, Dennis Alward, from 1915 to 1919. Attorney A. E. Wylie moved his law firm to the second floor of the building in November 1932. Prior to this Mr. Wylie's office was used

61

by the Clare County Credit Bureau, and also by Mr. Tatman as his private office after his retirement from the grocery business.

In 1943 Stanley Burdo purchased the north half of the building from the James Tatman Estate, combining it with the south half of the building which he purchased in 1936. Stanley's son Ben inherited the building and the hardware/furniture business in January 1947. Beginning in April 1968 the Clare Hardware and Furniture Company again became two separate businesses for a time. Ben Burdo owned and managed the Clare Hardware Company in the south portion of the building, while Dan and Bill Burdo owned and managed the Clare Furniture Company in the north portion. Ben Burdo retained ownership until 2006 when the building was deeded to his daughter Elaine Demasi. The Demasi's used the building for their hardware business. Vincent and Elaine Demasi sold the building in October 2006 to Dennis and Kathy Sian who continued the hardware business.

Sent., 12/2/1904; 6/9/1905; 1/11/1907; 6/19/1908; 3/6 and 12/4/1914; 1/30/1919; 1/24 and 9/26/1930; 11/25/1932; 2/1/1935; 3/6/1936; 7/15/1938; 4/25/1968

James F. Tatman
Photograph from the Clare Sentinel 1937

518 North McEwan
Doherty Building (1910-11)
Edward B. Gorr, Clare, architect and builder

Construction of this building began in 1904 after a fire in July of that year destroyed the wood frame building previously located here. By the end of 1904 only the foundation was completed. Construction did not begin again until 1910, and was completed in 1911. The building was constructed for Alfred J. Doherty. Upon completion of the building Mr. Doherty leased the first story to Elmer Anderson for his drug store business. The second story was leased to the John Q. Look No. 404 Lodge of the Masons. The Masons leased the second story of the building until 1931 when they moved to the old Doherty Opera House, three buildings to the north. Elmer Anderson purchased the building from Doherty in April 1921. Anderson ran his drug store business until his death in 1941. His daughter, Mrs. Jean Allen, assumed management of the business until 1947 while her brother was serving in the military and later attending school. Elmer's son, Elmer "Bud" Anderson, took over the operation of the store in 1948 from his mother Josephine. The building was deeded to the Anderson children in 1957. George Punches began managing Anderson's drug store in 1965 and purchased the business and the building in 1975. By 1983 and continuing to 1987 the building was occupied by Connie & Margaret's Hallmark Shop. The Emporium was using the building from 1988 to at least 1990. Margaret Punches bought the building in December 1998. Mood Makers beauty shop leased the building until 2012, followed by Fantastic Finds Antique Store, and then Millies Downtown gift store. Thomas and Kim Kleinhardt purchased the building in 2015. Millies closed at the end of the 2018, and Salon 518 opened here in 2019.

The Masons vacated the second story of the building in 1931. By 1934 Bowler & Bowler Attorneys & Counselors at law began using the second story. By 1947 and continuing to 1950 the Law Office of Joseph K. Naumes was using the second floor. In 1951 Miss Barbara Kane was occupying the residence on the second floor. From 1951 to at least the end of the year 1952 Dr. J. P. Calvird was occupying the office and residence on the second floor. The west half of the second story was used for the Clare Main Street office until 2012, while the east half of the second story is still used as an apartment.

The building retains its pressed metal ceiling on the first floor. The stairwell's first floor landing's tilework spells out "F & A M" for the Free & Accepted Masons which used the upper story from 1911 to 1931.

Sent., 12/2/1904; 10/14 and 10/28/1910; 1/13 and 7/7/1911; 4/28/1921; 3/16/1934; 5/30/1947; 5/26 and 10/20/1950; 5/4 and 9/14/1951; 12/2/1952; 5/5/1955; 2/12/1975; 5/25/1983; 10/13/1987; 3/14/1988; 10/30/1990.

Elmer and Josephine Anderson
Photographs from the Clare Sentinel 1906

520 North McEwan
McKinnon Building (1904)
O. M. Sutherland, architect

The front's original appearance is unknown. An exterior stairway to the basement was removed and cemented over in 1917. In the 1960s the building was remodeled to have a recessed entry with plate glass windows on both sides. The remodeling included brickwork below the windows and on the north and south ends of the building in a stacked bond pattern. Above the windows and doors was a broad flat canopy that extended across the entire façade. The building's upper facade was covered in undecorated paneling. Sometime after 2004 the façade was altered to contain a single center window, and the vinyl siding and pent roof added. At some unknown time the building was connected to the one to the north so the two could house the same business. The current windows and door were installed in 2012.

This building was constructed for Archie J. McKinnon in 1904. It replaced an existing wood building that was destroyed by fire in July of the same year. The building was originally leased to Elmer Anderson for his drug store business. He operated in the building until 1911 when he moved into the newly constructed Doherty Building immediately to the south. From late 1912 to early 1915 E. Burt Jenney leased the building for his banking business. In October 1915 the building became the Oil & Drum Co. office. The next month C. W. Calkins both opened and closed his store business. In December of the same year M. C. Fife opened a restaurant in the building. In 1917 Allen and Manee opened a meat market. Harris and Hirt moved their hardware store to this building in May 1928.   In April 1936 the building was deeded to Archie McKinnon's son, Kyle McKinnon. By 1945 Kenneth and Jay Hendrie were using the building for their Hendrie Brothers Market. The property was acquired by Margaret McKinnon in January 1948. The Hendrie Brothers partnership was dissolved in 1950 with Kenneth Hendrie retaining ownership of the business.   William Lewis purchased it from Kenneth Hendrie in 1952, and continued the meat market and grocery business under the Bill Lewis Market name. In 1953 the property was deeded to John and Martha Murphy (Martha Murphy was formerly Martha McKinnon), who owned it until September 1954 when they sold to Alfred J. Doherty II.   Robert Fielder opened Fielder's Shoe Store in October 1955. Marlin and Betty Alexander took over the shoe business from the Fielders in 1956, and it became Alexander's Shoes. Alfred J. Doherty II's wife Helen sold the building to Herschel Jewett in September 1979. James Mester purchased it in July 1983. As early as 1981 Jan-Dor Fashions, which was owned by Keith and Doris Benmark, was leasing the building. The Benmarks purchased the building at an unknown date, and owned the building until March 1989 when he sold to Christopher Miller. The building was leased to Sam's Brothers in 1989. The Edward Jones and Co. office of Mark J. Smith was using the building by 1995, and continued here until at least 1998. Mr. Miller owned the building until April 2004 when he sold to Diane Demo-Sadler and Vivian Demo. Starting in 2004 it has been used for the Apple Tree Lane Gift Shop business.

CHSY., 1950; 1961; 1982; 1987; *Sent.*, 8/4 and 12/4/1904; 10/11/1912; 10/8, 11/17 and 12/10/1915; 9/6 and 10/4/1917; 4/28/1921; 6/2/1950; 6/20/1952; 11/1/1956; 3/24/1960; 5/16/1968; 2/11/1981; 5/2/1989; 7/18/1995; 7/7/1998.

Hendrie Market, 1950
*Photograph from the
1950 Clare High School
Yearbook*

Alexander's Shoes, 1961
*Photograph from the 1961
Clare High School Yearbook*

East side of 500 block of North McEwan looking east, Circa 1970
Photograph from the Forrest Meek Collection

522 North McEwan
W. P. Lewis Cigar Factory (1904)
O. M. Sutherland, Clare, architect; D. J. Fox, builder

The storefront originally had its doorway located at the façade's south end and there was one large plate glass window to the door's north, extending across the front. The door and window both had transoms. The current storefront's brickwork and recessed entry has been in existence since at least 1950, but could date to as early as 1941 when the building was remodeled due to a fire. The east (rear) concrete block part of the building was added in 1952.

This building was constructed in 1904 for William P. Lewis to house his cigar store business. It replaced a wood frame building that was destroyed in a fire in July of the same year. After Lewis' death in January 1913, Bill Adams purchased the cigar store business. In February of the same year the east end of the building was leased to Shumway and Rogers for their barber shop. Jay J. Green began leasing the building in January 1927, and opened the Jay Green Clothing Store for men. William P. Lewis's wife Alphia Lewis sold the building to Clyde Harris in March 1934. Mr. Harris sold the building to Jay J. Green in June 1951, and the business name was changed to the J. J. Green Clothing Shop. The building was deeded to Jay J. Green's son Jay in 1962. He eventually changed the name of the business to Green's Clothing & Shoe. By the late 1980s the business was called Green's Shoes. The building had been used by the Green family for their clothing and shoe store for over sixty years. The early 1990s saw the building being leased to Diane Sadler for her Apple Tree Lane Gift Shop business. Diane Sadler purchased the building from Maxine Green in December 1998. The west end of the building was partitioned off in 2012 for use as barber shop, while the remainder of the building was used for the Second Hand Treasures retail store. Starting in 2015 Maxwell Flowers began using the entire building

CHSY., 1950; 1957; 1964; 1966; 1987; 1988; 1993; S*ent.*, 7/14, 8/11 and 12/2/1904; 1/3 and 2/7/1913

Jay Green's Clothing Store, 1950
Photograph from the 1950 Clare High School Yearbook

524 North McEwan
Doherty Opera House (1890)
Fred Hollister, Saginaw, architect

The section of the façade which contains the second-story windows is the only portion of the building which has not changed since its original construction. Some changes have occurred above and below this section of windows. Originally a balconet was located below the center second story windows. The original parapet had a brick pediment with a flag pole at its peak on the south end capped by a cornice with dentil bed molding extending to the north. The present recessed squares on the parapet were only located below the cornice. Cresting was located on top of the cornice. Below the pediment was a recessed circle with three windows in the lower half and small squares in the upper. The pediment was removed and the present look of the parapet was constructed in 1926. The street level front originally contained two storefronts, each with a center entry flanked by display windows. By 1910 the door to the south unit was located at the south end of the façade. In 1960 a marquee was added, spanning the entire façade and across the south half of the building to the north. By the 1970s the façade had a single door in the center with large plate glass windows on either side of it. The present street level façade was constructed in 2007. Historically the interior of the second story was accessed via a stairway located in the center of the building immediately to the north. The second-story interior retains the appearance it had when the Masons occupied it prior to 1990.

This building was constructed for Alfred J. Doherty. The first floor store units were completed in 1890 and the second floor Opera House was finished in 1891. The Opera House was designed to seat 700 people. The north unit of the first floor was leased to O. S. Derby for his furniture business, while the south unit initially housed the clothing store of H. Razek. In May 1891 Edward A. White was using a portion the Razek store for his jewelry business. In December 1892 S. C. Kirkbride took over the Razek store unit for his dry goods business. Since Kirkbride was also the postmaster for Clare, the post office was also located in his shop. S. C. Kirkbride operated his dry goods store until at least 1897, but it is uncertain when it actually closed. The Post Office stayed in the south unit until 1931 when it was moved to a larger building on East Fourth Street. By the mid-1900s J. E. Doherty's hardware and furniture business was occupying the former Derby store space. By 1911 M. B. Gallagher was using the north unit for his hardware and farm implement business. The process of converting the Opera House to a public meeting place was begun in 1912 and finished in 1914. In January 1931 the Alfred J. Doherty Estate deeded the building to his son Alfred J. Doherty, Jr. At the same time the Masons began using the former Opera House as the city's Masonic Temple. The Kroger Grocery and Bakery Company leased the building's south unit from 1935 to 1939. Sometime after that Mr. and Mrs. Kenneth Cox moved their Clarified Bakery into the south unit. The Coxes sold the bakery to Lon M. Galloway in June 1946, but bought it back in August 1947. In July 1957 Helen Doherty, Alfred J. Doherty Jr.'s wife, sold the building, in two parts: the second story to the Clare Masonic Building Association, and the first to Gay's 5 & 10 Store and Kenneth and Gertrude Cox. Gay's 5 & 10 had been leasing the building prior to their ownership. Gay's 5 & 10 Store purchased the second story from the Masons in October of 1979. Part of the agreement was to lease the second story to the Masons for ten years. The Cox interest in the building was sold in August 1983. The store became part of D & C Stores in the early 1980s and continued in business until the 1990s. James and Evelyn Gay and Richard Gay sold the building to Equity Investment Corporation in June 1992, and Equity Investment sold it to Isabella Bank and Trust in December 1992. In the early 2000s the Stone Soup gift shop leased the building. The Corporate Title business, owned by Isabella Bank, used the building in 2007-08, then moved to Mount Pleasant. The office was vacant for a number of months before Raymond James Financial Services began using the building in 2009. It has since been replaced by Isabella Bank Investment & Trust Services.

CHSY., 1950; 1978; 1989; 1990; *DPress.*, 4/18, 8/15 and 10/3/1890; 5/22/1891; S*ent.*, 12/30/1892; 7/5/1895; 3/30/1906; 6/28/1907; 1/28 and 4/15/1910; 5/7/1913; 1/9/1914; 5/21/1926; 5/17 and 5/31/1935; 8/19/1938; 6/7 and 8/2/1946; 8/8/1947; 7/14/1960; 11/17/1982.

Doherty Opera House
Drawing from the Clare Sentinel
72

532 North McEwan
Clare County Savings Bank (1887)
Fred Hollister, Saginaw, architect; A. A. Shaver, builder

The only area that has changed since its original construction is the first story of the façade and the building's east elevation. The structure originally had cresting at the top of the north and west elevations. The original segmental-arch-head entryway was located in the center of the building's façade. This entryway served both the north and south units of the building and led to a stairway to the second floor. To the south of the entryway was a large plate glass window. To the north of the entryway was a large circular three-over-two window with turned mullions, polychrome header bricks and raised stonework framing it. (See the photograph on page 184) After the 1920s when the bank relocated to 431 North McEwan, this window was removed and replaced with a plate glass window that matched the window on the south unit. The present lower façade and the east elevation were constructed in 1993 after Isabella Bank and Trust purchased the

Charles W. Perry, Clark H. Sutherland, William Wolskey (left to right)
Founders of the Clare County Savings Bank
Photographs from the Forrest Meek Collection

building. The building retains its historic Detroit Safe Company vault door, although not in its original location. The second story retains the rooms used for the Masonic temple.

This building was constructed in 1887 by Alfred J. Doherty. It was designed to house the Clare County Savings Bank in the north unit of the building's first floor, offices to the east side of the bank on the first floor, the Doherty Hardware business in the south unit of the first floor, and offices on the second floor. When Doherty built the Opera House building immediately to the south, access to the Opera House on the building's second floor was gained through the stairway in this building. The unit on the east side of the bank was used as a tailor shop in 1893 and 1894. By 1899 this area was used as an office. Also, in 1893 and 1894 the rear of the hardware store was used for a tin shop. The tin shop was relocated to the second floor above the hardware store before 1899 and continued there until at least 1906. Alfred Doherty sold his interest in the hardware business in 1903 to his sons Frank and Floyd Doherty. Floyd sold his interest to Frank in 1904. In 1907 the bank expanded its office space to include the whole north half of the building's first floor. Prior to 1909 Arthur Lacey's law office was located in this building. In 1909 a law partnership was created between Arthur Lacy and Joseph Bowler. Mr. Bowler would use Arthur Lacy's office and Mr. Lacy would represent the business in the Detroit area. By 1910 the Doherty Hardware Store was replaced by a harness shop, and in 1914 that was replaced by the Roy Joslin Lunchroom. In the winter of 1916 Mr. Joslin operated a seasonal bowling alley in his lunch room. In 1917 the Lunchroom was sold to Ralph Stevens. After the bank moved out in the early 1920s, J. E. Doherty opened his plumbing and undertaking business in the north unit of the first floor; he purchased the building the following year. Ora Dawson moved his cigar factory to the second floor above J. E. Doherty in January 1923. Two months later a fire caused some damage to the building. The Vogue Dress Shop began occupying the west end of the plumbing store space in 1927. The undertaking business was moved to the east end of the building and the plumbing supply store moved to the basement. Sometime before the late 1920s J. E. Doherty was co-owner of the building with Alfred J. Doherty I. After Alfred Doherty's death J. E. Doherty became the sole owner in the early 1930s. The J. E. Doherty & Son business operated here until at least 1943. He eventually sold to Fred Doherty. By the 1950s Clarified Bakery was leasing the first floor south unit. In the late 1950s the building went into foreclosure, and it was purchased by Alfred J. Doherty III in 1960. Harold Hughes Law office was working out of the building in 1959. By the mid-1960s the law firm was changed to Hughes & Trucks. In July 1965 Richard Nivison had taken over the Hughes & Trucks office space. Also in 1965 the Yarn Mart began business here. Lenny's Hair Styling was occupying the building's north unit by 1976. Sometime in the 1980's, D & C Variety store was using the first floor south unit. The building was sold to Isabella Bank and Trust in March 1993 and they occupy the entire first floor. The second story has been vacant since the late 1980s.

Dem., 4/1/1887; *Sent.*, 7/16/1903, 6/2 and 7/21904; 5/31/1907; 6/25/1909; 11/13/1914; 2/19/1915; 1/28 and 3/21/1916; 3/8/1917; 3/31 and 10/7/1921; 1/5 and 2/16/1923; 4/11/1927; 5/17/1935; 7/16/1943; 8/27/1959; 5/16/1963; 2/4, 7/1 and 8/26/1965; 2/18/1976.

604 North McEwan
Doherty Hotel (1922-24)
Clarence Cowles, Saginaw, architect; William J. Morris
Company, Midland, and O. W. Jenkins Company,
contractors; 1965 façade renovations (windows)
Additions: 1947; 1960 (Seiter Brothers, contractors);
1990; 2001.

The original hotel building has seen considerable change since its construction. The areas between the first floor piers had large plate glass windows, with transoms above. By the 1940s the transom windows were covered and by the 1960s the present windows installed. The windows in the upper stories were originally set into the brick façade without the vertical window banks. The second-story windows originally had arched tops, like the one that survives in the center of the south side. The present windows, set in vertical banks of windows with metal panels beneath, were installed in 1965. The middle bank of windows on the building's south elevation shows the window openings as they originally appeared. The stonework below the windows of the original structure where added in 2012 and replaced areas of stucco.

Additions have also been made to the building. The first was a sixteen by twenty-four-foot addition on the building's east side whose construction began at the end of 1924. In 1947 a thirty-five by thirty-foot addition to the building's banquet room, known as the Wedgewood Room, was constructed also on the building's east side. The one-story addition to the north of the original structure was constructed from 2012 to 2013.

In 1960 a separate hotel annex building was constructed to the northeast of the original hotel, and the large marquee sign along McEwan Street was added at the same time. In 1990 the annex was joined with the original hotel by means of a wing containing an indoor pool and thirty-three additional rooms. An additional sixty rooms were added in 2001 to the east and west of earlier additions.

The Hotel Doherty was built by Alfred J. Doherty for the purpose of providing Clare with a high class hotel that would replace the Calkins Hotel that, located on the same site, burned in 1920. Construction started in 1922 by the William J. Morris Company of Midland, but when they could not finish the building within the agreed upon time they were replaced by the O. W. Jenkins Company, who completed the remainder of the construction in 1924. Mr. Doherty served as the hotel's president from 1924 to 1928. The company that owned the hotel was incorporated in 1925. Son Alfred J. Doherty II became president in 1928 and served in that capacity until 1956. In an effort to capitalize on the growing tourist traffic Doherty constructed a set of ten one-story cabins. Also, under his ownership the lunch room which was located in the southwest corner of the building was converted to a cocktail lounge in 1942. The banquet room was enlarged and renamed the Wedgewood Room in 1947. The present neon sign located on the top of the building was installed in 1948. The cocktail lounge was remodeled in 1950 and renamed the Emerald Room. The City Library, which had been located in the northwest corner of the building's first floor since the hotel's opening, was asked to find new quarters in 1950. The space, in the north end of the main floor, was remodeled and became the Early American Room, the hotel's main dining room, in 1951. William Bicknell served as president from 1956 to 1969. During his leadership the hotel was expanded to include a separate annex located to the northeast of the main hotel, along with an outdoor pool. The cabins were torn down at this time to make room for the addition. Alfred J. Doherty III was president from 1969 to 2006. In 1990 he constructed another addition which joined the annex to the rest of the hotel, and added an indoor pool. His sons Dean and James, became co-presidents in 2006 with Dean later becoming sole president. The addition of sixty rooms on the east and west ends of the building, and the 2012 dining room expansion on the north end of the original hotel building complete the present look of the hotel.

Sent., 12/30/1921; 1/13/1922; 4/11 and 9/26/1924; 1/30/1942; 6/20/1947; 4/2/1948; 3/24 and 8/25/1950; 2/16/1951; 10/15/1959; 6/16/1960; 7/8/1965; Alfred J. Doherty III, Interview, 9/30/2009.

Doherty Hotel, 1924
Photograph from the Forrest Meek Collection

622 North McEwan
Dr. Kuno Hammerberg Monument (2002)
Brewer-Bouchey Monument Co., Saint Louis, MI

Sited on an area of red brick paving between the sidewalk and street at the northwest corner of the Hotel Doherty's block long frontage, this is a small black granite bench style monument whose base displays the inscription: IN MEMORY OF/ DR. KUNO HAMMERBERG M.D./ 1901 - 2002. The monument was placed here in honor of Dr. Kuno Hammerberg after his death in 2002.

Dr. Kuno Hammerberg was a much loved family practitioner, who practiced medicine in the Clare area for close to fifty years. Born on July 10, 1901, in Michigan's Upper Peninsula, he came to Clare in 1934 after graduating from Northwestern University Medical School in Chicago. The monument is placed in front of the location were Dr. Hammerberg practiced medicine the entire time he was in Clare. His office was in a wood framed building, originally a house, constructed prior to 1893. By 1899 it housed the Clare Sentinel newspaper. In 1910 it was used for a millinery business, and by 1923 it was a store. Prior to Dr. Hammerberg moving into the building it was used by a plumbing store. Dr. Hammerberg practiced medicine in this building until the 1970s. The building was torn down in 1978.

9/16/2002 Clare City Commission Minutes.

Dr. Kuno Hammerberg Office Building
Photograph from the Forrest Meek Collection

307 North McEwan
Clare Hay, Grain and Bean Company Elevator (1918)

This structure was built in 1918 by Chatterton & Son, and replaced a two-and-a-half-story Clare Hay, Grain & Bean Company grain elevator located on the same site. Chatterton & Son owned the elevator until E. G. Johnston purchased it in 1926 and operated the business under the same name. In 1939 or 1940 the name of the business was changed to the Johnston Hay, Grain & Bean Company. Sometime before 1953 it became the Johnston Elevator. Ed Johnston's son Joe took over the business in 1952, and sold it to the Cutler Dickerson Company in 1987. Gabe and Jonathan Seibt along with John Merillat purchased the grain elevator in 2016.

Sent., 8/8/1918; 5/7/1926; 6/5/1953.

South of Third St.
Great Lakes Central Railroad Crossing

This is a gated railroad crossing at road level. It is unknown when the gates and lights were added to the site, and although the rails, ties and other hardware are not original, the site is located on the original main line of the former Flint & Pere Marquette Railroad, built to Clare in 1870. Sometime between 1906 and 1910 the F & PM was absorbed into the Pere Marquette Railway. In the mid-twentieth century the Chesapeake & Ohio Railroad, later CSX Transportation, took over the railroad's operations. In the early 1990s the Tuscola & Saginaw Bay Railroad took over operations. The Tuscola & Saginaw Bay would change its name to the Great Lakes Central Railroad in the early 2010s.

The original rail line had a single set of tracks, with a combined freight and passenger depot located on the west side of McEwan just to the south of the tracks. The Toledo & Ann Arbor Railroad built to Clare in 1887, intersected the Flint & Pere Marquette tracks just west of the downtown. Where the tracks intersected, a new Union Depot was constructed. The depot at McEwan Street was converted to a freight depot. Sometime between 1884 and 1893 the number of tracks crossing McEwan was increased to three, with the center track being the mainline. The three tracks crossed McEwan until sometime after the mid-1900s when the sidings were removed

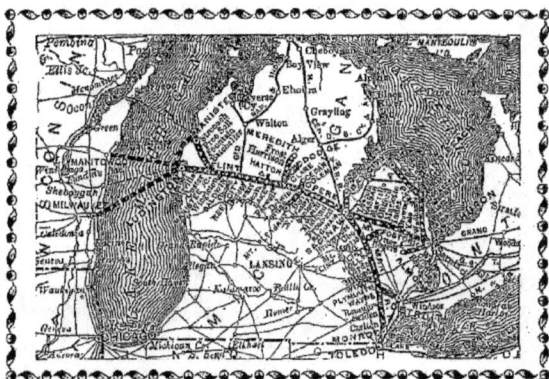

Flint & Pere Marquette Railroad Map
Clare Sentinel, September 4, 1896

leaving only a single set of tracks intersecting Clare's main street. The freight depot south of the tracks was torn down sometime after the middle of the twentieth century.

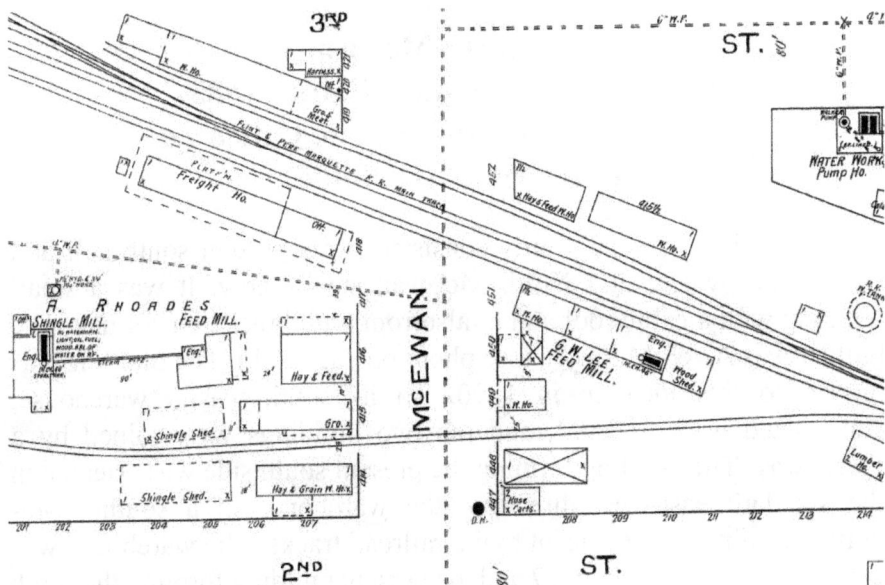

Railroad Crossing at McEwan Street
1894 Sanborn Fire Insurance Map

321 North McEwan
Clare County Savings Bank, (1885)
Michigan Creamery Co. Office
A. W. McIntyre, builder

   This building originally only consisted of its present south half and was located where 524 North McEwan stands now. It was a small building with a gable roof and a falsefront with bracketed cornice. The builder was A. W. McIntyre (see photo on page 158). The building was moved to this location in 1890. To its south was a warehouse, constructed prior to 1893, and the two buildings were joined by a breezeway. The building forming the present south side was oriented in the standard east-west direction, the warehouse in a southeast-to-northwest direction, adjacent to the railroad tracks. The warehouse was torn down after a fire in 1917 and the present building forming the south side stood alone after that. At the time of the fire the building was owned by Alfred J. Doherty, and used by Jay Wyman and Patrick O'Toole for their produce business. An addition forming the north part of the building was made between 1923 and 1934. A red face brick front with plate glass window was added in 1951 along with glass block windows on the south elevation after the building sustained fire damage in the spring of that year. By the 1960s the north part of the building was expanded again. The west addition to the building's north half was constructed at an unknown date.

Michigan Creamery Co. Ad
Clare Sentinel,
May 27, 1910

The south portion of this building was constructed in 1885 by bank owners Perry, Sutherland & Wolsky for use as the Clare County Savings Bank and was located where 524 North McEwan is located now. The building was sold to Albert Van Brunt in February 1887 when the bank relocated to its new location immediately to the north at 532 North McEwan. Van Brunt operated a grocery store out of this building for three years. In 1890 Alfred J. Doherty purchased the lot from Van Brunt in order to build his new opera house. The building was then moved to its present location at 321 North McEwan.

After this it is unclear who owned the building or when ownership changed. Sometime before 1893 the building was connected to a warehouse to the south. In 1893 and 1894 the building was used as a harness shop. In 1899 the building was used as an electrical supply store, and 1906 saw the building functioning as a bean warehouse. In 1909 the Michigan Creamery Company bought this building and the connecting warehouse. This portion of the building was used as the company's office. The building was used as a gasoline filling station in 1923 and continuing into the 1950s. Herb Leonard's D-X Service Station operated here from 1940 to 1949. Aube's Service used the building for a short time at the end of 1949 before Merritt Oil Company's Cities Service opened in 1951 and closed in 1959. The Clare Party Store was opened in 1964 by Mrs. Ruth Nivison. Jon and Vicki Warren, purchased the building from the Tuscola & Saginaw Bay Railway Company in 1994, and continued to operate it as the Clare Party Store. Trackside Market started business here in April 2017.

CCP., 9/26/1884; *CHSY.,* 1966; *Dem.,* 3/4/1887; *DPress.,* 4/4/1890; *Sen.,* 1/22/1909; 8/28/1917; 3/11 and 12/23/1949; 6/5/1951; 10/22/1959; 5/21/1964.

Michigan Ceamery Company, on left, circa 1910
Photograph from the Forrest Meek Collection

**Cities Services
Filling Station,
circa 1955**
*Photograph from the
Robert Knapp
Collection*

Clare Party Store, 1965
*Photograph from the 1965
Clare High School
Yearbook*

405 North McEwan
Beemer's Saloon (1900)

The building's original brick walls were covered with the present steel and wood in 1987. The east front door was originally inset and centered, with two fixed sash windows on either side of it. It was once crowned with a storefront cornice. The present steel siding on the second story is covering two windows on the south elevation and two windows on the façade. Brickwork above the second story windows formed three recessed horizontal rectangles with two recessed circles in between them. A cornice with dentil molding once capped the façade of the building. A one-story addition to the west end of the building was built between 1923 and 1934, but has since been replaced by a concrete block one. Until the 1970s a one-story barber shop abutted the building's south elevation.

This building was constructed by Oliver Beemer in 1900 for his saloon business. Oliver Beemer sold the building to George Benner in January 1911. During the early days of Prohibition, the building was used as a billiards room. Benner sold the building to Floyd Shoup in August 1920, and he converted the building into an ice cream and butter creamery under the name Clare Creamery Company. In the fall of 1925, the Clare Creamery Company relocated to a new building on the northeast corner of Fourth and Beech Streets. Fred Shoup sold the building to John Dionese in February 1927 and Dionese opened a restaurant. In 1935 after Prohibition had ended John Dionese converted his building from a restaurant back to a bar. Since then this building has always been used as a bar. John Dionese deeded his building in September 1938 to Virginia Dionese. Prior to 1950 the building was being used as Bill's Tavern. In 1950 Paul P. Dionese became the new manager, and continued to use the Bill's Tavern name. George's Tavern was operating out of the building in the mid-1960s. The Village Pub replaced George's Tavern in 1985 and continued until 1986. In November 1986 Virginia Hartzler (formerly Virginia Dionese) sold the building to Wilbur and Betty Adams. Gary and Cheryl Ruckle purchased it in April 1987, but began leasing it the year before for their Ruckle's Pier Bar and Grill business. RPYC Investments owned the building starting in September 2000, and continued to operate under the Ruckle's Pier Bar and Grill name.

Sent., 8/10 and 12/7/1900; 9/16/1920; 9/11/1925; 3/18/1927; 7/5/1935; 7/28/1950; 12/15/1966; 8/22/1968; 1/2/1985.

405 North McEwan, circa 1970
Photograph from the Robert Knapp Collection

407 North McEwan
Ramey Building (1926)

The original appearance of the building has changed a few times since its construction. At one point the building had an inset door on the north corner of the façade, while a large fixed sash window filled most of the remainder of the façade's street level. In 1948 the façade was altered to include glass blocks and a brick front. By the 1970s the door had been moved closer to the center and flush with the façade, and a smaller window was located to the south of the door. The present façade was built in 1987.

This building was built by Earnest Ramey in 1926 to replace a diner at this location that was destroyed by a fire in the same year. Ramey sold the building in April 1927 to Roy Joslin, who continued the restaurant business. Burton J. Sanford purchased the building in July 1936. Mr. and Mrs. Joe Murphy purchased the Beagles Café in 1945 and opened Murphy's Café. Ray Menthen purchased Murphy's Café in 1947 and opened Menthen's Café, which operated until 1961. The following year D & L Bar and Café opened and continued until at least 1979. The building was sold to Mary Atwood in December 1977. She owned it until November 1979 when Elizabeth Berrant purchased it. Dani Fuson purchased the building in October 1986 for her Downtown Dani's Restaurant, and was open until at least 1997. Gary and Cheryl Ruckle purchased the building in March 1999 in order to expand their Ruckle's Pier Bar and Grill business which they owned in the building immediately to the south. RPYC Investments, purchased the building in September 2000, and continue to operate under the Ruckle's Pier Bar and Grill name.

Sent., 4/2 and 6/11/1926; 4/8/1927; 7/3/1936; 10/12/1945; 6/6/1947; 10/19/1961; 10/11/1962; 6/13/1979; 16/16/1986; 3/11/1997.

West 400 Block of North McEwan looking northwest
Ramey Building, third building from the left, circa 1970
Photograph from the Forrest Meek Collection

409 North McEwan
Western Auto Store (1957)

Ella Autry built this building in 1957 to replace a building she lost to a fire in January of the same year. She continued her Western Auto Store business in this location. By the early 1970s Mrs. Autry was leasing the building to Louis Montini, who opened the Clare Print and Pulp store. Ella Autry sold the building to Elvin Autry in September 1978. Louis Montini bought it in February 1980. He owned it until Peter Montini purchased it in September 1993. The Clare Print and Pulp store continues to operate here.

Sent., 8/15/1957

415 North McEwan
Downtown Clare Professional Building (1972)

This building has changed very little since its original construction. The only change to the façade is the addition of the window and awning above the door. The window and awning were added at an undetermined time and replaced a plain unornamented panel.

This building was constructed by the 415 Corporation in 1972 for use as an office building. It replaced a building that burned in January 1957. Between 1957 and 1972 the property was used as a parking lot for the Groves Brothers Five and Ten Store immediately to the north. The 415 Corporation owned the building until March 1993 when Barbara Young purchased it. She owned it until September 2005 when the Four Fifteen North McEwan Company, purchased it. The building sat vacant for a number of years. Thomas and Kim Kleinhardt purchased the building in 2015 and opened The Lofts as a mixed-use apartment and office building in 2017.

417 North McEwan
Groves Brothers Five and Ten Store (1957, 1963)
Sanford Mott, contractor

The south two-thirds of the building was built in 1957, the north one-third, with front slightly recessed, in 1963. The original appearance of the building has been altered very little since its construction. The north one-third of the building was added in late 1963 at the same time that the building immediately to the north was constructed. Prior to this the lot where the addition was located served as a parking lot for the surrounding buildings. Originally archways through the side walls connected the addition and the adjacent building to the north. It is unknown when these archways were enclosed. The original awning was flat and showed all the brick work on the parapet. The present pent roof was constructed at an undetermined time. The signage for the Grove Brothers store was located within the framed brick area of the parapet, and consisted of individual letters. The present electric lighted sign was installed in 2003.

This building was constructed in 1957 by James Groves to replace a building at the same location that burned in January of that year. The building initially housed the Groves Brothers Five and Ten Store. James Groves built the north addition to the building in late 1963. By late 1977 George and Betty Graham were leasing the building for their furniture store. In March 1978 James' wife Arlene sold the building to the Grahams. Betty Graham sold it to David and Virgil Graham in December 2007. The Continental Home Center began operating out of this building in 2003.

CHSY., 1960; 1964; *Sent.*, 4/25/1957; 10/31/1963.

Doherty Building, circa 1920
Located at 411-425 North McEwan
Burned by fire in 1957
Photograph from the Robert Knapp collection

425 North McEwan
Gambles Store (1963)

This building was built as an addition to the Gambles store located next door to the north and originally had no separate front entrance. The windowed façade then had a projecting flat-top canopy in common with the building to the north (427). In the original construction there were interior openings to the buildings both to the north and south.

The present storefront was constructed in 1984 when a separate store first occupied this building only. At the same time a firewall was constructed separating this building and the building to the south. The opening connecting 425 and 427 to the north was also closed at some point, but it was reopened in 2012 when Ray's Bike Shop began using both buildings. A wooden log awning covering the entire upper façade above the windows was constructed in 2007 but removed in 2012. The current windows and doors and the shed-roof extension on the west elevation date from 2012.

This building was constructed in 1963 by Roy N. Beltinck at the same time as the addition to the building to the south (a previous building burned in 1957, and the site served as a parking lot until the present building was constructed). It initially housed an extension of the Gambles store located in the building to the immediate north (427). Roy N. Beltinck's wife Marion transferred ownership of the building to her sons James, Roy J., and Charles Beltinck in March 1969. James and Charles later sold their interest in the building to Roy J. Beltinck, and Roy sold the building to Emerson Hampton in June 1980. By the mid-1980s Charles and Martha Stuckert were operating a furniture store out of this building. Emerson's wife Eileen Hampton sold the building to Charles and Martha Stuckert in August 1984. In 1984 The Stuckerts were running a Montgomery Ward store in this building, but the following year had changed to Stuckert's Home Decorating Center. The Stuckerts sold to Roger and Emily Chase in July 1996. The Chases owned the building until September 1996, when they sold it to William and Pamela Wilson, who operated the Wilson Decorating Center. The property was deeded to Pamela Loar Wilson, and by December 2003 Joe Perras and Pamela Loar-Perras owned the building. Red Hook Properties purchased the building from Joe Perras in September 2007, and the building then housed Artistic Engraving and Marketing. This business closed and the building sat vacant for a number of years. It was sold to Oberloier Smith Properties Inc. in April 2012, and in the same year Ray's Bike Shop began using the building.

Sent., 10/31/1963; 11/14/1984; 12/11/1985; 7/9/1996; 11/5/1996.

Gambles Store in center, circa 1970
Photograph from the Forrest Meek Collection

427 North McEwan
Dawson Building (1890)

The storefront and lower façade reflects extensive renovations dating from 1947, 1957, and later. The present storefront doors and windows were installed in 2012. The rest of the second-story front is clad in vertical metal sheeting installed in 2002.

The present configuration of the storefront was the result of remodeling work done by Roy Beltinck in 1947. The original street level contained a center inset door with large windows on either side. Much of the present appearance of the building is the result of repairs made to the building due to damages sustained when the building to the south was destroyed by fire in 1957. An earlier fire in 1912 caused interior damage to the building, but did not damage the façade. The original façade had a storefront cornice below the existing sillcourse. The second-floor front windows had rounded brick caps with keystones. Also, even with the tops of the windows was a rough cut stone stringcourse. The façade was capped with an ornate cornice with decorative modillions. The partition walls on the second story were removed in 1896, and the entire floor was converted to a hall. The one-story twenty by twenty-four foot addition to the west end of the building was added in 1936.

427 North McEwan, circa 1945
Photograph from the Robert Knapp Collection

This building was built by George Dawson in 1890 for his saloon business. Dawson sold to William Wolsey in February 1897. As of May 1899 the store space housed a grocery. James Duncan bought the building in September 1899 and continued the grocery store business. He ran the second-story hall as Duncan Hall for dancing and social gatherings. Some time prior to 1906 Mr. Duncan closed the grocery store and opened a saloon, but in 1909 he converted it back to a grocery store. In May 1912 A. W. Thorpe leased the building and purchased Duncan's grocery stock. Earl Foss leased the building beginning in 1930, and opened a bakery. This was the third bakery opened in the city at that time. In 1936 the Clare Auto Parts Company occupied the newly erected addition on the west end of the building. Michael Chiaoutis and Peter Theodoris opened their Rainbow Grill here in 1939, and closed it the following year. After forty-two years of ownership the building was sold to Emery McLaughlin by the James Duncan Estate in July 1941. Emery McLaughlin sold the building to Roy N. Beltinck in February 1944. Roy Beltinck was the owner of the Gambles store, and had been operating out the building starting in 1941. Beltinck sold the Gambles business to Emerson Hampton in 1967. Mr. Hampton ran the Gambles store until he closed it in 1976. The following year he opened an Ace Hardware Store here. That business closed two years later. The building was deeded to James, Roy J., and Charles Beltinck by Marion Beltinck in February 1969. James and Charles sold their interest in the building to Roy J. Beltinck at an unknown date, and Roy sold the building to Emerson Hampton in June 1980. By the mid-1980s Charles and Martha Stuckert were operating a furniture store out of this building. Your Putting Us On Custom Sportswear was using the building from 1987 to 1898. Just Kidding childrens clothing store was here in 1990. T. I. Investments leased the building from 1992 to 1994. The following year Rock Road Express computerized engraving and photo imaging was here and occupied the building until mid-1997. Emerson Hampton's wife Eileen sold the building to Charles and Martha Stuckert in June 1996. The Stuckerts sold the building to Roger and Emily Chase in July 1996. Roger moved his Photographic Reverie & Framing business here in 1997, from the building at 104 West Fifth, and operated it until at least 1999. The Chases sold it to Bradley and Brittney Humphrey in November 2003. McEwan Street Real Estate purchased the building from the Humphreys in October 2007. The building was sold to Oberloier Smith Properties Inc. in June 2012, and in the same year Ray's Bike Shop began using the building.

Cour., 9/25/1896; *DPress.*, 4/11/1890; 9/2/1890; *Sent.*, 5/14/1909; 5/10/1912; 4/28/1939; 5/16/1941; 3/28/1942; 4/25/1947; 4/25/1957; 11/24/1987; 5/30/1989; 2/6/1990; 8/18/1992; 11/21/1995; 6/3 and 6/10/1997; 7/6/1999.

429, 431 North McEwan
Clare County Savings Bank (1922)
Cowles & Mutscheller, Saginaw, architects
W. J. Morris, Midland, contractor

This building was originally designed for use as a bank and had a vault form. An October 28, 1921, *Clare Sentinel* article describes the interior of the building as follows:

> Upon entering the building from Main Street we come into the entrance lobby 6x18 feet. After closing the outside door we encounter two more in this space, the first being an iron gate in the center and another door in entering the public lobby. At the left is a door which leads to the president's office, also the stairs leading to the offices above. At the right of this will be located the consultation room, but no entrance to this can be made from the lobby. As we pass to the public lobby we find a room 45x50 feet

with 22 foot ceilings. To the right is the office of the cashier, while just beyond to the west is the working space of the employees, enclosed with counters artistic gratings. To the left of these is a large spacious space in the center of which will be desks and supplies to the accommodation of the patrons. The desks and counters of this room will be of a pink Tennessee marble as well as four foot of wainscoting. Above this the walls will be finished in a unique panel effect. The floors of the entire building will be of terrazzo covered with linoleum in working places. Back of the public lobby and in the center we find the large vault which extends from the basement up to about 11 feet above the main floor, the basement section to be used for storing valuable papers of the bank. The upper part which opens to the main floor is divided in two sections the north half will be used for depositing money and the south for safety deposit boxes. The entire vault will be burglar proof. To the left of the vault will be found a ladies room at the rear of which is the toilet and storage rooms, while to the right and back of the vault is the customer's room. To the right of the vault the room serves as a passage to the locker and toilet rooms of the bank and the stairway to upper rooms. Here will be situated the directors' room and a small store room for supplies. These will face the public lobby to the east and fitted with pivot swinging windows. The same dark walnut finish will be carried out in these offices.

The building's Neoclassical front was largely rebuilt in 1939. Originally the central third of the façade was recessed and the central entry with its console bracket-supported flat-top classical lintel flanked by terra cotta-clad Ionic columns that ran up to the entablature. Above the entry was a triple-unit window. The columns on either side of the recess adjoined a broad slightly projecting pier on either side, and there was a similar pier at each outer corner of the façade. Shallow recesses between the piers on either side each contained a double window in the

Clare County Savings Bank, circa 1925
Photograph from the Forrest Meek Collection

ground and second stories of the same dimensions as the existing windows around the corner on the north façade, the second-story ones capped by the same ornamental terra cotta panels as the surviving ones on the north elevation. The north elevation's second-story windows in the recessed central section were much longer than the present windows, their sills located nearly at the level of the sills of the present low ground-story windows. A four-sided clock was added to the northeast corner of the building in 1929 but removed in the 1960s (in 2013 a reproduction of the 1929 clock was placed in its original location on the northeast corner of the building). The set of four triple windows on the second- story façade were added and the windows on the north elevation shortened when the building was remodeled in 1939. During this remodeling the street-level front was rebuilt with plate glass windows across the entire façade of the building and an inset door in the center. All the windows on the façade and north elevation were replaced with vinyl windows in 1993. The EIFS on the street level façade was added in 2006. The large plate glass windows on the façade had been removed prior to this at an unknown date. The building's second story retains a portion of the original egg-and-dart cornice and plaster medallions from the bank's interior. The basement also contains the Diebold vault door from the building's banking days.

This building was built by the Clare County Savings Bank in 1922 to house their bank business. The property was purchased in 1913 and the bank planned to start construction 1915. Architectural plans were drawn at this time by Cowles & Mutscheller (Clarence Cowles and George Mutscheller) of Saginaw, but the rising cost of building materials caused the delay in construction. The bank fell into receivership during the Depression and was deeded to the receiver, Allen Graham, in 1932. In December 1937 Isaiah Leebove, chairman

Kroger Grocery Store, circa 1940
Photograph from the Robert Knapp Collection

of the board of the Mammoth Producing and Refining Corporation, purchased the building from Graham. Leebove was murdered at the Doherty Hotel in May 1938 and the property was acquired by Mammoth Producing and Refining in September of the same year. Two months later Cornelius Wood purchased the building. Remodeled, it then housed a Kroger grocery store. In 1948 the building was leased to Marvin Witbeck for his Witbeck IGA grocery store. Marvin Witbeck leased the building for about ten years. From the early 1950s to at least

1960 a bowling alley was operating in the building's second floor. Witbeck's IGA moved in 1961 to a larger new building on the north end of Clare. Fellers Department Store later leased the building. The south unit was used by the Butcher Shop in the mid-1960s, while at the same time Worldtronic used the north unit for an occupational training school. Michigan Bell occupied the entire first floor from September 1966 to 1980. After the death of Mr. Wood, the owner since 1938, the property was deeded to his son, Cornelius Wood Jr., in July 1977. The second story of the building was used by Western Auto Assoc., as a second location for their store, from 1967 to 1971, Then by Deborah Lynn's Department Store in 1972, and Green's Bargain Center in 1974.

After Michigan Bell moved out of the first floor the south unit was used by the Custom T-Shirt and Garment Shop in 1981, Your Putting Us On from 1982 to 1986, David Allen's AAA office in 1989, the Leprechaun's Gift & Gadget store in 1990, Susan Koch's New Horizons Travel Agency from 1992 to 1996, Manpower in 1998, and the Clare Chamber of Commerce from 1999 to 2014. After the Chamber of Commerce, the south unit was first used by Wells Fargo Investors and then Brad Martin's State Farm Insurance Agent office.

The north unit of the first floor, after Michigan Bell move, was first used by the Aadvark hobby shop. By 1983, Suzanne James Flowers was sharing the store space with the Aardvark. This arrangement existed until the mid-1980s. Your Putting Us On moved from the south unit to the north unit from 1988 to 1989. The Design Spectre interior design business run by Tina Benchley was opened in 1989 and lasted for one year. Since then the Superior Title & Settlement Agency has been occupying the north unit.

Ronald and Barbara Kunse purchased the building in September 1990. In September 2004 the F.A.C.E. (Facing Alcohol Concerns through Education), purchased the property from the Kunses, and occupied the second story. The Clare County Review newspaper used the second story until 2020.

Sent., 3/14/1913; 8/20/1915; 5/4/1916; 10/28/1921; 7/28/1922; 12/10/1937; 12/9/1938; 6/2/1939; 5/7/1948; 12/18/1953; 12/1/1960; 12/7/1961; 9/30/1965; 2/10, 4/28 and 9/29/1966; 11/23/1967; 3/10/1971; 2/2/1972; 4/3/1974; 9/19/1979; 5/14/1980; 8/5/1981; 11/17/1982; 11/7/1984; 3/27/1985; 11/18/1986; 9/27/1988; 5/2 and 8/8/1989; 3/13 and 9/18/1990; 8/25/1992; 6/4/1996; 7/21/1998; 11/16/1999; Gerry Witbeck, Interview, 11/11/2009.

501 North McEwan
Davy and Company Store (1904)
George Barrus, Loomis, foundation
Bovey and Wood, Mount Pleasant, brickwork

This building still retains much of its original appearance, although some changes have occurred. The ten-foot deep entry recess was built, and the entire interior of the building reconstructed after a 1926 fire. The panels covering the transom windows were installed sometime in the late 1960s or early 1970s. A display case on the south elevation was added in 1914, and the windows on that side were bricked up in the 1960s.

This building was constructed in 1904 for Lew E. and Vernal R. Davy for their Davy & Company dry goods and clothing business. This building stands on the site of a wood building at the McEwan/Fourth corner and also includes what was the south third of an older building immediately to the north as its north half. Lew E. Davy was the manager of Clare Davy & Company store here, while his brother Vernal managed the company's Reed City store. In 1910 John H. Wilson bought an interest in Davy & Company and it became the Wilson and Davy Company, selling the same line of goods as previous. In 1924 Lew and Vernal Davy purchased the stock of the Wilson and Davy Company and changed the name to Davy's. At the same time F. L. Fleming purchased Wilson and Davy's shoe department and started the Fleming Shoe Company in the basement of Davy's building. Fleming's Shoe Store operated in this building until it closed in 1962. Vernal Davy sold his interest in the building to his brother Lew in January 1925. A fire in 1926 gutted the building but left the exterior standing. Except for changes to the entrance the newly remodeled building continued to look the same on the outside. Glen C. Folkert purchased the building and business from the Davy Estate in October 1963 and opened the Clare location of his Mill End Stores chain. The building and business were deeded to Folkert's daughters, Deirdre Folkert and Jacklyn Fairbairn, in December 1989. The Mill End Store business closed in 2009. The Venue at 501 has been using the building as an event space since 2015.

Sent., 12/24/1903; 5/26 and 12/2/1904; 11/19/1909; 2/11/1910; 8/21/1914; 9/22/1922; 1/8 and 3/12/1926; 2/3/1939; 11/22/1962; 9/12/1963.

Davy and Company, 1904
Photograph from the Forrest Meek Collection

505, 509 North McEwan
Mussell/Elden Building (1895)
Designed by architect (unnamed) from Saginaw

The present south storefront underwent a major remodeling in 2008 that brought its appearance back to something similar to the original. The oriele window above it lacks the ornamental cresting it once displayed. The north storefront was rebuilt in its present form in 1957; prior to that it looked very similar to the present appearance of the south unit. In 1957 the second story oriel window in the north half was removed for safety reasons. An outside stairway leading to the basement on McEwan Street was removed in 1920. The building retains its Gardner Elevator Company freight elevator, which is located in the building's southwest corner. Both the north and south halves' first story retain their pressed metal ceilings.

The building was constructed in 1895 as a joint effort between Lew Davy, Robert Mussell, and William Elden. The local newspaper noted the plans for the building were by a Saginaw architect, but did not list the name. The building was originally three storefronts in length, but the southern unit owned by Lew Davy was renovated and combined with his new building to the south in 1904. It was originally intended to be three stories in height, and another unit to the north was planned by Ed White but both never came to be. The present south unit was built by Robert Mussell for use as his drug store, which he relocated from the third building to the north. Robert's wife Anna operated the drug store for many years after Robert's death in 1902. By 1912 Forest Shumway

Robert Mussell Drug Store Storefront, circa 1900
Photograph from the Forrest Meek Collection

was operating a barber shop in the basement of this unit. After about thirty-three years of business which started at 515 N. McEwan, Mrs. Anna Mussell sold the drug store business in 1916 to Floyd Kirkpatrick. A fire in March 1917 gutted the interior of this unit of the building, but it was rebuilt and in use before the summer of the same year. Anna Mussell reacquired the drug store from Floyd Kirkpatrick at the end of the year 1931. Anna Mussell sold her drug store business to E. H. Wright in April 1936. In May 1946 Roy Cimmerer purchased the drug store business from Mr. Wright and the part of the building housing it from Anna Mussell and opened his Economy Drug Store. Roy Cimmerer owned the store until 1976 when his son Robert and Robert's wife Gayle Cimmerer took over operation of the business. Robert Cimmerer obtained this part of the building in 1983 after his mother's death. Roy's Economy Store closed in 1983 and was replaced by Cimmerer's Pharmacy. Folkerts Coffee Creations purchased this part of the building in December 2007, and Deidre Folkert purchased it in June 2008. Coffee Talk 505 opened in 2009 but closed in 2012. After being vacant for a short time the Revive coffee shop used the south unit of the building. Heart of Michigan Café opened in 2015, and the name was changed to 505 Café in 2019.

The north section of the building was constructed at the same time as the other two units for William Elden to house his bazaar store. The 1917 fire in the Mussell section burned the roof of this part as well and resulted in extensive water damage. Thomas Holbrook leased this part of the building for his bazaar business prior to the fire and continued after. In the late 1920s the Red Front Cash and Carry Store was located here. By 1929 Fred Morgan was operating his store under the Your R Grocer name. The following year the name was changed to The Food Store and then again to The Food Shop. William Elden continued to own this north section until June 1934 when he sold to his son Norris Elden. Elden sold it in November 1947 to Frances Ellen Hall, Mary Morgan and Anne Marie Danielson. Fred Morgan passed away in 1940, and his son Robert and Robert's wife Mary took over the operation of the store. Morgan Grocery closed in September 1948. In October of the same year Household Appliance Company, owned by James Wood, was leasing the unit. It is unknown when Anne Marie Danielson and Mary Morgan sold their interest in the unit, but Frances Ellen Hall and her husband John sold it in 1953 to A. J. and Helen Doherty II. A. J. Doherty III inherited this part of the building from Helen in March 1957. The Houshold Appliance Company moved out in 1972 and was replaced by the Little Miss & Master Shoppe. The store was next occupied by Mandy's Discount Fabric which opened in February 1974. In the mid-1980s the Mill End Store, located at 501 North McEwan, expanded its business here and sold shoes until the 1990s. Doherty sold the building to Deirdre Folkert in June 2008. Spider Submissions Gymnasium began leasing the second story of the building in 2009, but vacated it the year after. In 2012 Made with Loving Hands Arts and

Craft Consignment Shop became the sole occupant of the north unit of the building, and was later replaced by the Pere Market gift shop. Amanda Steffke Photography opened here in December 2019.

The photographer L. C. Hulbert in May 1914 took over the photography studio of M. W. Cartwright, but it is unknown which part of the building they occupied. From November 1898 to November 1907 Thurston Undertaking was located on the second floor of the north part. Courier Printing was located in the west end on the second story's south part. When Thurston Undertaking moved out in 1907, the dentist Dr. H. E. Neeland occupied their old office. Later Dr. Sanford and Dr. McKnight also had offices in the second story. The Upper Rooms Sleep Suites was opened in 2019 in the second floor.

Sent., 2/22, 3/15, 8/23 and 8/30/1895; 11/15/1907; 8/16/1912; 5/8/1914; 6/20 and 7/20/1916; 3/22 , 5/24 and 7/19/1917; 8/26/1920; 9/17/1926; 9/28/1928; 3/1/29; 8/11/1930; 2/20 and 12/4/1931; 11/15/1935; 5/1/1936; 5/28/1937; 9/17/1948; 4/11/1957; 11/15/1972; 7/20/1973; 1/30/1974; 5/30 and 9/26/1984; 7/24/1990.

Roy's Economy Drug Store, circa 1970
Photograph from the Mary Ann Shurlow Collection

511 North McEwan
White Jewelry Store (1887)

The building was built in a manner that a second story could eventually be added. Joining the building with the Davy/Mussell/Elden building to the south and adding a second story were planned in 1895. This was not done, but instead a ten-foot addition was built on the west end of the building in the same year. Another one-story addition on a concrete slab was constructed between 1910 and 1923. This addition was half the width of the building and was located west of the south end of the building's west side. The building received a final addition sometime after 1934 that brought its west and north sides out to the present dimensions. The present upper front façade with its pent roof was constructed in 1965.

This building was built in 1887 by Ed White to house his jewelry business. White sold his jewelry business to M. D. Ellis in April 1905, but then bought it back from Ellis in July of the next year. Ed's son Carl joined him in the business in December 1913, the business name becoming White and Son. In August 1916 Ed White sold his jewelry business to Cyrus Mummon, who signed a five-year lease on the building. The building was sold to Frank and Margaret McKnight in September 1925. The Clare Electric Company was using the building at the end of the 1920s. In the early 1930s the Gas Corporation of Michigan was leasing the building. The Johnson Electric Shop occupied the building in the mid-1930s. From 1937 to 1941 the Gambles Store was using the store front. In May 1941 Dr. Frank McKnight moved his dental practice here from the second story of the building immediately to the south. The building was remodeled after the death of Dr. McKnight, and in March 1965 Barb Krell opened Barb's Infant and Gift Shop. Margaret McKnight sold the building to Barb and Robert Krell in July 1966. By 1972 the property had been foreclosed on. Kenneth and Patricia Jones purchased it in October 1973. Cloze N-Stuff Women's Apparel operated in the building from 1974 to the early 1990s. The Joneses owned the building until August 1994 when they sold it to Sandra Bailey. Edward, Ramona, and Linda Prichkaitis purchased the building in April 1996 for their "Main Street" location of their Drapery Boutique business. The Prichkaitises owned it until November 2007, when they sold to Lawrence and Linda Witbeck for their Radio Shack store. The business was sold to Chris Lewis in 2015, and later renamed Clare Electronics.

CHSY., 1967; 1975; 1989-1991; *Dem.*, 3/11/1887; *Sen.*, 2/22 and 6/14/1895; 4/21/1905; 7/6/1906; 12/26/1913; 6/1/1916; 4/26 and 11/29/1929; 11/7/1933; 4/5/1935; 12/24/1936; 2/25/1938; 3/28/1941; 3/11 and 6/10/1965; 11/29/1972; 7/16/1975; 10/2/1990; 4/16/1996; 10;19/1999.

Barb's Infant and Gift Shop
After the 1965 remodeling
Photograph from the Clare
Sentinel, June 10, 1965

513 North McEwan
Bogardus Building (1916)

The building front was substantially altered around 1965 when the stonework and present display windows were installed. The present entry occupies its historic location at the façade's north end. The interior retains its original pressed metal ceiling with egg-and-dart molding. Concealed by the canvas awning in the upper façade is concrete lettering that spells out "S BOGARDUS" in the center of the dark brick.

This building was constructed in 1916 by Simon Bogardus for his grocery store business. Bogardus operated his store for an unknown time, and then his son-in-law N. L. Tibbils operated a jewelry store here until 1941. In August 1941 Consumers Power Company began leasing the building. Eva Bogardus deeded the building to her daughter Hilda Tibbils in August 1945. Howard Evert leased the building for his jewelry business beginning in November 1957, after Consumers Power vacated the building. Howard Evert purchased the building from Hilda Tibbils in December 1965, installing the present stone front. Lawrence

Evert obtained the property in August 1974, and continued the Everts Jewelry business. Rodger Hicks, continued the jewelry business under the Hicks Jewelers name. He purchased the building in November 1987, but leased it starting in 1982.

CHSY., 1964; 1975; 1980; 1994; *Sent.*, 6/1 and 6/28/1916; 8/1/1941; 11/28/1957; 1/6/1982.

Everts Jewelers, 1958
Photograph from the 1958 Clare High School Yearbook

515 North McEwan
C. B. Wood Building (1942)

This building was constructed by Dr. C. B. Wood in the spring of 1942. Mammoth Producing Corporation was the first business to lease the building in 1942. Michigan Consolidated Gas operated out of this building from 1944 to 1964. Russ's Record Shop was leasing the building from 1965 to 1995. The property was deeded to Winston and Neil Wood in September 1990. The Woods sold to Rose Coon in August 1993, then sold to Robert Coon and Patricia Tyler in September 1996. The building was sold to Kenneth Plonski and Brenda Harshman in October 1996, for their Bluebird Café & Deli, but then deeded back to Coon and Tyler in November 2001. Mary Faith Lund bought the building in February 2002 and sold it to James Grawey in August 2005. In August 2005 Debra Gadberry purchased the building. In the mid-2000s the building was being used by Rustic Creations, and prior to that Fantastique Bridal and Formal Wear store was operating here. Thomas and Kim Kleinhardt, purchased the building in May 2009. The

Kleinhardts opened their 515 Gallery in late 2010. A highly decorative colored glass tile mosaic was added to the building's west elevation in 2012.

CHSY., 1972; *Sent.*, 7/3/1942; 7/4/1944; 12/3/1964; 8/19/1965; 7/18/1995; 12/17/1996; 3/18/1997; 5/22/1970.

OPEN
FOR BUSINESS
in our new location
515 McEwan St. Clare
(Formerly Mich. Consolidated Gas Office)

Watch For **Grand Opening**
(Coming soon)

RUSS COON WILL DEVOTE FULL TIME TO OPERATIONS AT THIS NEW LOCATION

RUSS' RECORD SHOP
515 McEwan St. Clare

Russ's Record Shop
Advertisement
Clare Sentinel,
August 19, 1965

Experience a taste of Old World Charm in downtown Clare!

Bluebird
Cafe & Deli

Bakery • Cafe
Specialty Foods

Coffee & Donut 99¢

★ DAILY SPECIALS
★ HOMEMADE SOUPS & BREADS
★ FINEST IMPORTED MEATS
★ FRESH BAKED GOODS DAILY

The Finest Gourmet Beverages
ESPRESSO • CAPPUCCINO
TEA ASSORTMENT

515 N. McEwan, Clare • 386-4914
INSIDE SEATING AVAILABLE OR CARRYOUT

Bluebird Café & Deli
Advertisement
Clare Sentine,l January 14, 1997

517 North McEwan
Lossing Building (1886)

The original building on this site had two stories. In 1886 the two-story building was moved back to the west and a new one-story front section added to the east facing McEwan Street. This façade had a similar appearance to the building immediately to the south at that time. It had an inset center doorway with angled glass windows extending out on both sides of the door and display windows to either side. The front had transom windows above the door and windows, and a dentil cornice above the transom windows. Sometime between 1906 and 1910 the two-story section of the building was either lowered to or replaced by a one-story structure. The façade was altered in 1947 to look as it appears in the photograph on page 119. An opening to the building to the north was constructed in the winter of 2012. The façade of the building was altered in 2016 to resemble more of the pre-1947 look of the building.

The original building on this site could have been built as early as 1871. It was a two-story building that was later moved to the west and the present one-story structure added to it in 1886. This one-story section was added while Dorothy Lossing owned the building. Ed White leased the building for his jewelry business in 1886, but then moved to his new building three doors to the south the next year. Mrs. Lossing owned the building until February 1888 when she sold it to Martha Mason. In July 1889 Martha Mason sold the building to Theo Boge for his shoe and boot repair business. Theo Boge left Clare in October 1891, selling the building to Edward Waller in February 1894. Between 1891 and 1914 the building housed a shoe repair shop. D. Crouse ran the shop in 1905-07, and William Lange from then until 1914. Edward Waller sold the building to Allen E. Mulder in August 1905. Thomas Lynch purchased the building from Mulder in May 1914 and owned it until May 1916 when he sold to Arthur Dorney. Dorney sold the building to James Bicknell in August 1919. Bicknell owned the building for eight months, selling it in April 1920 to Jonathan Jones, who sold it twenty days later to Thomas Holbrook. Prior to Thomas Holbrook's purchase W. F. Broderick was leasing the building. Mr. Holbrook moved his bazaar business here from the Mussell/Elden Building four doors to the south. The Ruth Belle Beauty Shop was operating here in the early 1940s, but would be replaced by the American Beauty Shop by 1947. In 1947 Bliss and Fisher opened The Vogue Dress Shop in the east end of the building, while the American Beauty Shop operated in the west end. Mr. and Mrs. Floyd Rosier bought The Vogue Dress Shop in July 1949. They sold in July 1953 to Mr. and Mrs. Wayne Spenny, who continued the ladies apparel business. The Vogue Dress Shop closed in December 1954, and the store was replaced by Jean's Dress Shop in 1955. Jean's Dress Shop owned by Jean Makin, was operating in the building until early 1958. Thomas Holbrook's wife Cora sold the building in January 1958 to Donald and Octavia Jones. By April of the same year Jones Floor Covering was operating out the building, and continued until 1984. Jackson Mair purchased the building in December 1982 and owned it until April 1992 when it was purchased by John Seibt. At the same time ownership of the building transferred to Willard Bell. Glory Be ladies fashion was operating from 1985 to 1986. The Helium Connection was open in 1986 and 1987. In 1988 Wee Pets 'N Things used the building. Karen's Bridal Gallery and Boutique leased the building from the late 1980s to the early 1990s. In May 1994 Willard Bell transferred ownership back to John Seibt, The next month Victor and Patty Lemm purchased the building. The Hometown Variety store operated out of the building from about 1994 until at least 1999. Aaron Lund bought the building in March 2001, and sold it to Meng Mei Wong and Ling Li Wong in October 2003 for their Panda Chinese Restaurant. The Cops and Doughnuts Bakery purchased the building in December 2011 and began using it in the winter of 2012 for the restaurant part of the business. It has since been changed to sell gifts and apparel.

CPress., 4/29/1887; *CHSY.*, 1960; 1971; 1989; 1993; *Dem.*, 12/31/1886; *DPress.*, 10/2/1886; *Sent.*, 2/22/1907; 2/10/1913; 2/27/1914; 6/3 and 6/24/1920; 11/12/1943; 10/10/1947; 2/20/1948; 7/8/1949; 7/10/1953; 12/9/1954; 2/10 and 6/2/1955; 7/18/1957; 1/9, 4/3 and 4/24/1958; 5/2/1984; 8/21/1985; 3/11 and 3/25/1986; 4/28/1987; 3/8/1988; 1/17/1989; 8/8/1992; 10/25/1994; 11/23/1999.

American Beauty Shop/Vogue Dress Shop, circa 1950
Photograph from the Robert Knapp Collection

521 North McEwan
Foss Bakery (1907)
Clark and Son, builders

The building's second-story front still appears as it did when it was originally constructed. The original street level façade had recessed entries at the north and south ends, with plate glass windows between, and transom windows above. In 1922 a twenty-five by thirty-five foot addition was constructed on the west end of the building. The present street-level storefront was constructed in 1961. In 2009 an opening was created to the building immediately to the north, and an additional opening was constructed to the building to the south in 2012. The building retains its historic freight elevator, an American Radiator Company coal burning boiler, and about thirty pieces of historic bakery equipment.

This building has always contained a bakery. It was constructed in 1907 for J. E. Foss' bakery business. In March 1941 the sons of Jennie Foss (J. E. Foss's wife), Earl and Ernest Foss, took over the operation of the business and ownership of the building. Earl sold his interest in the building in December 1959. Charles Palshan purchased the business from Mr. and Mrs. Ernest Foss in March 1965. Ernest Foss had been involved in the operations of the bakery since 1916. Charles Palshan and his wife Maxine leased the building from 1965 until August 1986 when they purchased it. They sold it in April 1991 to Kenneth Mackenzie. Mitzi Mitchell purchased the building from Mackenzie in May 2001 and owned it until March 2006 when she sold to Antoinette Jablonski. In July 2009 Jablonski leased the building to a group of nine Clare city police officers, who changed the name from Clare City Bakery (which it had been called since at least 1896) to the Cops & Doughnuts Bakery. Cops & Doughnuts, purchased the building in August 2010.

Sent., 8/30, 11/1 and 12/6/1907; 10/27/1922.

517, 521 and 523 North McEwan Street (left to right), circa 1970s
Photograph from the Forrest Meek Collection

523 North McEwan
Rhoades Block (1908)
E. B. Gorr, Clare, architect; William Holbrook, Clare, masonry; Geek Brothers, Clare, contractors

This building appears almost exactly as it did when it was originally constructed, the only difference being the absence of the balustrade and ornamentation on the top of the facade. These were taken down sometime in the late 1930s or early 1940s. The twenty by twenty-four foot addition was constructed on the west end of the building in 1949. The north side of the building was bricked over after the Dunlop Building to the north burned in the 1970s. In 2009 an opening was created through the walls of this building and the building immediately to the south. The building retains its original metal ceiling. The basement's east wall shows the bricked over opening which once was the coal chute located on McEwan Street.

523 North McEwan Storefront, circa 1930s
Photograph from the Robert Knapp Collection

The pressed metal ceiling was a product of the Eller Manufacturing Company of Canton, Ohio, and its components are listed as being Colonial in style (with one exception) in the company's 1910 catalog. The ceiling is formed from the following components: Cove model No. 1813, with what appears to be Inside Leaf No. 51 and Mitre Leaf No. 51 ½ at angles; Panel No. 432, twenty-four by twenty-four inches; Panel No. 433, twelve by twenty-four inches, and Panel No. 434, twelve by twelve inches; and Gothic Filler No. 855 around the edges next to the cove.

This building was constructed in 1908 by Andrew Rhoades for the purpose of housing his grocery store business. It replaced a wood frame building that was destroyed by fire in 1907. Mr. Rhoades operated his grocery store until December 1917. The following month B. H. Demarest leased the building for his Demarest Cash Bargain Store. In December 1920 Andrew Rhoades sold the building to William Bicknell, who owned it until 1968. From 1931 to 1939 the Chaffee Grocery was operating here. In June 1939 Lyle Smith leased the building for his Modern Food Market business, in April 1941 Murl Houghton for his Houghton Drug Store business, and in July 1965 Charles Clark for his Clark Drugs business. William Bicknell sold the building to Edward Hardy in April 1968 and he owned it until November 1976 when he sold to Charles Clark. Downtown Drugs was leasing the building in 1982 and operated well into the 1990s. William Barz purchased the building in December 1984 and Kevin Stevens bought it in April 2008 for his Kevin's Carpet business. This business closed the same year and the building was deeded back to William Barz. In August 2009 the Cops and Doughnuts business, which is located in the building immediately to the south, purchased the building, and is used for its dine in customers.

CHSY., 1958; 1964; 1982; 1989; 1996; *Sent.*, 10/9/1908; 12/13/1917; 1/10 and 1/24/1918; 11/13/1931; 6/2/1939; 4/4/1941; 4/23/1949; 7/15/1965; Eller Mfg. Co., *Eller's "Perfect-Fit" Steel Ceilings. Catalog No. 20*, 34, 86, 125, 150, 165.

Rhoades Block, 1908
Photograph from the Clare Sentinel, October 9, 1908

525 North McEwan
Her Place (1985)

This building replaced the Dunlop building (Clare's first brick building), which burned in the 1970s. This building was constructed in 1985 by Willard and Ruby Koch to house the Her Place women's clothing store. Ruby operated the business until 2008 when her daughter-in-law Michelle took over management the business. Her Place closed in 2020.

Sent., 7/31/1985

601, 603, 605 North McEwan
Dunwoodie Building (1907)
E. B. Gorr, Clare, architect; Barris and Linsea, builders.

This building was constructed in 1907 by James Dunwoodie as a multi-unit retail building. The center unit was originally leased to J. Gardner for a music store, and the north unit was leased to Mr. Thurston for his picture framing, undertaking, and cabinet business. The center unit housed a clothing store by 1910 and, by 1916, the Princess Theater. In April 1909 Frank Ballinger leased the south unit for his grocery store business. In August of the same year William Ryan purchased Ballinger's grocery business. The south unit was vacant in 1910, but prior to 1916 Simon Bogardus leased it. The Consolidated Light and Power Co., run by F. B. Doherty, moved into either the south or center unit in April 1912. F. E. Doherty had a vulcanizing business in the basement of this building that he relocated to another building in July 1913. The building was sold to William Caple after the death of Mr.

Dunwoodie in 1916. From 1916 to 1922 Caple began selling the three units.

Caple sold the south unit to Norris J. Brown only five days after he purchased the building. Brown deeded the property to his son, Wells Brown, in September 1920. The Central Gas Company was using the building in the early 1920s, and the A & P Tea Co. used it in the mid-1920s. Wells Brown sold this unit to Murl Houghton in June 1937 for his Clare Drug Company business. Vanderwark's Grocery was advertised as using the building 1942. In September 1945 Mr. Houghton leased the unit to Miss Louise Loeffler for her Louise's Flower and Gift Shop. Prior to her lease, it was used by James Hoskins, owner of Jim's Recreation. William and Dorothy Maxwell purchased this unit in October 1971, but began leasing it as early as 1947 for their Maxwell Flowers business. They sold the building to Ronald & Barbara Kunse in April 1992. Carolyn Murphy, purchased this unit in January 1997. Maxwell's Flowers used the building until the mid-2010s. The Clare Candy Company opened in the west end of this unit in December 2014. Brewin' on McEwan opened here in 2015.

The center unit was purchased in April 1922 by John Asline. Asline, whose Princess Theater opened in this location by 1916, continued his theater business here until he opened his newly constructed Ideal Theater immediately to the north in 1930. Mr. Asline sold the center unit in August 1936 to Roy Cimmerer. Uncle Tom's Recreation was in business here in 1937. It operated until 1947 when it was replaced by Russ Moody's Tavern and Restaurant. Bill's Tavern began operations here in 1961 which replaced Bogies Tavern. Jerry's Bar was open from the mid-1960s to 1972. Wild Bill's Pub began leasing the building in 1973. Roy Cimmérer's wife Minerva sold the unit to William & Carol Carlton in April 1978. The Carltons sold to William and Dorothy Maxwell in June 1978, but the Maxwell's were using the building as early as 1975. Until the 2010s Maxwell Flowers business operated out of both the south and center units. William and Dorothy Maxwell sold to Ronald & Barbara Kunse in April 1992. Carolyn Murphy purchased this unit in January 1997. The center unit was occupied by Friends and Coffee coffee shop in the 2010s, and later by Brewin' on McEwan micro-brewery and restaurant. The south and center units continued to be used together when The Blind Tiger Pub & Eatery opened in May 2017. Dave and Donna Maxwell purchased the business in 2018 and changed the name to Timeout Tavern. The center section's west elevation shows the original appearance of the door opening on the north end of the section with two short windows to the south, all set in segmental-arch-head openings capped by heads formed by three rowlock courses.

Caple sold the north unit to William Reardon in August 1919. In April 1921 the Thurston Undertaking business moved out to a larger location and Charles Gould of Gould Undertaking Co. began leasing this unit. William Reardon sold the unit to Levi Cimmerer in July 1921. In November 1921 Gould Undertaking Co. was renamed Friz Undertaking Co. Andrew Friz purchased this part of the building in March 1926 and at the same time also purchased the stock and undertaking business of Charles Gould. Friz leased the unit to Mr. and Mrs. Tom Ramey, owners of the Ramey 5¢ to $5.00 Store, in December 1941. Andrew Friz owned the unit until August 1945 when he sold it to Carl Schmitt. In November 1949 Ernie Bryant and Neilan Cradit's The Sports Shop began operating out of this unit. The unit was leased to the Moyer's Store in December 1951. In April 1954 Carl Schmitt sold it to Dr. John White, who used it for his optometry practice. Dr. White owned the unit until April 1971 when he sold it to Dr. Alan Scott.

The basement of the building under the south unit contained the Clare Public Library from November 1950 until 1961. The Yarn Mart began to lease the former library space in November 1962. It was then leased by Bob Chapman of Chapman Business Machines from October 1966 until the early 1970s.

CHSY., 1950; 1951; 1958; 1974; 1985; *Cour.*, 6/14/1907; *Sent.*, 5/7, 7/26 and 11/1/1907; 4/16 and 8/27/1909; 4/19/1912; 7/18/1913; 1/20/1916; 4/17/1919; 4/28, 7/1 and 11/14/1921; 11/10/1922; 4/9/1926; 3/26 and 8/20/1937; 12/12/1941; 3/13/1942; 8/31 and 9/28/1945; 3/14 and 7/11/1947; 11/11/1949; 11/10/1950; 12/14/1951; 7/16/1954; 8/31 and 10/26/1961; 11/15/1962; 11/14/1963; 10/20/1966; 12/2/1970; 11/8/1972.

607, 609 North McEwan
Ideal Theater (1930)
R. V. Gay, St. Johns, architect
Roeske Wobig, Saginaw, contractor

The present ground-floor movie theater façade, presumably dating from a renovation done in the 1940s or early 1950s, is Moderne in style. The theater entrance comprises three aluminum framed glass doors, with a side light to the north, all set within a broad slant-sided recess between enameled metal panel-faced walls containing display cases for movie posters, two on each side. Projecting over the sidewalk above the entry is a blue-green, yellow, orange, and white-colored triangular-footprint metal marquee illuminated by bulbs and neon lighting. The marquee is topped in each face by a yellow metal sign panel containing raised, neon-lit letters spelling out the theater name, IDEAL.

The ground-story storefront to the north has a deeply recessed entry at the left (south) and display windows facing the entry and street. An angled plate glass window extends from the door and meets another

John Asline
Photograph from the
Clare Sentinel
October 28, 1932

plate glass window on the façade. The window bulkheads and north corner pier are faced in whitish rubble stonework, which has been in place since at least 1961, while the wooden door, with large glass light, and metal window trim appear to date from c. 1950 or a little earlier.

This building was constructed in 1930 for John Asline. Mr. Asline owned the Princess Theater in the center unit of the building immediately to the south, but was looking for a larger building to house his movie theater business. Continuing the theater business, James Olson leased the theater in November 1933. Olson bought the building from John Asline in December 1938. The theater was closed for approximately one year prior to October 1968. At that time mayor and service station owner Willard Koch, Carl Stephenson, owner of Stephenson Funeral Home, and Dr. Elmer. C. Shurlow, osteopathic physician and operator of the Clare Nursing Home, purchased and reopened the Ideal. Stephenson and Shurlow eventually sold their interests to Koch. Tom Koch, Willard's son, took over management of the theater in 1996.

The building also contains a small storefront on its northeast corner. The Cotton Radio Hospital was the first tenant. They occupied the space for less than a year when they were replaced by Clare Realty Co. By the 1940s the business name was changed to the Art Damoth Agency, and he conducted business here until at least 1954. Marion's Record Shop moved here in December 1957. Russ's Record Store started business here in 1959. They added another business, Russ's Paint Store, within this unit in 1964. Both businesses operated here until 1965 when they moved to 515 North McEwan. Virginia's Drapery Shop was here in 1967. The Art Damoth Agency returned to the building in 1969. Damoth used this building as his insurance office while at the same time operating his real estate business in the building immediately to the north. The following year Art Damoth was sharing his office space with Forrest Meek and his The Redman Agency. By 1971 both agents were working for the Redman Agency. From mid-1971 to 1973 Art Damoth was the sole agent for the Redman Agency. Mike Hebner's Shamrock Real Estate Office operated here from 1973 to 1975, Northern Realty in 1976, Campbell-Morse Realty from 1978 to 1979, and Gateway Realty from 1979 to 1986. Best Insurance was running their business here from 1987 to 1988. Books R Us was here in 1989. The Clare Area Chamber of Commerce opened their office here in 1993, and operated until 1998 when they moved to 427 North McEwan. Covet Cut and Color started business here in 2012.

CHSY., 1961; *Sent.*, 3/21 and 5/30 and 9/8/1930; 5/8/ and 5/15/1931; 7/10/1942; 2/26/1954; 12/5/1957; 12/3/1959; 4/2 and 10/1/1964; 4/29 and 8/19/1965; 6/29/1967; 10/23/1968; 7/30/1969; 12/16/1970; 1/6, 4/7 and 7/7/1971; 2/14 and 3/14/1973; 11/26/1975; 2/18 and 10/13/1976; 5/24/1978; 10/10 and 10/24/1979; 6/3/1986; 6/23/1987; 12/27/1988; 9/19/1989; 5/25/1993; 9/11/1998.

Redman Agency, Inc./Art Damoth Agencies Advertisement
Clare Sentinel, December 16, 1970

611 North McEwan
R. J. Whitney House (1873)

This building has seen some change over its history but its basic character remains evident. The predominant feature of the building is its side-gable roof with subsidiary front-facing gable present from the building's construction. The original structure was the gabled section closest to McEwan Street. Whether or not the one-story rear section is original is not known, but it is shown in the 1884 birdseye view. In 1905 the present stone foundation was placed under the house. Other than the removal and addition of a porch on the façade, the building did not change until 1953. At that time the porch was removed and larger windows installed on the façade. The present appearance of the building was due to a major renovation in 1995. That is when the street-level storefront was constructed, and the one-story addition on the west end was expanded.

This building was constructed in 1873 by R. J. Whitney. It was built to be used as a residence, but it is unclear if this was Whitney's primary residence or a rental property. The property was sold to George Bellnap in June 1873 and sold by Bellnap to Peter Callam in November 1878. Alfred J. and Alice Doherty purchased the building in May 1879. This was not the first home that the Doherty's lived in after arriving in Clare, but it was the first one they owned. They lived here until May 1883, when they began renting to William Goodman. A. J. and Alice Doherty owned the house until August 1883 when they sold it to Elizabeth Phinisey. Mrs. Phinisey died in approximately 1888 and left the house to her daughter, Ova Phinisey. Ova married Floyd Kane in 1904 and they sold the house to Thomas Holbrook in May 1905. Isaac Hampton purchased the house in March 1916 and sold it to William Caple in January 1917. Up until this point the building was used as a residence, but Caple used it for his insurance and real estate business. In September 1921 Mr. Caple sold his business to the Clare Insurance and Realty Company, which purchased the building in December of the same year. The building was next purchased by Mabel Lockwood in June 1928. She used the building for her millinary store. Dr. Burton Sanford purchased the building in April 1931 and along with Dr. F. C. Sanford moved their medical practice here in 1935. Prior to that the building was used by the Johnson Electric Shop. The Sanford's medical office served the public here until at least 1942. In December 1952 W. James Olson purchased the building and the next month began leasing it to Arthur Damoth for his real estate and insurance business. The Damoth Agency was merged in 1958 with Bernard Wyman of the Mount Pleasant Agency in January 1958, and the named was changed to the Wyman-Damoth Agency. The name was changed to United Agency in 1960 and operated in the early 1960s. Arthur Damoth purchased the building in November 1963 along with Donald Holbrook and Anne Irene Olson. Beginning in 1965 and until 1972 Art Damoth used this building for his Art Damoth Real Estate office. James Sykora bought the building in March 1971. The Central Travel Agency, owned by Joe Cascarelli, began leasing the building in August 1973 and he eventually purchased it in November 1985. The business name would change to Central Michigan Travel Services in 1975, and Central Travel and Cruise Center in 1987. Julia Cascarelli bought the building in December 1986 but sold it to Edward Kosciuszko in December 1988. It was foreclosed on in February 1989. Steven and Kristi Gollish, purchased the building in January 1990. The Leprechaun Shop gift shop, which was owned by the

Gollishes, operated out of the building beginning in 1990 and continued into the early 2000s. After the Leprechaun Shop closed, the building was leased to Gates Computer and Gaming, which operated for a short time in the mid-2000s. The building since has had several renters which have all used the building for a short time. Kap's Koins coin shop, started using the building in 2013.

CHSY., 1961; *Sent.*, 5/27/1883; 10/28/1904; 5/26/1905; 1/18/1917; 9/30/1921; 2/2/1934; 5/24 and 10/11/1935; 12/18/1942; 1/2 and 3/13/1953; 3/26/1954; 1/16 and 2/3/1958; 7/7/1960; 4/13/1961; 7/29/1965; 7/14/1972; 8/15 and 8/22/1973; 5/14/1975; 3/25/1986; 8/11/1987; 5/29/1990; 6/4/1996.

Mabel Lockwood Millenary, circa 1930
Photograph from the Robert Knapp Collection

613 North McEwan
White House Restaurant (1935)
Kern Brothers, builders

Other than the two additions to the west end of the building the structure has changed little since its original construction. The first eight by ten foot addition which is immediately to the west of the main section was constructed in 1937. Another small addition for restrooms on the building's west end was added at an unknown date. The metal roof was installed in the 2010s.

This building was constructed in 1935 on property owned by Thomas Holbrook. The diner was first operated by Mr. and Mrs. Roy Schultz. From 1935 to the present this building and an adjacent house, that was located to the northwest, had been sold together as a unit. The adjacent house was destroyed by fire in 2013. Holbrook owned the property until September 1939 when he sold it to Curtis and Dolores Hearnes. The property was deeded to Dolores Hearnes in June 1952 through her divorce from Curtis. Dolores Hearnes eventually remarried and became

Dolores Kuhlman. Benjamin & Joan Harrell purchased the property from Dolores Kuhlman in November 1991. They sold to William and Monica Baranski in September 1995. Denise Jenks, purchased the property from the Baranskis in October 2003.

Sent., 9/17/1937; Denise Jenks, Interview, 8/19/2009; John Jabour, Interview, June 2011.

West side of the 600 block of North McEwan looking northwest
Circa 1970
613 North McEwan in right center
Photograph from the Forrest Meek Collection

Significance Section

The Clare Downtown Historic District meets national register criterion A at the local level for serving, over the years from the late nineteenth century to the 1960s and later, as Clare's commercial center, offering stores, banks, hotels, and professional offices; its governmental center, the location of city hall and the post office; and its social and recreation/entertainment focal point, with standing buildings that housed lodge halls and entertainment spaces, including an opera house and movie theaters. The district also meets criterion A for its association with the area's agriculture through the elevator and various stores that served the agricultural community and its associations with the area's oil and natural gas industry during the early years of the industry from around 1930 to the 1960s.

The district also has significance under criterion B for four buildings that are directly associated with Alfred J. Doherty, a businessman and community leader who played a direct and key role in a broad range of projects and activities to improve the city from the 1880s until his death in the 1920s.

The district also meets criterion C for its variety of late-nineteenth and early and mid-twentieth-century architecture that includes public buildings and a church as well as commercial buildings. The district is particularly rich in commercial buildings of Neoclassical-inspired design but also contains notable Late Victorian, Commercial Brick, and International style/Mid-century Modern buildings.

The Founding of Clare

The Huron, Ojibwa, and Ottawa Indians preceded white settlers in what is now Clare, Michigan. Although they never settled here they did use this and the surrounding area for hunting. When the Isabella County Indian Reservation was created in 1855 near what is now Mount Pleasant to the south, the Isabella-Houghton Lake Indian Trail was also carved out. The trail was used to travel from the Chippewa River in Isabella County to the south to Houghton Lake farther north in the northern Lower Peninsula. This trail would eventually become part of what is known today as Old US-27, and it traveled through the future downtown Clare.

The future site of Clare remained a wilderness into the 1860s. The area contained large stands of white pine, and this drew the attention of lumbermen beginning in the 1860s. On September 1, 1863, Ammi W. Wright, a leading lumberman from Saginaw, purchased land that included what is now the part of the downtown district east of the present day McEwan Street. Five months later, on February 10, 1864, Bay City lumberman William McEwan purchased two tracts of land located on what is now the west side of McEwan Street. Ammi Wright purchased his land from the Flint & Pere Marquette Railroad Company, while McEwan purchased his using military warrants which he bought from Private Admiral Bumpus and Sergeant William Rand, two veterans of the War of 1812. On September 13, 1864, McEwan purchased Ammi Wright's tract of land; McEwan thus came to own the entire site on which the central part of Clare developed. McEwan began operations in Clare in 1868, including the construction of a lumber camp located to the southwest of the present downtown Clare, and the land which makes up the central part of Clare was cleared in 1868 and 1869. William McEwan had his home, as well as a sawmill, in Bay City. The logs harvested from the Clare area were floated southeast down the Tobacco River, then north on the Tittabawassee and Saginaw Rivers up to Bay City.

As mentioned earlier Ammi Wright purchased his land from the Flint & Pere Marquette Railroad. The Flint & Pere Marquette was organized in 1857 and was granted lands by the United States government in exchange for constructing a railroad from Flint through Saginaw to Ludington, Michigan. The east part of the line between Flint and Saginaw was completed late in 1862. The long stretch west from Saginaw, through lands that were nearly entirely wilderness, was completed to Ludington in 1874. The part of the line from Saginaw west as far as the future site of Clare was to be completed in 1870. The line crossed the Isabella-Houghton Lake Indian Trail, which was later improved into an Isabella-Tobacco River State Road, near the McEwan lumber camp by the end of 1870.

With the railroad and the State Road intersecting on his land, McEwan believed this would be an excellent location for a new town. He hired Peter Callam and John W. Calkins to survey an area of eighty acres spanning the railroad line for the new town. McEwan's plat of the village site, the first in Clare County, was filed on December 30, 1870. The original plat of the town of Clare extended from one block south of First Street on the south to one lot north of Seventh Street on the north and from the third lot west of Maple Street on the west to three lots east of Hemlock Street on the east. The Flint & Pere Marquette Railroad dissected the town at an angle from the southeast to the northwest. Roughly one-third of the townsite was to the south of the tracks and two-thirds to the north. Historically the commercial area developed in the heart of the town along McEwan Street, the industrial area along the railroad line, and the residential area surrounding both.

The Clare Business District

By the end of 1870, Clare, named for the county in which it is located, comprised a small collection of buildings. Four boarding houses, mainly serving the railroad crews constructing the Flint & Pere Marquette Railroad and local woodsmen employed in lumbering, were located south of the railroad tracks. These boarding houses were owned by Pettibone, McKinnon, Markley, and Slater. One of McEwan's surveyors, Peter Callam, constructed Clare's first store along First Street. This store also housed the first post office, with Callam serving as the first postmaster. Henry Trevidick constructed a drug store the same year on the southeast corner of Fifth and McEwan Streets. These buildings, in addition to a handful of houses and McEwan's lumber camp, were all that made up Clare at the end of 1870.

The next year thirty more buildings were added to the settlement. The area south of the railroad tracks would contain warehouses and support industries. It would have the reputation of being known as 'the other side of the tracks.' The town would mainly grow to the north where most of the important commercial buildings and the residences were located. The area south of the tracks, however, would develop first. The early development of the area south of the railroad tracks can be attributed to the prevalence of marshy land located to the north. Much filling was needed to make the land north of the tracks usable; logs and sawdust along with more suitable fill were used to raise the grade.

The 1870s was a time of rapid growth for the new town. Lewis Randolph, Albert Lotis and Alfred Louch opened blacksmith shops in 1871, 1872 and 1875, respectively. Louch was responsible for the construction of the stage coaches which ran from Clare to Mount Pleasant. The stage line was operated by Saxton in 1873 and by the Parrish Brothers from 1873 to 1879. The stage was the main means of communication with the closest significant town, Mount Pleasant, located sixteen miles to the south, until a railroad line connecting Coleman, located on the F. & P.M. east of Clare, with Mount Pleasant was constructed in 1879.

In the same location as his blacksmith shop at the southwest McEwan/Second corner, Alfred Louch operated his "Live and Let Live" livery stable. Behind him E. Smalley operated his wagon-building shop in 1877. On the opposite side of McEwan between Second Street and the railroad tracks stood a group of warehouses. Two of these were operated by Pratt & Company and supplied Pratt's lumber camps. Lumbering was a huge industry in the Clare area during the 1870s. Pratt's company alone paid out $75,000.00 yearly in expenditures in the Clare area, with most of this money staying in the village. The lumbering activities, with their payroll and related expenditures, supported the town and encouraged growth.

The Sterns House hotel was located on the east side of McEwan south of Second Street. This side of the street also contained J. W. Calkins hardware store, Peter Callam's grocery store (1870), and the shop of A. A. Shaver, furniture maker (1873), on the southeast corner of First and McEwan Streets. In addition, a saloon operated by A. Beebe (1872) was located on the west side of McEwan between Second and First Streets.

The Flint & Pere Marquette passenger and freight depot was located on the west side of McEwan just south of the tracks. On the other side of the tracks to the north was the Nicholls House hotel, which changed its name to the Anglo-American House before it burned in 1879. On the east side of McEwan just north of the tracks was another hotel, the Alger House (1871). To the north of the Alger House were O'Callaghan's grocery store (1878), George Lee's store, Fred Lange's bakery (1874), George Halstead's barbershop, and Jefferies meat market. These buildings, including the ones located on the west side of McEwan between Fourth and Third Streets, with the exception of the Alger House and O'Callaghan's, were all destroyed by fire in 1878.

Farther north on the east side of McEwan Street between Fifth and Fourth Streets was the William Ross grocery (1872), followed to the north by Grace Whitley's dry goods store (1878), S. Bowdish's drug store, and R. Crawford's grocery store. In the same block on the east side of McEwan, from south to north, were located J. C. Rockafellow's general store and later post office (1875), P. Campbell's boot and shoe shop, 'Deacon' Cooley's harness shop, and William Elden's jewelry store (1879) at the southwest corner of Fifth and McEwan Streets.

In 1878 the *Clare County Press* published the following description of the village of Clare:

> Clare is the name of a bright little village situated midway between Saginaw and Reed City, on the Flint and Pere

Marquette Railway, one of the most extensive railroad lines passing through the state, reaching from Toledo, on Lake Erie, to Ludington, on Lake Michigan. Clare County is geographically nearly the center of the state, on the high table of the water shed and is noted for its healthful climate, its extensive timber operations, and unsurpassed agricultural lands. The Clare village has some seven hundred inhabitants, and is increasing. The business places comprise about a dozen dealers in dry goods and groceries, three hotels, three saloons, two drug stores, two millinery stores, a jewelry store, a clothing store, a picture frame store and undertaking establishment, a hardware and furniture store, two boot and shoe shops, a harness shop, a blacksmith shop, a carriage shop, a foundry and machine shop, two shingle mills, a grist mill, a planing mill, sash and door factory, a grain elevator, and numerous small industries incident to every village. The Congregationalists have a good church building, and flourishing society, and the Methodists Episcopal Society have a new church just completed, which do credit to a larger town. There is a graded school in charge of competent teachers, red ribbon and white ribbon temperance societies, three lawyers, three doctors ... With good churches, good schools, good society, good facilities for the transaction of business, and cheap lands in abundance, Clare is destined at no distant day to become an important center of industry and trade.

Despite Clare's growth in the 1870s, it was a very rough town to live in. There were frequently shootings and unruly behavior within the town. The need for hiring a marshal was apparent to the townspeople, but in order to do that the town must become an incorporated village. This action was opposed by both William McEwan and the Flint & Pere Marquette Railroad. Combined they owned about sixty percent of the platted town. Incorporation for them would mean paying taxes on their properties. The townspeople won out in the end. The voters approved the establishment of village government, and on January 13, 1879, the State of Michigan incorporated the Village of Clare.

On the down side, the later part of the 1870s proved to be the end of Clare's chances to become the county seat. The first Clare County seat was located in the neighboring village of Farwell. The circumstances behind a fire which destroyed the county building in Farwell in 1877 are unclear. Some people suspected arson, and many of those people believed it was set by people from Clare who wanted the county seat moved to their town. However, Clare is not centrally located in the county, but instead near its southern edge. In the end neither Clare nor Farwell would be the seat of county government. Early in 1878 a committee appointed by the county board of supervisors selected an undeveloped location close to the county's geographical center near Budd Lake. After this centrally located site was approved by county voters, the owner, the Flint & Pere Marquette Railroad, platted a village and donated a courthouse square site to the county. The site, named Harrison after President William Henry Harrison, has served as Clare County seat since 1879.

Despite losing the county seat plum, the village of Clare continued to grow during the 1880s. During the decade Clare transitioned from a pioneer lumber boomtown to an established village with a more diverse economy. By the middle of the decade Clare County's pine forests would be depleted and its lumbermen moved on to other forest lands farther north and in states farther west. The growing amounts of cleared land gave rise to agriculture.

In 1881 Clare's first Opera House was constructed on the site of the burned Nicholls House, and the Doherty Hardware Store on the east side of McEwan between Fourth and Fifth Streets opened. In 1883 Robert Mussell built his drug store on the west side of McEwan between Fourth and Fifth Streets, and the Zemon-Sable store, the Osborn & Randall Roller Mill, E. H. De Vogt photography, Bicknell's Home Delivery Dairy, and H. E. Lambeck's tailor shop all opened.

The first brick commercial building, Dunlop's Medical Hall, was constructed on the southwest corner of McEwan and Fifth Streets in 1885. The Clare County Bank opened in a location on the opposite side of McEwan from the Medical Hall in the same year. The year 1885 also saw additional new businesses, the L. T. Olds Dairy, W. Scott Emory, cigar manufacturer, and John Dennis' meat market, established.

A second railroad serving Clare, the Toledo, Ann Arbor & North Michigan Railroad, was completed north to Clare in 1887. The line was located to the west of the downtown just outside of the platted town. The old Flint & Pere Marquette passenger and freight depot was abandoned and a new Union Depot serving both lines constructed in the same year where the two lines crossed. The Flint & Pere Marquette added a number of sidings to serve local businesses in Clare in the period between 1884 and 1893. The 1884 birdseye view shows only the single main line track running through town. Eleven years later the 1893 Sanborn map shows three sets of tracks crossing McEwan Street and four crossing Beech Street. As time progressed the railroad added multiple sidings to serve the needs of the industries located along the tracks.

After only six years of operation the Husted Opera House burned in 1887, and was not rebuilt. The year 1887 also saw the Maxwell and Bryant blacksmith shops, H. O. Squires restaurant, E. L. Squires ice house, and the Harris & Herrick grocery opening for business. In 1887 the Clare County Savings Bank, after two years in their wood-framed building, constructed a new two-story brick building on the southeast corner of Fifth and McEwan Streets.

Clare also made great strides in infrastructure in the 1880s. Wood water mains were installed in 1886, and gas-operated street lights along with Clare's first telephone lines were introduced in 1887. And, after much debate and all volunteer help, McEwan Street from the Little Tobacco River to Sixth Street was topped off with a clay cap to provide a more solid driving surface.

To demonstrate the amount of growth taking place in Clare in the 1880s the *Clare County Press* published a new, glowing summary description of the Clare community in 1887:

Clare, an incorporated village of 1,200 inhabitants, located near the geographic center of the lower peninsula, at the probable junction of the F. & P. M. and T., A. A. & N. M. R. R., 50 miles from East Saginaw, 39 miles from Reed City and 15 miles from Mt. Pleasant. It has 2 churches, 1 graded union school, 2 weekly newspapers, 3 hotels, 3 livery barns, 13 grocery and provision stores, 5 dry goods and clothing stores, 1 furniture store, 3 hardware stores, 4 drug stores, 2 boot and shoe stores, 2 meat markets, 1 manufacturer of beef and chicken broth, 1 bank, 1 planing mill with sash & door factory, 1 planing mill, 1 foundry, 3 shingle mills, 2 lumber mills, 1 grist mill, 4 blacksmith shops, 1 photography gallery, 1 dentist, 5 physicians, 2 lawyers, 1 lodge I.O.O.F., 1 lodge I.O.O. Foresters, 1 lodge Chosen Friends, 1

Bird's-eye View Drawing of Clare, Michigan

lodge G.A.R., 7 millinery shops. The contiguous country is the very best agricultural land. The Tobacco River flows near the village with grayling and trout in the waters. Homes can be procured for the thousands with moderate means. The best place in the state to locate manufacturers.

O. H. Bailey & Co., Boston Mass, 1884

The start of the decade of the 1890s began with a change in its form of government. In 1891 the village of Clare petitioned the state legislature to approve a charter incorporating it as a city. With a population of 1,174 citizens Clare became the smallest incorporated city in Michigan, a title it held until the following year when Harrison was incorporated as a city.

The new decade also saw the introduction of electrical service into the village. In 1890 Alfred J. Doherty's Doherty Electric Light Co. was operating a small electric plant at a dam on the Tobacco River. Doherty strung line from this initial plant to his hardware store and several nearby stores in 1890 and the next year extended service to his new Doherty Opera House building. In 1894 Doherty with other investors founded the Clare Electric Co., which soon made electrical service available to the rest of the city. The first electric street lights along McEwan were turned on in

Alfred J. Doherty
Drawing from the
Clare Sentinel 1900

April 1895. They were lit at dusk and turned off at midnight. By July of the same year there was seven and a half miles of electrical wire strung providing electricity to the entire city. The downtown power lines were strung down McEwan Street in front of the buildings. In 1922, when damage from an ice storm necessitated the reconstruction of the power poles and lines, they were relocated to the back alleys.

Alfred J. Doherty was influential in bringing electricity to the city of Clare, but this was only part of his importance in the city's and downtown's history. He came to Clare from Belfast, New York, in 1878. From 1880 to 1883 he taught at the Dover School north of town. Doherty opened an insurance office in 1883 and worked at that until he opened his hardware business in 1885. He built Clare's second (and still standing) Opera House building in 1891. Doherty was elected to the State Senate in 1901 and re-elected in 1903 and 1905. He served as the Senate Republican Whip for both of his terms. At the end of his senatorial terms he was named as a possible gubernatorial candidate, but declined to run. He later served on the State Board of Agriculture and was eventually appointed as the director of the Michigan State Fair.

He served as one of the first statewide elected members of the Michigan State University Board of Trustees, serving from 1907 to 1919. He was responsible for the construction of eight business blocks in the downtown area (four of which still stand), the Doherty Hotel being the best known, and numerous residences. At one time before the turn of the twentieth century he owned the Clare Water Works, the Clare Electric Light Company, and the Clare Telephone Company. He was also part owner of the electric power plant on Mackinac Island. He served as mayor of Clare from April 1920 to April 1922. In the later days of his life he served as a lobbyist for the Pullman Railroad Car Company.

The 1890s saw the construction of several important early brick buildings in the downtown area. The no longer standing Wilson-Sutherland Building was constructed in 1890-91. It housed William Wolsky's dry goods business from 1891 to 1902. In the same year Alfred Doherty constructed his Opera House Building at 524 North McEwan. O. S. Derby's furniture, and Henry Razek's clothing store occupied the two first-floor units, while the Opera House occupied the whole second floor. A few years later S. C. Kirkbride's dry goods store plus the U. S. Post Office would replace the Razek store. The Davy/Mussell/Elden Building was constructed on the west side of McEwan between Fourth and Fifth Streets in 1895. It was built as a triple storefront building with Lew Davy's clothing store, Robert

West side of McEwan Street's 400 block looking northwest, Circa 1885
Photograph from the Forrest Meek Collection

Bird's-eye Photograph of Downtown Clare
Photograph from the Forrest Meek Collection

Mussell's drug store and William Elden's bazaar store occupying the first floor units.

The year 1900 saw the construction of Clare's largest commercial building, Alfred Doherty's six-storefront building on McEwan's west side between Third and Fourth Streets (no longer standing); (see photo on page 94) it took up most of the middle of the block. The first decade was also remembered for the impact of fires in the reshaping of Clare's streetscape. A fire on July 4, 1904, was the largest in Clare's history. The arson fire was set in a barn close to Pine Street between Fourth and Fifth Streets. The east wind pushed the fire toward the west and it consumed most every wood frame building on the block. The only buildings to survive along McEwan Street were three brick buildings, the Clare Hardware Building on the northeast corner of Fourth and McEwan Streets (502 N. McEwan) and the Doherty Opera House and Clare County Savings Bank Building located at 524 and 532 N. McEwan. These three masonry buildings still stand. All the buildings that replaced the burned-out wooden ones, and all future buildings in the downtown, were constructed with brick walls.

A 1907 fire caused extensive destruction along the west side of McEwan between Fourth and Fifth Streets opposite the area on the street's east side hard hit by the 1904 fire. The two wood frame

150

Photograph by A. S. Lyndon, Ann Arbor, MI, Circa 1907
Photograph from the Robert Knapp Collection

buildings on the north end of the block just south of the Dunlop Medical Hall burned along with most of the buildings on the south side of the block along Fourth Street. Within one year the two buildings along McEwan and most of the West Fourth Street buildings had been replaced.

Fires would continue to change the landscape of downtown Clare, but none was as destructive as the 1904 and 1907 fires. From 1910 on, nearly all new building construction along McEwan Street would come about as a result of individual buildings being destroyed by fire. The Wilson-Sutherland Building on the southwest corner of Fourth and McEwan (429-31 N. McEwan) burned in 1910 and the site remained vacant until 1922 when the still-standing Clare County Savings Bank Building was built on the site. The six-storefront Doherty Building on McEwan Street between Fourth and Third Streets burned in 1957. Its site was occupied by four new buildings built between 1957 and 1972. Clare's first brick building, the Dunlop Building, located at the southwest corner of Fifth and McEwan, burned in the 1970s and was eventually replaced by the Her Place Building in 1985. The McEwan Professional Building at the southeast corner of Fourth and McEwan was constructed in 1997 sometime after the Jackson Meat Market burned. The Subway store, on the northeast corner of Third and

McEwan Streets, constructed in 2000, was the exception. It was built on a vacant lot that had once contained a gasoline filling station.

The last significant building growth in downtown Clare occurred along West Fifth Street in the 1930s. The new Clare City Hall building, followed by the Post Office, proved to be the catalyst for further growth in the area. Three more buildings in the half block west of McEwan Street were added between 1937 and 1941.

Clare's downtown continued to prosper in the 1950s, with much storefront renovation taking place, but the 1960s and more recent years have proved to be more challenging. Since the early 1960s limited access highway construction bypassing downtown Clare has had negative repercussions on the downtown which was dependent on the tourist industry (see Commerce section below). In an effort to attract and retain businesses, Clare created its Downtown Development Authority in 1989. Despite the highway bypasses, which shunt most through traffic past the city's downtown, and the ongoing development of a large commercial area north of the city near a freeway exit, the city's downtown has retained a substantial amount of business activity including not only stores such as Clare Hardware that continue to serve local needs but also the Doherty Hotel and, in recent years, the Cops and Doughnuts store complex that are magnets for visitors as well as locals.

West side of McEwan Street's 500 block looking southwest, Circa 1920s
Photograph from the Robert Knapp Collection

Commerce

McEwan Street has always been the commercial heart of Clare. Initially most businesses located to the south of the railroad tracks, but the town would soon grow more to the north. McEwan Street between Third and Fifth Streets had the highest concentration of commercial businesses. West Fourth Street early on also had a high concentration of commercial activity, but not enough to rival McEwan Street. West Fourth Street would become less important as a commercial area toward the last quarter of the twentieth century. Beginning in the 1930s Fifth Street would rise as an important commercial area of the town.

Even before the platting of Clare in 1870, Peter Callam and Henry Trevidick were operating a general store and drug store respectively in Clare. As time went on, Clare would acquire the necessary businesses for the needs of its citizens. The 1893 Sanborn map shows six saloons, five dry good stores, ten grocery stores, three drug stores, four millineries, three barber shops, two jewelry stores, one hardware store, and an agricultural implements store, all within a three-block area of McEwan and a half block area of West Fourth Street. In addition, the town had several hotels, blacksmith shops, boot and shoe shops, restaurants, a livery, and a marble works. Other businesses within Clare would eventually include a photography studio and two undertakers. As time progressed and agriculture replaced the lumber industry, Clare would acquire more harness shops and implement and hardware stores. With the automobile came gasoline filling stations, automobile dealerships, and automobile repair shops. Most of the early business buildings were of wood frame construction, but by the early part of the twentieth century they had been replaced by brick.

Few buildings in Clare were constructed with multiple store fronts. Three buildings were constructed with two storefronts, two with three storefronts, and one with six storefronts. The Davy/Mussell/Elden Building was altered from three storefronts to two in 1904 when the Davy Building was constructed. The Doherty six-storefront building was lost to a fire in 1957.

The following list is a sampling of some of the businesses which operated long-term in the early to middle part of the twentieth century in buildings that survive to this day:

Bicknell's Department Store, 420 N. McEwan (1907-1966)
Davy & Company Store, 501 N. McEwan (1893-1963)
Anderson Drug Store, 518 N. McEwan (1911-1975)
Foss Bakery, 521 N. McEwan (1907-1965)
Clare Hardware, 511 N. McEwan (1904-present)
Mussell Drug Store, 505 N. McEwan (1895-1936)
Thurston Funeral Home, 509 N. McEwan (1898-1907), 605 N. McEwan (1907-1921), Odd Fellows Building (1921-1926), 114 W. Fifth Street (1926-1951), corner of Sixth and Beech Streets (1951-?)
Jay Green Clothing and Shoes, 522 N. McEwan (1927-late 1980s)
Whitehouse Restaurant, 613 N. McEwan (1935-present)

For clothing purchases in Clare, the most popular places to shop were Bicknell's Department Store and Davy's Clothing Store. Bicknell's Department Store was founded by Nathan Bicknell in 1907. Bicknell came to Clare in 1875 and started in business by opening a general store. As business improved, he was able to construct a brick store building in 1898, located at 418 N. McEwan. In an effort to expand his business he constructed another brick store in 1907 at 420 N. McEwan, and opened a dry-goods store there. This store was located immediately to the north of his general store building. Once the dry-goods store was opened his son James converted the older building to a grocery store while Nathan' other son William managed the dry-goods

East side of McEwan Street's 400 block looking southeast, Circa 1882
Photograph from the Robert Knapp Collection

store. William bought out James' interest in the business after the death of their father, and would operate the business until his death in 1966. Subsequent owners have continued to use the Bicknell Building for clothing-related businesses.

The other major clothing store in Clare was started by brothers Vernal and Lew Davy along with F. B. Smith in 1893. This business was operated out of the Wolsey Building located at the southwest corner on Fourth and McEwan Streets. Vernal Davy and F. B. Smith operated another Davy Store located in Reed City, Michigan, thirty-nine miles west, while Lew Davy operated the Clare store. Lew Davy moved his business to the newly constructed brick Davy/Mussell/Elden Building on the west side of the 500 block of McEwan in 1895. At the turn of the twentieth century Davy purchased the frame building immediately to the south of his brick building. He operated his business out of both buildings until he constructed a single brick building at 501 N. McEwan in 1904. Lew Davy purchased his brother's share of the business in 1925, and operated the business until his death in 1963. Glen Folkert purchased the Davy store building in October 1963 and operated it as the Mill End clothing store.

West side of McEwan Street's 400 block looking northwest, Circa 1940s
Photograph from the Forrest Meek Collection

McEwan Street looking southwest, Circa 1950
Photograph from the Robert Knapp Collection

The Mussell Drug store started by Robert Mussell in 1883, and was located in a brick building in the middle of the west side of the 500 block of McEwan Street. Mussell's business was growing and the need for a larger building was evident. In a joint effort with Lew Davy and William Elden, Robert Mussell constructed a two-story three storefront building, with Mussell's storefront in the center. With Robert's death in 1902, his wife Anna Mussell operated the drug store until 1936. Anna was one of the few business women to own and operate a business in the Clare community. She sold the business to E. H. Wright in 1936, who later sold to Roy Cimmerer in 1946. The building housed a drug store until 1983.

By 1906 local merchants were complaining about the competition from mail order catalogs – so much so that the *Clare Sentinel* printed an extensive article in their December 7, 1906, issue addressing the consequences of buying merchandise from catalogs instead of local merchants. What the response was to this article is unknown but it seems that most businesses adjusted and survived this crisis.

Like most other towns, Clare also witnessed an infusion of chain stores in the downtown in the 1920s and 30s. E. A. Anderson converted his drug store business at 518 N. McEwan to a Rexall Drug Store in the early 1920s. Murl Houghton opened his Walgreen's store at 523 N. McEwan on September 24, 1936; the store was previously the Clare Drug Company. The A & P Tea Company grocery occupied the south unit of 601 N. McEwan at the northwest corner of Fifth and McEwan Street, and later 412 N. McEwan. The south unit of 524 N. McEwan housed a Kroger Grocery and Bakery starting in 1935 and then moved to 429 N. McEwan in 1939. No. 429 N. McEwan became the location of an IGA Store in 1948. The Gambles department store occupied several different buildings in downtown Clare starting in 1934. Other chain stores that located in the city's downtown included the Western Auto Store located at 409 N. McEwan and the Firestone Store located at 406 N. McEwan.

Chain stores were one threat to the long-term vitality of the downtown's independent merchants. Another and perhaps greater threat in Clare's case was the replacing of the old main roads that passed through the city's business district with limited access highways that bypassed the business district entirely. Prior to the freeway development, downtown Clare stood at the intersection of several important highway routes. US-27 (now US-127), a primary north-south route in Michigan's Lower Peninsula, followed McEwan Street through the downtown. US-10, which provided a connection between Detroit and the Saginaw Bay cities of Saginaw, Bay City, and Midland and also led west to Ludington and ferry connections across Lake Michigan to Wisconsin, followed Fifth Street through town, intersecting US-27 at the corner by the Doherty Hotel. US-10 led a few miles west to State Route 115, which serves as a gateway to the northwestern Lower Peninsula's Lake Michigan resort areas. The city's location at this important route junction made it an important stopping off point for travelers. The downtown relied for a substantial part of its livelihood on restaurant, hotel, and gas station business and other retail sales to visitors. In 1961 the US-27 (now US-127) freeway and a US-10 freeway running east from Clare were completed, and in 1975 the US-10 freeway running west from Clare was completed. These entirely bypassed downtown Clare, resulting in the closing of all the gasoline service stations and most of the restaurants in the downtown area.

Eventually a new commercial area, known locally as "Hamburger Hill," developed at Clare's far north end near the US-127/10 exit. Here gas stations, restaurant and hotel franchises, along with other stores, have opened to serve both the traveling public and local residents. The growth of this new commercial area has resulted in substantial business loses in the downtown area.

Banks

The first known bank in Clare was established by Wheaton and Perry and was operating as early as 1879. The Clare County Savings Bank, which opened in 1885, was started by William Wolsky, Clark Sutherland, C. W. Perry, and Louis Weisman. It was originally located in a small building on the northwest corner of the lot where 524 N. McEwan is now located. In 1887 Alfred J. Doherty built a new building for his hardware business on the southeast corner of McEwan and Fifth Street. Doherty occupied the south half of the building and the bank leased the north half.

The Clare County Savings Bank bought the lot at the southwest McEwan/Fourth corner in March 1913 as a site for a building of its own. By 1916 the plans had been drawn up, but rising building costs delayed the project. The new building was constructed in 1922.

Despite the bank's history of prosperity and excellent management, the Clare County Savings Bank suspended business on May 21, 1932. An investigation showed that at the time of the

Clare County Savings Bank, Circa 1885
Photograph from the
Robert Knapp Collection

bank's closing the Clare County Savings Bank held $40,000 in assets in the building, $140,000 in mortgages, $528,000 in bonds, but only $32,000 in cash reserves. The cash reserves were well below state law requirements. The investigation also exposed the fact that bank officials had been conned by a traveling bond salesman who promised big returns on oil investments, but the bonds were actually worthless. The bank never reopened but the building, with its front remodeled but still showing much evidence of the Neoclassical design, remains in use today as an office building.

Two additional banks opened in July 1903. One was Dr. J. W. Dunlop's private bank housed in his no longer standing Medical Hall Building. How long this bank operated is unknown. The other bank that began then was the Citizens Bank. It was established by Fred Lister, John R. Goodman, George Benner and Charles H. O'Donald, with ten thousand dollars capital. The bank was originally located at 515 N. McEwan, but in 1907 it moved to the building on the northeast corner of McEwan and Fourth Streets (502 N. McEwan). By 1908 the bank had doubled its capital and, receiving a state charter, became the Citizens State Bank. About the same time Fred Lister, the bank president, died of cancer. William Haley became the new bank president. During William Haley's tenure as president, Dr. A. E. Mulder, J. W. Calkins, Mrs. A. E. Mussell, W. H. Virtue, and N. A. Bloom all served on the Board of Directors. Mr. Haley eventually sold his interest in the bank to Albert E. Sleeper, who was then the acting State Treasurer, and would later serve as Michigan's governor in 1917-20. James S. Bicknell became the bank's cashier in 1911 and two years later the bank president.

In contrast to the Clare County Savings Bank, the Citizens State Bank did very well financially. They purchased the 502 N. McEwan building they were leasing in 1917. In 1929 the building was completely renovated and given a white stone Art Deco façade (the building is still standing but the exterior no longer reflects the 1929 appearance). Due to its investments in the local oil industry the bank remained sound through the 1930s. The bank sold the building in 1961 and relocated to a modern new building on the west side of the 800 block of McEwan Street (outside of the district). The Citizens State Bank would operate in Clare until 1979 when it was absorbed by Chemical Bank.

Offices

Three early twentieth-century buildings and one mid-twentieth-century building in downtown Clare have second stories that were devoted to office space. Those buildings are the following:

109 W. Fifth, Holbrook/Mair Building (1941)
502 N. McEwan, Clare Hardware Building (1902)
505, 509 N. McEwan, Mussell/Elden Building (1895)
506 N. McEwan, Tatman Building (1904)

One of the more noteworthy Clare citizens who had his office in the downtown was dentist Dr. A. E. Mulder. Dr. Mulder worked as a dentist, but also served in the past as president of Clare's School Board and as Clare's mayor. He had his office at 502 N McEwan from 1942 to 1953, when the building was owned by Citizens State Bank. The Mammoth Oil Company also had offices in the 502 N. McEwan building from 1937 to 1942 after it had been previously located at 431 N. McEwan. In 1942 Mammoth Oil moved to 515 N. McEwan, and in 1961 move back to 502 N. McEwan, where it stayed until the late 1970s.

Albert Thurston had his undertaking business on the second floor of 509 N. McEwan, and the Clare Courier Newspaper operated out of 505 N. McEwan. A. Ray Canfield, publisher of the Clare Courier, also served as the secretary of Michigan's Democratic Party from 1907 to 1919. Between 1915 and 1919 Dennis Alward, another local politician, served as Michigan's Republican Party Secretary, and had an office on the opposite side of McEwan at 506 N. McEwan.

Dr. H. E. Neeland, Dr. Sanford and Dr. McKnight all had offices upstairs in the building at 509 N. McEwan. Attorney A. E. Wylie located his law firm at 506 N. McEwan.

Donald Holbrook, Clare County's Prosecuting Attorney from 1937 to 1942 and later Circuit Court and Appeals Court judge, had his law firm's office in the 109 W. Fifth Street building starting in 1941. He also shared the second floor at various times with the Freeman Oil Company, Higelmire and Associates, and Gibraltar Construction.

Hotels

The first hotels in Clare were the Markley, McKinnon, Pettibone, and Slater boarding houses constructed in the 1869-70 period to serve the railroad work crews building the Flint & Pere Marquette through the area. Markley's was located on Vernon Hill, which lies immediately to the south of the present downtown; the locations of the others are unknown. None remain standing.

The first real hotels were constructed in 1870 and 1871. Caleb Sterns built his hotel on the east side of McEwan just to the south of Second Street and along the Little Tobacco River. The Nicholls Hotel was built on the west side of McEwan just to the north of Third Street, next to the Flint & Pere Marquette depot. It was described as being "one of the most excellent houses in this section of the state," but to what it was being compared in this then thinly settled part of the world is unclear. The third hotel constructed was the Alger House. This hotel was located on the northeast corner of McEwan and Third Street, directly across the street from the Nicholls Hotel.

The Nicholls Hotel would eventually change its name to the Anglo-American House before it burned to the ground in 1879. The Alger House would go through a variety of owners between 1873 and 1881. Sometime between 1884 and 1893 the building was cut into three parts and moved off the lot. The Sterns House, which later became the Commercial House, closed sometime after 1897.

The Exchange Hotel was located along the east side of McEwan between Third and Fourth Streets in the 1880s. A portion of the building was moved to the south side of Fourth Street to the west of McEwan sometime after 1884; renamed the Lackie House, owned by Archibold Lackie, it advertised a stove in every room and a livery in back. Later sold to Henry Orth from Saginaw and renamed the Central Hotel, it then became the Clare Inn sometime before 1934 and remained in business past mid-century until destroyed by fire.

The Toledo, Ann Arbor & North Michigan Railroad was built to Clare in 1887, intersecting with the Flint & Pere Marquette Railroad at the west end of town. The new Union Depot was constructed that same year where the tracks intersected and the old Flint & Pere Marquette Depot along McEwan was abandoned. The relocation of the depot resulted in the construction of a hotel close by. The Stevens House was built near the depot on the north side of Fifth Street. Although built to

161

Sterns Hotel
*Photograph from the
Robert Knapp
Collection*

Nicolls Hotel
*Photograph from the
Forrest Meek
Collection*

Exchange Hotel, on right
*Photograph from the Robert
Knapp Collection*

Alger House
*Photograph from the
Forrest Meek
Collection*

be a first-class hotel, the Stevens mostly served railroad men. Plagued with financial problems and changing management several times, the Stevens House closed sometime between 1899 and 1906. Another hotel near the depot on the south side of Fifth Street called the Thompson Hotel opened sometime between 1910 and 1923. This hotel, like the Stevens House, did not attract a high-quality clientele. Despite this it was able to remain in business into the mid-1900s.

None of these early hotel buildings have survived.

In 1891 the first hotel in Clare to put on metropolitan airs, J. W. Calkins' Calkins House, opened at the northeast corner of Fifth and McEwan. The Calkins House was a three-story brick structure. Its main floor, elevated five feet above ground level, contained dining and reception rooms as well as the office, and also a Western Union Telegraph office, where railroad and ship tickets to all points could be purchased. A large bar and a "Tonsorial Parlor" along with a wash room and laundry were located in the basement. The second and third floors, reached by broad flights of stairs, contained spacious and luxuriant parlors and sleeping rooms accessed by well-lit hallways. Each room contained an electric call bell connected to the hotel office. The entire

Calkins Hotel, Circa 1907
Photograph from the Robert Knapp Collection

building was heated with steam heat and lighted by electricity. In addition, a carriage would transport guests back and forth from the railroad depot.

The Calkins, Clare's leading hotel during its thirty-year existence, burned in January 1920. J. W. Calkins did not plan to rebuild, and plans by a Detroit businessman, W. E. Currie, for what he called the Blue Moon Hotel did not materialize. Clare's business community and many leading citizens viewed the lack of a quality hotel in town as a major drawback to the city's moving forward as a progressive community.

One year after the loss of the Calkins Hotel the city and Clare Chamber of Commerce reached an agreement with Alfred J. Doherty, the city's wealthiest and most influential citizen, to construct a high-class hotel. The agreement was that the Chamber of Commerce would purchase the site of the old Calkins House and turn it over to Doherty, and Doherty would be given tax incentives for five years in return for building a hotel with a value of at least $60,000.00 on the site.

Two contractors later and at a cost exceeding $200,000.00, the Doherty Hotel was completed in April 1924. It contained four stories, with sixty sleeping rooms and several suites. Thirty-six of the rooms contained either a tub or a shower, the rest contained only a sink, but all had hot and cold running water. In addition, the hotel featured an elevator, billiard room, cafeteria, dining room, ballroom, two store spaces, and quarters for the public library.

After the hotel's opening skeptics opined that a small city like Clare could never support such a large hotel, and Doherty's investment would never pay off. The hotel was such a success, however, that by the end of 1924 Doherty was already expanding his kitchen. The hotel remains in operation today and has had to expand several times over the years. In 1933, at the end of Prohibition, the hotel was issued the third liquor license in the state of Michigan, and the first outside of Detroit.

The main reason for the popularity of the Doherty Hotel was its location at the intersection of key highways. At the time the Doherty Hotel was constructed, the major roads coming through Clare were State Highway M-14 (McEwan Street), which ran north and south, and State Highway M-20 (Fifth Street), which ran east and west. Both were still dirt roads at the time. The key to drawing automobile traffic from the south to the northern vacation areas was the paving of these two roads.

Interior of Doherty Hotel Lounge, Circa 1930
Photograph from the Robert Knapp Collection

In the mid-1920s there was tremendous competition between communities for state funding to pave roads. In addition, there was talk that M-14 would be rerouted and bypass Clare altogether. In 1925 Clare natives Dennis Alward, A. Ray Canfield, and Alfred J. Doherty began lobbying Washington D. C. to have M-14 designated as a military road between Lansing and Camp Grayling, the state's National Guard training camp, located sixty miles north of Clare, which would make it eligible for federal funding for concrete paving. With the help of Congressman Roy Woodruff, they were successful, but it was not until 1932 that the pavement actually reached Clare. In 1926 M-20 became US-10, and M-14 became US-27 (now US-127), and the Doherty Hotel then stood at the intersection of two major federal highways heading north connecting downstate cities with popular northern recreation destinations. As a result, most tourist traffic from southeast and south-central Michigan traveled through downtown Clare on its way north. In addition, Clare was approximately halfway between Michigan's southeast cities and northern vacation areas, which made Clare – and the Doherty – popular dining and overnight locations before the remainder of the journey north.

The most famous guest to frequent the Doherty was Henry Ford. Ford owned proving grounds to the west of Harrison, and would stay at the Doherty when in the area. In addition, during Clare County's oil and gas boom in the 1930s and 1940s many oil men used their Doherty Hotel rooms for offices.

COTTAGE ANNEX, HOTEL DOHERTY, CLARE, MICH.

Doherty Hotel Cottages, circa 1935
Postcard image from the Robert Knapp Collection

With the rise in tourist traffic coming through Clare after the paving of US-27 and US-10, additional motels and cabins began springing up. Some of these included the Lone Pine Cabins, the Manor Inn Rooms and Cabins, and Roy McKinnon's Tourist Cabins. These were mostly located along US-27 and US-10, but never presented any competition to the Doherty Hotel. The Doherty Hotel also constructed ten cottages of their own east of the hotel building in 1930.

In fact, except for the period during the Depression, the Doherty Hotel has always been a very successful hotel. The first real decrease in business occurred in 1961 when the US-27 bypass was constructed around Clare. This decrease in business was nothing compared to when I-75 was completed to its connection with US-27 well north of Clare in 1975, taking much of the Detroit area traffic headed north away from US-10 and Clare. Despite these setbacks the Doherty Hotel survived and has also expanded several times since 1975. At present the hotel is run by the fourth generation of Dohertys and remains a popular dining, hotel, and conference location.

The Doherty Hotel received both state and national recognition for both its food and service in the mid-1900s. State recognition came from a March 14, 1954, article in the *Bay City Times*, the July 1958 issue of the *AAA Motor News*, and a February 1959 article in the *Detroit Free Press*. National recognition came in the 1960 edition of the *Duncan Hines Adventures in Good Eating* dining guide, along with articles in the January 1960 and February 1963 issues of the *Ford Times* magazine.

Car Dealerships/Garages

Alfred Doherty's son Floyd is believed to have owned the first automobile in Clare. He purchased a Cadillac in 1908 and drove it back to Clare. His father was known to have driven an Oakland, but likely kept it in Lansing where he served as a state senator.

For its size Clare had a good selection of automobile dealerships. On East Fifth Street Walsh & Gordon sold Plymouth and Chryslers, while Corman Motor Sales dealt in Oldsmobiles. Woodward Auto Sales sold Hudson and Essex at 103 West Fifth. Zemmer Motors sold Chevrolets on East Fourth Street, and Thompson & Wilkinson sold Willy-Knight, Overland, Whippet, and International trucks from their implement store on West Fourth Street.

Ike Hampton operated his Ford dealership in the still standing building at 412 N. McEwan starting in 1915. The building housed a garage and showroom until at least 1934. Hampton purchased the building immediately to the south (406 N. McEwan) in 1923 in order to expand his dealership. After Ike Hampton's death the building was sold to Floyd and Clarence McGuire and Eugene Campbell, who operated the Firestone Home and Auto Supply Store. Arthur Ulrich operated his Pontiac dealership from the same location in the 1950s.

Newspapers

The Clare County Press, Clare's first newspaper, began publication in 1878. Prior to this, Clare was served by the Farwell Register from nearby Farwell, seven miles west, which started publishing in 1871. The Clare County Press was started by Alvardo F. Goodenough. Dennis E. Alward became editor of the paper in 1880, and purchased it the same year. Alward owned the paper for eight years and during that time shortened the name to the Clare Press. Marvin D. Eaton started a second paper, the News-Argus, in December 1884, and it became the Clare Democrat in 1886. The Democrat eventually merged with the Press, and the combined paper became the Clare Democrat and Press.

CLARE COUNTY PRESS.

VOL. II.   CLARE, MICH., FRIDAY, JULY 25, 1879.   NO. 12.

The Clare Press.

JOB PRINTING
Of all Kinds at the Press Office. Nice New Type.

THE PRESS
Is the Best Advertising Medium in Clare county.

VOL. IX.   CLARE, MICH. FRIDAY, SEPTEMBER 10, 1886.   NO. 19

The Clare Democrat.

Vol. 5.   CLARE, MICH., APRIL 5, 1889.   No. 16.

The Clare Democrat and Press.

ESTABLISHED, Democrat, Dec., 1884. Press, April, 1878.   CLARE, MICH., FRIDAY, FEBRUARY 7, 1890.   NEW SERIES NO. 28

E. D. Palmer and R. G. Jefferies started the Clare Sentinel in 1892, and later purchased the Clare Democrat and Press. The Clare Sentinel was known as a Republican paper and had no Democrat opposition until 1895. That was the year A. Ray Canfield moved to Clare from Harrison and started the Democrat-leaning Clare Courier. It was housed on the west end of the second floor of 505 North McEwan Street. In the battle of newspapers the Clare Sentinel won out, and published long after the

Vol. I.   CLARE, MICH., FRIDAY, JULY 5, 1895.   No. 2.

Clare Courier, which changed its name to The Clare County News in 1922 and went out of business shortly thereafter.

E. D. Palmer eventually sold his interest in the Clare Sentinel to R. G. Jefferies, and Jefferies eventually sold the paper to Edgar G. Welch and Philip A. Bennett. Welch and Bennett operated the paper from a building located on the east side of the 600 block of North McEwan Street. In 1907 they constructed a new building at 114 W. Fourth Street and moved the printing operations there.

THE CLARE SENTINEL

Volume 1.   CLARE, MICH., FRIDAY, JANUARY 13, 1893.   Number 7.

THE CLARE SENTINEL
AND THE
DEMOCRAT-PRESS.

Established 1878.   CLARE, MICH., FRIDAY, DECEMBER 28, 1894.   New Series: Vol. 3, No. 6

The Clare Sentinel.

Established 1878.   CLARE, MICHIGAN, THURSDAY AFTERNOON, AUGUST 7, 1902.   New Series: Vol. 10, No. 37

Welch and Bennett sold the Clare Sentinel to Erastus Palmer and Enoch Andrus in 1910. The next year Mr. Palmer sold his interest in the paper to Andrus, who retained ownership until 1921. John P. Jones and Malcolm Feighner next became owners. Two years later Benjamin Parish purchased Jones' interest. Benjamin Parish died on June 27, 1934, but his wife Florence retained his interest in the newspaper.

The Clare Sentinel and printing business of Malcolm Feighner and Florence Parish continued to grow and necessitated a move to a larger building. This move took place in 1938 when the business was relocated to 112 W. Fourth Street, the building immediately to the east of their previous location. This building served as its home until after 2000. The Clare Sentinel stopped publishing in April 2012.

Agriculture

From the earliest surveys of Michigan, the northern portion of the state had always been considered to have poor soil for the growing of crops. Clare County, including the area surrounding Clare, was covered with White Pine forests, which were considered to grow in sandy and infertile soil. This was the opinion of experts even as late as the beginning of the twentieth century. The November 18, 1906, issue of the *Detroit Free Press* quoted University of Michigan professor of forestry Filbert Roth as saying, "Since 1875 Michigan has fooled away over $1,500,000 trying to sell for agricultural purposes the so-called cut-over pine lands. The first thing for the people to understand is that all lands are not suited for the plow; that the light soil of the upper half of the lower peninsula and of the upper peninsula is, broadly speaking, a natural forest reserve rather than an agricultural country." The opinion of Professor Roth may have been true for the north and northwestern part of Clare County, but the southeast portion of the county, including much land around Clare, proved to be good for agricultural purposes.

Throughout its history only about forty percent of the land in Clare County was used for agricultural purposes. Of all the agricultural land in the county, forty-four percent was located in the four townships in the southeast quarter of the county: Arthur, Grant, Hatton and Sheridan. The City of Clare was the major commercial center for this area of the county, and also for parts of northern Isabella County to the south.

Because of the small amount of land used for farming, Clare County was not a major producer of any agricultural products when compared to the more heavily producing southern counties. But the one area in which Clare County led the state was the number of large farms located within the county. From 1910 to 1950 Clare County led the state in the number of farms with 1,000 or more acres. From 1910 to 1940 it placed anywhere between second place and fifth place in the number of farms between 500 and 1,000 acres. In 1930 Clare County had one of only thirteen farms in the state that measured 5,000 acres or more. Most of these large farms were devoted to raising livestock, with cattle and sheep being the major animal types.

The number of large farms was evidence that commercial farming in Clare County could be profitable. Many of the owners of these large farms were outside investors and did not reside within the county. Men from Saginaw, Chicago, Detroit and northern Ohio were owners of these commercial farms. The reason can be found in the cost of farming in Clare County. In 1900 the value of farm land in Clare County was $8.00 per acre, the ninth lowest in the state. Between 1900 and 1910 the total value of farm land increased by 214.8%, the twelfth highest increase of farm values of any county in the state.

With livestock being a major agricultural activity in the county, clover and timothy were major crops. Other crops produced in the county included potatoes, beans, peas, corn, sugar beets, oats, barley, and rye. In general most crops grew well, but not in abundance. Most crop yields from 1900 to 1950 were at or slightly below the state average. Flooding was not a problem within the county, while an abundance of creeks and a high water table provided enough water to sustain crops in the dry times.

Early Mills and Elevators

Most of the grain-handling facilities located in the town of Clare have historically been located near the railroad tracks. There were two exceptions to this. First, a flour mill was built on the Tobacco River in 1879. This mill was destroyed in 1886 by flooding resulting from a heavy downpour that washed out crops, railroad grades, bridges, mills, and roads. Then in 1892 Mr. Varney built a flour mill on the Tobacco River at about the same location as the present Shamrock Lake Dam. The mill eventually went out of business and was removed. What remained at the site washed out in the 1910s.

In 1876 T. P. Horning and Reist built Clare's first grist mill, but it was destroyed by fire the next year. In 1879 the Horning-Schaeffer flour and grist mill was built at a location north of the Flint & Pere Marquette tracks on West Fourth Street. This was eventually destroyed and replaced by the W. E. Hubel flour mill sometime between 1894 and 1899. The flour mill was sold and became the Kirkbride & Co. Flour Mill in 1903. By 1910 the building no longer existed.

By 1893 Andrew Rhoades was operating a feed mill along with his shingle mill located on the west side of McEwan south of the Flint & Pere Marquette tracks. The complex consisted of the two one-story mills along with two one-story shingle sheds, a one-story hay and feed warehouse, a one-story hay and grain warehouse, and the Rhoades

Kirkbride and Company Mill
Photograph from the Forrest Meek Collection

Grocery Store. By 1899 the shingle mill was expanded and converted into a hub and heading mill, but the feed mill was never enlarged. The feed mill was discontinued sometime between 1906 and 1910. In 1910 the complex retained only one feed warehouse.

The G. W. Lee Feed Mill was in 1893 located on the east side of McEwan Street. This was another one-story mill with an attached

Burch and Wyman Grain Co. Elevator
Photograph from the Forrest Meek Collection

one-and-a-half-story warehouse. An additional one-and-a-half-story hay and feed warehouse was located on the north side of the railroad tracks.

By 1899 the G. W. Lee Feed Mill was replaced by Clare's first grain elevator, which was operated by J. T. Horning. This was a three-story structure; it was sold to Burch and Wyman in 1905. They immediately made modifications to the building to include field bean handling and coal retail. They also purchased the F. B. Doherty lime, cement, and coal business. By 1910 the elevator was being operated as the Clare Elevator Company. This grain elevator was torn down in the 1970s.

The Clare Roller Mill was built in 1903 by William Callam. The mill was operated by an electrical turbine water wheel at the dam on the Tobacco River. By 1923 it was being operated as the Clare City Mills, and producing twenty tons of feed per day. The building was torn down in 1937 to make room for a Gulf Oil Company gas station.

Clare Roller Mills
Photograph from the Forrest Meek Collection

The Survivor: The Chatterton-Johnston Elevator

Clare's second grain elevator was erected in 1905. This elevator was built by J. D. McLaren on a spot just south of the A. S. Rhoades mill complex. It was a two-and-a-half-story structure with warehouses for hay and barrel heads. The elevator was purchased by Chatterton and Son in 1917, and renamed the Clare Hay, Grain & Bean Company elevator. The following year the original two-and-a-half-story elevator was torn down and replaced with the present three-and-a-half-story elevator located at 307 N. McEwan. In the same year the warehouse just to the north of the elevator was expanded. The elevator was sold to Ed G. Johnston in 1926. The name of the business was retained at the time of the purchase but was eventually changed to the Johnston Hay, Grain and Bean Company in 1940, and has since been changed to the Johnston Elevator. Ed Johnston's son Joe took over the business in 1952. The elevator was sold to the Cutler Dickerson Company in 1987.

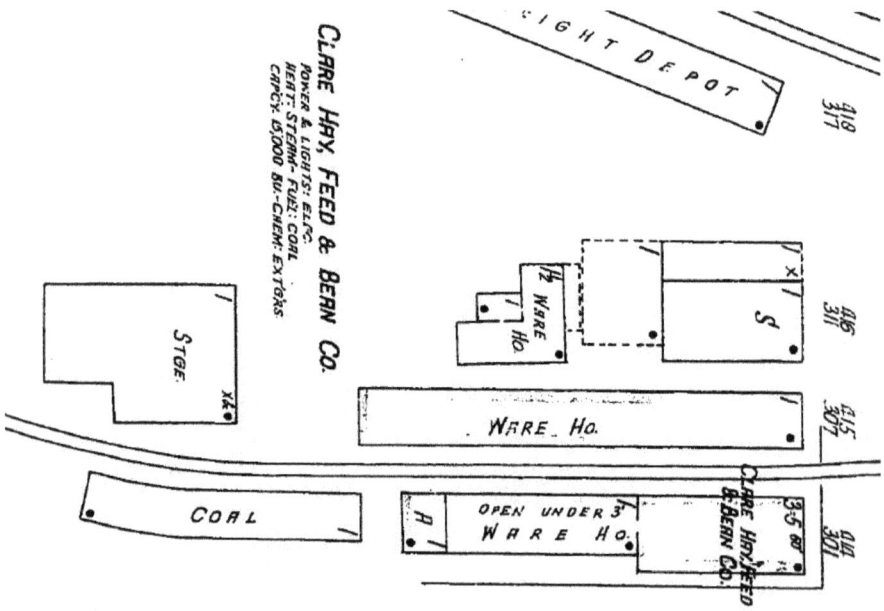

Clare Hay Grain and Bean Co., Elevator in lower right corner
Drawing from the 1923 Sanborn Map

By the turn of the twentieth century Clare had, for the most part, completely transitioned from an economy dependent on the lumber industry to one based on agriculture. As a result of the success of the local agriculture, Clare began to advertise itself as "The Market City" in 1909. The following year the *Clare Sentinel* reported sales of agricultural products in excess of one million dollars. Of that one million dollars, grain production accounted for thirty-one percent, livestock (alive and dressed) twenty-eight percent, and dairy products (wholesale cream and butter) twenty-five percent.

G. O. Fullerton & Son (left), and Johnston Elevator Co. (right)
Photograph from the Forrest Meek Collection

Agriculture-related Stores

During this time businesses began to spring up in support of this industry. A list of Clare businesses from 1902 shows very few stores catering to agricultural enterprises. Besides five hardware stores, John McKerracher's harness shop is the only farm-related business listed. Sometime after 1907, John Gardener would own an agricultural implement business on the north side of west Fourth Street. This implement store was sold to L. H. Thompson in 1912, and sometime in the mid-1900s became the Brewer Implement Store. At an unknown location W. B. Webb and Mortimer Gallagher owned the Clare Hardware and Implement Company. They relocated to 506 N. McEwan in 1914 after purchasing the Calkins Hardware building.

Oil Industry

The earliest history of exploration in Michigan for oil and natural gas is very poorly documented. It is possible that early discoveries in Ontario east of Sarnia in the early 1860s may have led to some exploration in the nearby areas of Michigan's St. Clair County across the border from Sarnia, and wells driven in that area in the 1887-90 period reportedly produced small amounts of crude oil that were refined and used for lubricating buggy and wagon axles. Drilling for water or for brine in certain parts of the state resulted in oil and natural gas discoveries, and since the state was located close to areas in Ontario, Ohio, and Indiana that were already producing oil and gas by 1900, there was ongoing interest in the subject and expectations that oil and gas in marketable quantities would be found. A first successful strike in Saginaw, fifty miles southeast of Clare, in 1925 quickly led to further strikes in that area and to larger firms beginning to explore more widely where the geology suggested. Drilling in what came to be the Mt. Pleasant field, ultimately one of the largest producers, located relatively close to Clare, began in 1927 and early in 1928 came an important strike that ushered in a boom in the oil and natural gas industries across the central part of the Lower Peninsula from Saginaw, Bay City, and Midland on the east to Mt. Pleasant, Alma, and Clare in the center and to Muskegon on the west. Exploration and new discoveries across the region proceeded rapidly during the 1930s.

In the Clare area the first discovery was of the McKay gas field in Grant Township in 1929. Additional oil and gas fields were developed in the west and northwest part of the county and to the south in adjacent Isabella County during the 1930s and 40s and later. The discovery of oil in the Clare area had a greater positive economic impact on the city of Clare than the tourist industry. To a large extent it insulated the city from the effects of the Great Depression.

With the oil and gas discoveries representatives of Michigan and national oil companies flocked to the scene. In the early oil boom days few oil men actually opened local offices. Most ran their operations out of rooms at the Doherty Hotel. The Strange Oil and Gas Company was one of those businesses headquartered at the Doherty Hotel. There were, however, exceptions: the Freeman Oil Company had offices in the

Doherty Building in the 400 block of North McEwan Street and also in the second story of the Holbrook/Mair Building at 109 West Fifth Street. Merritt Oil also had an office in Clare, though at a location unknown today. Additionally, William Teeter opened a real estate and oil lease exchange office in February 1930 in the building at 502 North McEwan Street.

The key player in the county's oil industry in the 1930s and later was the Mammoth Petroleum Company, established in 1930 and reconstituted as the Mammoth Producing & Refining Corporation in 1933. Isaiah Leebove and Carl ("Jack") Livingston, both with backgrounds in the Oklahoma oil industry, and Sam Garfield, who had strong connections with Detroit's largely Jewish criminal underground, the Purple Gang, created the company after coming to Clare in 1929 seeking opportunities in this area located so close to previous discoveries. Leebove also had strong connections with New York's criminal underworld. Mammoth Petroleum/Producing & Refining was more than just your average oil exploration and drilling company. It was an oil company that served to launder money for Detroit's Purple Gang crime syndicate. Mammoth Oil had its first known office in Clare in the second story of the Citizens State Bank Building at 502 N. McEwan, the northeast corner of North McEwan and Fourth Streets, in April 1937. In December of that year the company acquired the former Clare County State Bank Building across the street at 431 N. McEwan. For the area's oilmen and investors, including those affiliated with Mammoth, the Doherty Hotel continued to serve as a key social gathering place. On May 16, 1938, the hotel's bar became the site of the murder of Isaiah Leebove by Jack Livingston, his former business associate in Mammoth, who felt Leebove had cheated him of his fair share in Mammoth profits. In 1942 Mammoth moved its office to the newly constructed building at 515 N. McEwan, remaining there until it purchased the Citizens State Bank Building in 1961. Mammoth Oil operated from this location until it closed its Clare office in the 1970s.

Social History/Entertainment and Recreation

Clare like most other communities had its share of social organizations. From the Sanborn maps it can be noted that the Women's Relief Corp. operated a dining hall on the northeast corner of Sixth and McEwan Streets from c. 1894 to 1899. The Grand Army of the Republic (G.A.R.) occupied for a time Duncan Hall located on the second floor of 427 North McEwan.

Two groups which had a long presence in Clare's downtown were the Masons and the Independent Order of Odd Fellows (IOOF). The Masons met in the north unit of the second floor of the Wilson-Sutherland Building, located at the southwest corner of Fourth and McEwan, from c. 1893 until the building burned in 1910. The Masons then relocated to the second floor of the newly constructed Doherty Building at 518 North McEwan and remained at this location until 1931 when they remodeled and moved into the old Doherty Opera House. In 1989 after meeting in the former Opera House for fifty-eight years the Masons moved to the former Seventh Day Adventist building on East Fifth Street (outside of the district).

The IOOF is first known to have met in the south unit of the second floor of the Wilson-Sutherland Building in 1893. The following year they moved to a building in the middle of the east side of McEwan Street between Sixth and Seventh Streets. By the turn of the twentieth century the IOOF had moved out of this building and it was being used by the Knights of Pythias. The IOOF relocated to the second floor of Alfred J. Doherty's new six-storefront building. After fifty-seven years of meeting in this location, the IOOF was forced to relocate when the building burned in 1957. Their new lodge was constructed north of the downtown on Wilcox Parkway in 1958.

The American Legion met in the second floor of City Hall when the new building, officially known as the Clare City Hall and Memorial Building and dedicated to those who served and died in World War I, was completed in 1934. The building was designed to house second-story space for the American Legion.

The Clare Library Association and the Clare Study Club were two groups comprised of mostly women which advocated for the advancement of education in Clare. The two groups were influential in accumulating a 300-book library in the early twentieth century which was initially housed in the Union School. The school and library were lost in a 1921 fire. The Clare Library Association once again rallied to collect books and was able to establish a library within the Doherty Hotel once the building was completed in 1924. In 1950 the Doherty Hotel asked the library to relocate in order to use the space for a dining room. The library first relocated to the basement of the Dunwoodie Building across the street on the west side of McEwan, and operated there until 1961 when it relocated to the northeast corner of Fourth and McEwan. The library continued to grow and found it necessary to expand into a larger building, which it did in 2007, relocating to 185 East Fourth Street.

Even though the village of Clare was platted in 1870 and had seen rapid growth, it was not until 1881 that it saw the opening of its first Opera House. The Husted Opera House was constructed in 1881 at what is now 415 North McEwan. It was a three-story building with the opera house located on the third floor. The building was destroyed in an 1888 fire that damaged nearly the entire block of buildings. With the loss of the Opera House, Clare was without a place of entertainment. The G.A.R. Hall filled some of the void, but it was not equipped for the needs of the Clare citizens. Coming to the rescue in 1890 was Alfred J. Doherty. His Doherty Opera House at 524 N. McEwan, located adjacent to his hardware store, opened in 1891, with the 700 seat opera house located on the second floor of the building.

Repertory troupes who came to the Doherty Opera House traveled a circuit which included Farwell and Harrison. The Doherty Opera House also offered local drama talent, particularly that of the Clare Dramatic Club, consisting of Floyd Doherty, Alberta Long, Julia Harris, Sarah Malcolm, Mrs. Robert Mussell, Frank Colburn, T. S. Dorsey, C. H. O'Donald, R. G. Jefferies, Grant Defoe, and Frank Louch. Music was provided by the Kirkbride orchestra. Some of the club's productions were "The Dutch Recruit," "Among the Breakers," "A False Marriage," and "Imogene or the Wicked Witch." Probably the most unusual production put on at the Opera House was by Professor D. M. Bristol in 1893. His "Equescurriculum" included thirty horses.

After the opening of the Doherty Opera House, the G.A.R. Hall continued to hold productions. In fact in 1890 and 1891 a traveling troupe held shows of "Uncle Tom's Cabin" in both the G.A.R. Hall and the Doherty Opera House within sixty days of each other. However, the

179

Doherty Opera House began acquiring the better shows and the G.A.R. Hall was converted to a gymnasium for the local citizens.

Business was booming for the Doherty Opera House at the turn of the twentieth century. The interior was completely redecorated in 1901. In 1903 the Opera House tried its hand at motion pictures. The Colonial Motion Picture Company scheduled a showing of the "The Great Train Robbery" movie. The movie and projector were, however, destroyed in a fire in Alma prior to the movie's showing in Clare.

The motion picture industry continued to be bad news for the Doherty Opera House. The mid-1900s and early 1910s saw the opening of several small motion picture theaters in Clare. The Star Theatre, the first to open in 1906, was located on West Fourth Street. It was owned by Whitney and Sutton, and showed one- and two-reel movies. The theater had a large white sheet on one end of the room and benches for patrons to sit on. In 1907 Dr. Dunlop opened the Oriental Theatre on the vacant second floor of his Medical Hall on the southwest corner of Fifth and McEwan Streets. The theater, bought by E. N. Whitney in 1910, became the Vaudette. The Star Theatre became the Temple in 1908 and then, bought by Fred Northquist in 1911, became the Palace Theatre.

On July 4, 1912, the first full-time theater was opened in Clare. The Princess Theatre, owned by the Princess Photo Company, was located in the center unit of the Dunwoodie Building on the northwest corner of Fifth and McEwan Streets. The theater showed three-reel movies and illustrated songs daily.

As motion pictures became more popular, the Doherty Opera House could not compete. In March 1913 the Opera House's seats were sold off and work began to convert it to a public meeting room. In 1931 the Masons were leasing it for their Masonic Lodge.

What became downtown Clare's primary movie theater was built in 1930. In that year John Asline, then the owner of the Princess Theater, constructed the Ideal Theater at 609 N. McEwan. The theater could seat five hundred people, and was equipped with the most up-to-date projectors. The Ideal still serves Clare to this day.

Other recreational activities included roller skating on the second floor of 506 N. McEwan, and bowling on the second floor of 431 N. McEwan after the building was no longer used for banking purposes.

Churches

On September 8, 1872, the Rev. Austin Hull Norris and State Superintendent of Congregational Churches, the Rev. Leroy Warren, arrived in Clare to promote the establishment of a Congregational church in the village. The following Sunday evening the Rev. Norris held his first worship service in a small building in the south part of town that was being built for a school building. The church was officially recognized by council on December 22, 1872. The small congregation first met at the school building, but the Rev. Norris was determined to have a proper church building. He learned that William and John McEwan had set aside lots number eleven and twelve in block sixteen, on West Fifth Street, in trust for the Presbyterian Society. The Presbyterians, lacking an organized congregation, relinquished their claim on the property to the Congregationalists.

Construction of a Congregational church, the first church building in Clare, began in July 1873. The financial hard times of 1873 caused the money for the project to come in slowly, and as a result the building was not finished until the summer of 1874. The present brick Congregational church, completed in 1909, stands at the same site within the district.

Other denominations would also soon build in Clare – the Free Methodists, Methodist Episcopal Church, Baptists, German Lutherans, and Catholics all by 1900 – but their church buildings all stood outside the district.

Congregational Church, circa 1900
Photograph from the Forrest Meek Collection

Architecture

The Clare Downtown Historic District contains a concentration of commercial buildings that, dating from the later nineteenth to the mid-twentieth century, possesses architectural significance for embodying a variety of architectural styles and features. The district also contains several architecturally distinguished non-commercial buildings, including a church and public buildings.

Clare's Congregational Church, built in 1908-09, is significant as a central-plan auditorium type church whose domed Greek cross-form exterior reflects Early Christian (with Byzantine and Romanesque elements as well) church design – a highly distinctive design for a Michigan Protestant church building of the early twentieth century. The building is significant in architectural terms not only for its design but also for its high place in the career of its Saginaw, Michigan-based architect, William T. Cooper.

Two significant public buildings within the district are the 1930s City Hall and Post Office buildings. Clare's City Hall was constructed in the winter of 1933-34 under the direction of the Civil Works Administration (CWA). The CWA was a New Deal agency established to provide construction jobs to unemployed workers. The program began on November 8, 1933, and ended less than five months later on March 31, 1934. The Clare City Hall and Memorial Building (its official name when built) is a two-story brick building of simple Art Deco-influenced design that is notable for its exterior brickwork that includes panels of vertically laid soldier bricks, raised brick details, and accents in brick of different hue from the main body of the building – techniques that, without dramatically raising the cost of the building, provide a great deal of artistic variety and visual interest. Although the building has been substantially altered over the years, these visual qualities have survived for the most part and reflect solid honor on the architect, R. V. Gay (1895-1943) of St. Johns, who had an extensive career in central Michigan specializing in school and public buildings. Gay (R. V. was his given name) first worked for the Warren S. Holmes Co. of Lansing, school building design specialists, in the early 1920s and then briefly as a partner in Gay & Brezner before forming his own firm around 1923. His two largest projects were the Northern Michigan Tuberculosis Sanitarium (later Alpine Regional Center for

Developmental Disabilities) in Gaylord, 1936-39, and Midland High School in Midland, 1935-37. Gay had a Clare connection in that his wife, Florence (White) Gay, was from there – the two met in the early 1920s at the Warren S. Holmes Co., where both were serving as draftsmen, and Mrs. Gay later worked with R. V. Gay in Gay's architectural practice. Gay's obituary notes that he was "prominent in state and national American Legion circles."

The Clare Post Office was constructed in 1936-37. While a typical design for a Depression Era post office whose symmetrical unornamented modern design represents one of the eleven basic standard post office designs used by the Office of the Supervising Architect of the Treasury between 1934 and the early 1940s, the building exhibits the quiet understated refinement of design of most of these 1930s post office buildings. The Clare Post Office is also notable for containing a mural created for it when the building was new. It is Allan Thomas' mural, "The Mail Arrives in Clare-1871." Post office murals such as this were funded through the Treasury Department's Section of Painting and Sculpture, and commissioned both to provide artwork to local communities for the purpose of boosting the morale of people suffering the effects of the Great Depression and providing support for unemployed artists as part of the federal Depression-relief effort.

The earliest buildings within the Clare Downtown Historic District are three former residences. All of them were wood framed and of vernacular design that would be common to any late nineteenth-century rural Michigan community. Of them the 1882 Goodman House at 120 E. Fifth is the most intact.

The downtown's and district's two most important nineteenth-century buildings from an architectural standpoint are the adjoining Doherty Opera House and Clare County Savings Bank buildings at 524 and 532 N. McEwan, of Late Victorian design and built in 1891 and 1887, respectively. The buildings' broad upper facades complement each other in their use of rock-face stone trim, tall soldier brick arches over the windows, and paired windows beneath broad segmental arches. The bank building retains its broad projecting cornice supported by beefy brackets in groups of three. The Opera House has lost something through the removal of its decorative roofline treatment – a cornice with ornamental balustrade and gabled treatment at one end – and a small

Clare County Savings Bank (left), and Doherty Opera House (right),
Photograph from the Robert Knapp Collection

balustrade balcony that once fronted the center paired windows. Restoring at least the roofline treatment would have a dramatic visual impact on this key building and its block in the downtown.

The close design affinity between the two buildings stems from the fact that both were built for the same client, local businessman Alfred J. Doherty, and Doherty used the same architect, Fred W. Hollister of Saginaw, for both. Hollister (1847-1923) had a wide-ranging career across the Lower Peninsula and beyond over more than a half century. Born in upstate New York, he came to Saginaw as a youth and, working in other architects' offices beginning in 1864, entered into his own practice in 1870. Hollister had a general practice and designed everything from houses to commercial buildings and churches, but he was best known for his public and institutional buildings that included county courthouses in Isabella, Saginaw, Ogemaw, Gladwin, and Huron counties, 167 school buildings, according to an obituary, and large buildings at the Michigan Soldiers' Home in Grand Rapids, Michigan School for the Deaf in Flint, and Industrial School for Boys in Lansing.

Key features of the downtown district are its many Neoclassical buildings. These buildings by their number, size, and fine detailing visually dominate the McEwan streetscape and give the downtown much of its character. Neoclassicism is an architecture that prominently features elements directly or at least loosely based in classical Greek and Roman architecture, particularly columns, piers, pilasters, and cornices and entablatures. America's Classical and Greek Revival architecture, most popular from the 1820s to the 1840s, reflected one rebirth of interest in the architecture of ancient Greece and Rome, but went out of style in the 1850s. A new rebirth of interest in Neoclassical as a more restrained and simplified alternative to the highly decorative Victorian styles most popular in the 1850s to the 1880s was popularized by the very widely attended 1893 World's Columbian Exposition in Chicago, whose buildings presented a luxuriant display of imposing large-scale architecture predominantly of classical character.

Neoclassical styling was introduced to the Clare downtown in 1904 with the Davy Building at 501 N. McEwan, with its broad piers, second-story window bays outlined by piers and entablatures, and broad main frieze and console bracket-decorated cornice. The second-story piers' Ionic capitals and most of the Ionic capitals on the second-story window piers have disappeared over the years, but enough are left to serve as

Davy Building, 1904
Photograph from the Forrest Meek Collection
185

models for reproducing these important lost features that would further enhance the visual character of this notable building.

The large building to the immediate north at 505, 509 N. McEwan is also a prime example. It also has a console-bracket-detailed main cornice and a classical-trim-decorated bay window (a second bay window in 509 has been removed) and, while lacking the broad piers, instead features classical molded architrave-trim brick window surrounds on the second-story windows and also a molded brick egg-and-dart band forming the frieze's lower edge – both unusual touches not duplicated elsewhere in Clare's downtown. (see page 107)

Like the Davy Building, the Tatman Building at 506 N. McEwan also displays a simplified, abstract Neoclassicism that works well in commercial blocks of standard form with storefronts downstairs and office or living quarters upstairs. It has large brick piers with Ionic capitals of simplified, abstract form. A low corbelled brick architrave supports a broad plain frieze and a cornice with oversized squared-off modillions. The paired second-story windows have plain stone slab caps. Now housing a single large store, Clare Hardware, the broad-fronted building with its six groups of paired windows plus a single one at each end is one of the largest commercial blocks in the district. The building was designed by Clare architect O. M. Sutherland. Sutherland is also responsible for the design of two other brick buildings on the same block of McEwan, which were also rebuilt after the 1904 fire.

The 1911 Doherty Building next door to the Tatman at 518 N. McEwan is another outstanding Neoclassical store building. Its second story is adorned with a brick pier at each outer edge and fluted columns in the center. Piers and columns are crowned with highly detailed Ionic capitals rather than the more abstract form used next door, and the cornice displays intricately detailed console brackets and a dentil band beneath. The entablature's brickwork, also intricately detailed, uses corbelled work to form separate architrave and frieze bands and dentil-like details. The upstairs windows' flat-arch stone caps with raised keystones are another fine classical touch. This is another of local businessman Alfred J. Doherty's ornaments to his city.

The Cops & Doughnuts "complex" at 521 and 523 N. McEwan contains two more notable buildings of Neoclassical inspiration, both constructed in the wake of a 1907 fire. The Foss or Clare City Bakery building at 521 N. McEwan was constructed in 1907, the Rhoades

Building at 523 in 1908. The Rhoades Building uses a quoin-like treatment in the brick end piers, with masonry Ionic capitals of wonderfully abstract form, while the main cornice itself displays console brackets with conventional classical detailing above a decorative metal frieze. The storefront retains its old prism glass transoms. This beautifully detailed brick building was designed by another local architect, Edward Gorr. The Clare City Bakery Building, 521, has the most inventive front of any Neoclassical-influenced building in the district, using the brickwork to provide a highly abstract version of the classical vocabulary.

An important historic feature of the Rhoades Building is its highly intact original pressed metal ceiling, fabricated by the Eller Manufacturing Company of Canton, Ohio. Ornamental pressed metal ceilings (and wall finishes) came into great popularity in the late nineteenth century as a cheaper and more durable substitute for ornamental plasterwork. They were part of a much broader development of architectural metalwork of all kinds – ornamental metal building fronts; pressed metal exterior cladding in place of wood, brick, or stone; cornices; and roofing material – that reached a peak of use during the same late nineteenth and early twentieth-century time period. The pressed metal technology made possible an infinite variety and degree of complexity in designs – ornamental work that was far beyond what could be accomplished in plaster at an affordable price. Manufacturers of pressed metal ceiling and wall material were to be found in many parts of the nation, but Ohio in general and particularly Canton, Ohio, located near great steel mill centers such as Pittsburgh, Pennsylvania, and Youngstown, Ohio, became an important center for the industry. By 1900 Canton was the home of three leading manufacturers, the Berger Manufacturing Company, Canton Steel Ceiling Company (based in New York, but with the plant in Canton), and the Eller Manufacturing Company. These companies' early twentieth-century catalogs, each a thick volume containing hundreds of designs for whole ceilings and ceiling components – Berger's 1908 *"Classik" Metal Ceilings Catalogue Number 12* contains 420 pages – illustrate both the immense variety of designs and the artistic skill and creativity of the firms' designers and artisans. Eller's 185-page 1910 catalog states that the company, the successor to J. H. Eller & Co., was then in its twentieth year of making metal ceilings (Eller, Introductory,

4). Like Berger and some other large-scale manufacturers, Eller designated its designs by style, such as "Gothic," "Colonial," or "Italian Renaissance," the intent seeming to be to assist clients in selecting models for the various ceiling components that complemented one another. The Rhoades Building's ceiling mostly follows a design for an entire "Colonial" ceiling that, illustrated on the catalog's page 34, uses the same cove design along the edge outlining the same panels in three sizes. The Clare ceiling differs from the page 34 design, though, in using a filler of "Gothic" design for the flat area against the cove around the edges. The ceiling uses stock components illustrated on later pages in the catalog. It is a fine example of the pressed metal ceiling type during its prime years. Another excellent example of an Eller pressed metal ceiling exists in the former Lipsett Hardware Building, now the Pickford Area Historical Society Museum, in Pickford, Chippewa County.

What was once the downtown's most fully developed example of Neoclassical design, and still retains much of the original Neoclassical finish, is the former Clare County Savings Bank at 431 N. McEwan. The building originally displayed a shallow, recessed portico containing two two-story tall Ionic columns in the central third of the front. While the front was rebuilt without the portico and the banking room divided into two stories after the bank's 1932 failure, the buff brick front and

Architects Rendering of the Clare County Savings Bank
Drawing from the Robert Knapp Collection

long street-facing side retain much of their terra-cotta detailing, including the classical entablature and parapet cap, rosette medallions in the low attic, pier capitals displaying anthemions and other classical motifs, and the ornamental terra cotta panels above the side windows depicting acanthus leaves and other classical devices.

This building was designed by Cowles & Mutscheller of Saginaw, comprised of Clarence Cowles and George Mutscheller – Cowles also served as the architect for the Doherty Hotel, whose construction began in 1922. The building was designed in 1915, but not constructed until 1922. Born in Flint, Clarence Cowles (1869-1935) moved to Saginaw and opened his own architectural office in 1893. George Mutscheller (1882-1936) was born in Sturgis and moved to Saginaw by 1908, when he and Cowles formed the Cowles & Mutscheller firm. Saginaw historian/architectural historian Thomas Trombley states that, "In the first decade of the twentieth century, Clarence Cowles produced designs for a number of substantial private and public buildings. Although he employed many different historically inspired styles, his work is characterized by structural innovation and imaginative manipulation of space." Trombley lists among Cowles' own buildings two in Saginaw – St. Mary's Catholic Cathedral, 601 Hoyt, a Gothic building built in 1901, and the Forest Lawn Cemetery Comfort Station, exotic in its Moorish-inspired design. A 1915 article cited by Trombley reported that the Cowles & Mutscheller firm "has designed 1,600 buildings since its inception." He states, "In the teens, Cowles and Mutscheller designed some of their finest buildings." While the loss of the full Ionic column-decorated original front of the building is to be regretted, the building exterior as it stands today with much of the original intricate Neoclassical detailing in place remains a key architectural landmark in the district and downtown.

An architectural "style" dating from the early to the mid-twentieth century commonly found in Michigan downtowns is what has been called "Commercial Brick," a fashion in which references to historic styles of architecture are downplayed or omitted and the decorative qualities provided by the brickwork itself impart the "style." Rectangular panels of brickwork outlined by raised strips of header and rowlock or full stretcher and soldier bricks, as in the upper façade of 104 W. Fifth Street, are a characteristic Commercial Brick motif, with other forms such as panels of basketweave or herringbone brickwork.

Color variations – playing off two different hues of brick in the same façade – are also sometimes part of the Commercial Brick vocabulary. The 1907 Clare City Bakery Building, with its elaborate shadow-catching display of brickwork that presents more abstract than truly classical forms seems the prototype for Commercial Brick in downtown Clare. A prime example in the district is the 1933-34 Clare City Hall in which architect R. V. Gay used raised brickwork panels, strips and panels of soldier brickwork, and accents of brick of different hue to enliven a building of otherwise relatively simple exterior design. The buff brick upper façade of the 1930 Ideal Theater Building is the district's outstanding commercial building of Commercial Brick design. Its upper façade displays a variety of brickwork patterns – stacked headers forming raised strips flanking the window openings and framing the façade's three broad piers and forming vertical raised strips and panels in the centers of the piers, horizontal bands of alternating raised and recessed rowlock and soldier bricks spanning the tops of the window bays, and horizontal bands of headers alternately recessed and flush with the façade below the second-story window openings and below the parapet – that provide an interesting play of light and shadow.

The massive Bicknell Building at 418-20 N. McEwan, its larger north part built in 1907 and the shorter southern section in matching style resulting from the façade renovation of an older building in 1923, also fits into the Commercial Brick fashion despite its classical-inspired cornice with modillions and dentils. Its attic below the cornice displays recessed squares of brickwork with masonry blocks marking the corners and strips of headers outlining the panels on all sides. A three brick high corbelled band formed a cornice-like detail separating the attic from the tall storefront below. Horizontal header courses spanning the attic façade between the panels and blocks above and below them were made of a different color brick from the rest, giving the upper front a bi-colored look that is no longer present since the façade was painted in the 1970s. The historic photo of the building in *Clare 1865-1940* shows the now boarded-in middle level of the façade above the storefront filled with broad strips of large prism glass windows that made a strong contribution to the building's very striking appearance. A 1907 newspaper story lists "Bogart" of Saginaw as "architect" – who this was

Bicknell Store Building, circa 1923
Photograph from the Forrest Meek Collection

and whether architect in the modern sense or in the old sense of "chief builder" was meant is unclear.

During the 1920s "modern" architecture that purposefully rejected the historic styles of the past began to come into popularity in the United States. Modern design had its beginnings in the United States as well as Europe in the early twentieth century, but found more ready acceptance in Europe than it did in the United States. One early form of modernism, known as Art Deco, characterized by angular, blocky forms, was at its height of popularity from the 1920s into the 1930s. Although City Hall's brickwork and the Ideal Theater Building's upper façade's brick detailing both have something of an Art Deco feel to them, no buildings in the district truly exemplify Art Deco. But two buildings in the district do exemplified the slightly later Moderne style of the mid-1930s to the early 1950s with its smooth finishes and rounded rather than angular forms. One is the Ideal Theater's theater front with its colorful marquee, a 1937 renovation to the 1930 building, the other was the enameled metal panel-front building at 517 N. McEwan that forms the southern end of the Cops & Doughnuts buildings. The enamel from the 517 North McEwan building was removed in 2016 when the façade was completely remodeled.

In the first decades after World War II the International style, the high point of modern design in its crisp, clean lines and lack of ornament, became widely accepted in the United States. The dominance of the International style coincided with the prosperous period of the 1950s and 60s when much building and renovating of older buildings was taking place across the nation. The buildings at 102 W. Fifth and 417 N. McEwan with their stacked-bond brickwork built using elongated Roman brick and large expanses of shop windows set on low bulkheads are highly intact examples of the International style storefront design of the post-World War II era. The current front of 102 W. Fifth likely dates from a 1948 renovation after a fire, while 417 N. McEwan was built in two parts, the larger south end in 1957 and north end in 1963.

***West side of the 600 block of North McEwan, looking northwest,
Circa 1970***
Photograph from the Forrest Meek Collection

Bibliography

Barrera, Helen G. "Mom and dad designed structures all over the state" [R. V. and Florence Gay]. *Detroit Free Press,* March 28, 1988. Metro/State section, 12c.

Barrera, Helen G. File of information on life and career of architect R. V. Gay provided to MI SHPO 1988.

Bellinger, Scott; Roger Lintemuth, et al. *Michigan Oil & Gas Story: County by County.* Mt. Pleasant, MI: Michigan Oil & Gas News, Inc., 1991.

"Boom Clare." *The Clare Press*. Clare, Michigan. 4 February, 1887.

Central Michigan Community Federal Credit Union. Retrieved 2 April 2010. From http://www.cmcfcu.com/profile.html.

Christensen, R. O. Saginaw County Fairgrounds Main Gate, Saginaw, National Register nomination [Cowles & Mutscheller background].

"Clare A Million Dollar Market." *The Clare Sentinel*. Clare, Michigan. 16 December, 1910.

Clare Area Centennial Committee. *Clare Remembered*. Mount Pleasant, Michigan: Enterprise Printers. 1979.

Clare, City of. City Charter. Clare, Michigan. 1948.

"Clare, Clare County, Mich." *The Clare County Press*. Clare, Michigan. 11 October, 1878.

"Clare, 'The Market City.' " *The Clare Sentinel*. Clare, Michigan. 5 March, 1909.

Eller Manufacturing Company. *Eller's "Perfect-Fit" Steel Ceilings. Catalog No. 20*. Canton, Ohio, 1910. R. O. Christensen.

Greusel, John Hubert. "Problem of Renewing Michigan's Forests." *The Detroit Free Press*. 18 November, 1906.

Jackson, Kathleen, Photography Collection.

Knapp, Robert C. *A History of Downtown Clare, 1868-1958*. Manuscript. 2009.

---. *Clare 1865-1940*. Images of America. Charleston, SC.: Arcadia Publishing. 2012.

---. *Mystery Man: Gangsters, Oil, and Murder in Michigan*. Clare, MI: Cliophile Press, 2014.

---. Photography Collection.

Lingaur, Kenneth. *Downtown Clare Historic District Survey, Clare, Michigan, Clare County*. Manuscript. Pere Marquette District Library, Clare Michigan. 2011.

Meek, Forrest. *The Doherty Hotel*. Preliminary Draft. 1991.

---. *Michigan's Heartland 1900–1918*. Clare, Michigan: Edgewood Press. 1979.

---. *Michigan's Timber Battleground*. Clare, Michigan: Clare County Bicentennial Historical Committee. 1976.

---. Photography Collection. Mid-Michigan Community College. Harrison, Michigan.

---. *Time Line History of Clare, Michigan*. Manuscript in Pere Marquette District Library. Clare, Michigan. 1991.

Northeastern Michigan Development Bureau. *Clare County Special, The Land of Diversified Agriculture, The Last Good Land at a Low Price*. Bay City, Michigan: April, 1916.

"Saginaw Architect Called by Death" [Fred W. Hollister]. *Saginaw News Courier,* April 11, 1923.

Sanborn Company. *Sanborn Fire Insurance Maps*. Pelham, New York. 1893, Sheet 1. Proquest L.L.C. 2001-2008.

---. *Sanborn Fire Insurance Maps*. Pelham, New York. 1894, Sheets 2 and 3. Proquest L.L.C. 2001-2008.

---. *Sanborn Fire Insurance Maps*. Pelham, New York. 1899, Sheets 3, 4, and 5. Proquest L.L.C. 2001-2008.

---. *Sanborn Fire Insurance Maps*. Pelham, New York. 1906, Sheets 2, 3, and 4. Proquest L.L.C. 2001-2008.

---. *Sanborn Fire Insurance Maps*. Pelham, New York. 1910, Sheets 2, 3, and 4. Proquest L.L.C. 2001-2008.

---. *Sanborn Fire Insurance Maps.* Pelham, New York. 1923, Sheets 2 and 4. Proquest L.L.C. 2001-2008.

---. *Sanborn Fire Insurance Maps.* Pelham, New York. 1928-1934, Sheets 2 and 4. Proquest L.L.C. 2001-2008.

United States Dept. of Commerce and Labor. Thirteenth Census of the United States, Taken In The Year 1910, Volume VI, Agriculture 1909 and 1910, Reports By States, With Statistics For Counties, Alabama – Montana. Washington: GPO, 1913.

United States Dept. of Commerce. Fifteenth Census of the United States: 1930, Agriculture Volume I, Farm Acreage and Farm Values By Townships or Other Minor Civil Divisions. Washington: GPO. 1931.

---. Sixteenth Census of the United States: 1940, Agriculture Volume 1, First and Second Series State Reports, Part 1, Statistics For Counties, Farms and Farm Property, With Related Information for Farms and Farm Operators, Livestock and Livestock Products, and Crops. Washington: GPO, 1942.

---. United States Census of Agriculture: 1950, Counties and State Economic Areas, Michigan, Volume I Part 6. Washington: GOP, 1952.

United States Dept. of the Interior, Census Office. Census Reports, Volume Five, Twelfth Census of the United States, Taken In The Year 1900, Agriculture Part I Farms, Livestock, and Animal Products. Washington: United States Census Office, 1902.

All photographs unless otherwise noted are attributed to the author.

Appendix

Michigan Gazetteer and Business Directory Listings for Clare Michigan

A Gazetteer is a business directory based on geographic locations, and included some social and economic statistics. The Michigan Gazetteers featured listings from each of the known towns and cities in Michigan. Each municipality had a general description which included population, nearest large cities, railroads or closest railroad station, types of businesses, churches, and types of utilities that served the area. Also featured was an extensive list of businesses operating within the area. If a business wanted to draw attention to themselves they could pay extra to have their name bolded, or they could place on advertisement in the gazetteer. The following pages are the complete listings for the City of Clare found in the Gazetteer that were available on the internet. The Michigan Gazetteers shown here were published by C. F. Clark of Detroit, Michigan.

Author's Note

When compiling the Gazetteers there were a number of errors found in the original documents. Most of these errors were in the spelling of names. Efforts were made to correct these errors, but some may still exist.

Clare. A village of 700 inhabitants, is situated in the township of Grant, on the southern line of Clare County. It is a station of the F. & P. M. Ry., 50 miles above East Saginaw, and 5 east of Farwell, the county seat. Clare is a new and growing village. The first settlement was made in 1870. It has 3 saw and shingle mills, 1 planing mill, 1 flour mill, a Congregational church, and a large new school house with an attendance of 100 pupils. There are 2 hotels, Sterns' Stage House being the best. A stage leaves here daily for Mount Pleasant 15 miles south, fare $1.00. The principal articles of shipment are lumber, shingles, hoops, staves, and flour. Good water power is derived from Tobacco creek. Telegraph, Western Union, Express, American, Mail, daily. J.C. Rockafellow, postmaster.

BUSINESS DIRECTORY

Beebe A Byron, wines and liquors.

Bogardus Mrs Martha, millinery.

Boorne George, lumber and shingle mill.

Calkins John W, hardware.

Callam Peter, general store.

Cooley Wallace S, harnessmaker.

Crawford Robert, General Store, Main.

Davis Malcolm D, physician.

Donahue Patrick, cigars and liquors.

Elden Wm H, jeweler.

Ervey Albert M, shoemaker.

Halstead George, barber.

Hardy Llewellyn, station agent and telegraph operator.

Hardy Mrs Theresa, millinery.

Horning John T, shingle mnfr.

Horning Tobias P, flour and shingle mill.

Hustead Berton, blacksmith.

Jefferies George W, justice of the peace.

Jefferies Mrs George W, bakery.

Lamb & Son, (David W. and Rudolph W), foundry.

Lee George, grocer.

Louch Alfred, blacksmith.

McIntyre Arthur W, justice of the peace.

McKinley Rev J F (Methodist).

Maynard Thomas H, physician.

Nicholls John A, propr Nicholls House.

Norris Rev A H (Congregational).

Ort Henry, sash, doors and blinds.

Palmer Eugene, propr Alger House and livery stable.

Rider Ebenezer W, lawyer and planing mill.

Rockafellow John C, general store.

Shaver & McIntyre (Albert A Shaver, Arthur W McIntyre), carpenters and undertakers.

Slattery John B, liquors.

Slocum & Mason (James A Slocum, Jacob Mason), hop mnfrs.

Spring Edwards J, groceries, boots, shoes and express agent.

Sterns Caleb W, Propr Stern's Stage House and Livery, Main. (*See adv.*)

Stern's Stage House, C W Sterns Propr, Main. (*See adv.*)

Trevidick Henry, druggist.

Wheaton Elijah D, lawyer.

Whitley & Co (Grace Whitley, Harvey Deuell), general store.

Wright James A. shoemaker.

Sterns House

C. W. STERNS, Proprietor,

CLARE, - - - **MICHIGAN.**

This House is the Head Quarters for commercial and other travelers, and is run in connection with the Nelson House, Mount Pleasant. A daily stage and livery rigs run between the two houses, connecting with every train on the F. & P. M. R. R.

1879

Clare. First settled in 1870, has a population of about 700; located in Grant township near the southern line of Clare county, on the F. & P. M. R'y, 5 miles east of Farwell, the seat of justice, 30 northwest of East Saginaw, and 148 from Detroit. The village has two churches-Congregational and Methodist-a large school house with and average attendance of 100, two hotels, and a weekly newspaper. The shipments are shingles, hoops and staves, flour and wheat. This is the chief outlet and railroad shipping point for Mount Pleasant and the rich agricultural region contiguous to it, and is quite an important railroad station. Daily stage to Mt. Pleasant, 15 miles south; fare $1. Express, American, Telegraph, Western Union. Daily mail. J. C. Rockafellow, postmaster.

BUSINESS DIRECTORY

Alger David, lawyer.

Alger House, D & F Alger Propr.

Alger D & F (David and Frank), proprs Alger House.

Beebe A Byron, saloon.

Bicknell Nathan, Auctioneer and Commission Merchant, Business Promptly Attended to.

Bogardus Mrs. Martha, Millinery.

Bowdish Seth, drugs and groceries.

Calkins John W, hardware and stoves.

Callam Peter, general store.

Chamberlin M F & Sterns (Millard F Chamberlin, Caleb W Sterns), Proprs Sterns' Stage House.

Cooley Wallace S, harnessmaker.

Crawford Robert Sr, General Store, Grain and Provisions.

Davis Malcolm D, physician.

Elden Wm H, jewelry and fancy goods.

Ervey Albert M, shoemaker.

Goodenough Alvaro F, Editor and Propr Clare County Press.

Halsted George W, grocer and confectioner.

Hardy Llewellyn, station and express agent.

Hirzel Mrs. Jeannette, millinery.

Horning John T, grain dealer.

Horning Tobias P, Shingle Mnfr.

Horning & Schaffer (Tobias P Horning, Julius Schaffer), grist mill.

Jefferies Geo W, grocer and meat market.

Lamb Randolph, founder and machinist.

Lange Freidr, Baker and Confectioner.

Lee George W, grocery and meat market.

Louch Alfred, blacksmith.

McClure Neil, physician.

Mason Jacob, well driver.

Maynard Thomas H, physician.

Mutz James, gunsmith.

O'Callaghan John, grocer.

Ort Henry, planing mill and sash and door factory.

Post J & F L (John and Floyd L), Saw and Shingle Mill.

Render Thomas, wagonmaker.

Rockafellow John C, general store.

Ross Wm, General Store.

Shaver & McIntyre (Albert A Shaver, Arthur W McIntyre), carpenters and undertakers.

Slattery John B, grocer.

Slocum James A, hop dealer.

Sterns' Stage House, M F Chamberlin & Sterns Proprs, (*See adv.*)

Trevidick Henry, general store.

Wheaton & Perry (Elijah D Wheaton, Charles W Perry), lawyers.

Whitley Grace, dry goods, boots and shoes.

Wolsky Wm, clothing, boots and shoes.

1881

Clare. An Incorporated village of 850 inhabitants, was first settled in 1870, and located in Grant township, near the southern boundary of Clare county. It is a prominent station on the F. & P. M. Ry, at the junction of the branch to Harrison with the main line, 50 miles northwest of Saginaw, 39 east of Reed City, and 148 northwest of Detroit. Harrison, the county seat is 19 miles north. Clare has 2 churches-Congregational and Methodist-a graded public school with 125 pupils, a weekly newspaper, 8 hotels and several saw and shingle mills. Much of the contiguous country is covered with a heavy growth of pine and hardwood timber, but it contains some rich agricultural land, specially adapted to the culture of wheat and grass. The shipments and shingles, hoops, staves, flour, wheat, and general produce. Among the recent improvements are a new town hall and a grain elevator. Express, American, Telegraph, Western Union. Mail daily. J. C. Rockafellow, postmaster.

BUSINESS DIRECTORY

Alger House, L Hardy Propr.

Alward Dennis E, editor and propr Clare County Press.

Bebee & Davis (Abiram Bebee, Malcolm D Davis), druggists.

Bicknell Nathan, Auctioneer and Commission Merchant, Business Promptly Attended to, Bicknell Blk.

Bicknell R A & Co (Richard A Bicknell, James S Bicknell and Martha Bicknell, Special), General Merchandise, Bicknell Blk.

Bogardus Mrs Martha, milliner.

Calkins John W, Hardware, Stoves, Tinware, Crockery, Grain and Produce, Pressed Hay, Feed, etc.

Callam Peter, general store.

Clare County Press, D E Alward editor and propr.

Cleveland P J, shingle mnfr.

Cooley Mrs Wallace S, fancy goods.

Dwyer Daniel R, harnessmaker.

Ervey Albert M, shoemaker.

Goodenow Charles N. harnessmaker.

Gulick Rev J (Methodist Episcopal).

Halstead George W, grocer.

Halsted George W, barber.

Hardy Llewellyn, Propr Alger House.

Horning Tobias P, Lumber and Shingle Mnfr and Grocer.

Husted Julius B, Propr Lumberman's Home.

Jefferies M R, groceries and meats

Jenks Jay C. exp and station agt.

Kelley Peter, gunsmith.

Lange Frederick, baker.

Lee George W, grocer.

Lossing Mrs D J, milliner.

Lossing M J, Surgeon Dentist, Bicknell Blk. (*See adv.*)

Louch Alfred, wagonmaker.

Lumberman's House, J B Husted Propr.

Mason Mrs M M, milliner.

Morris James, wagonmaker.

Nichols Lambert A, grocer.

O'Callaghan John, grocer.

Perry Charles W, lawyer.

Rockafellow John C, general store.

Sailsbury Wm, barber.

Schaffer & Reist (Julius Schaffer, Jacob Reist), Flouring Mill.

Shaver Albert A, furniture.

Slattery John B, grocer.

Sterns Caleb W. propr Sterns' Stage House.

Travis J J, physician

Tucker Mrs Hattie, dressmaker.

Wolsky Wm, clothing, boots and shoes.

Clare. An incorporated village, was first settled in 1870, and located in Grant township, near the southern boundary of Clare county. It is a prominent station on the F. & P. M. R. R., 2½ miles from the junction of the branch to Harrison, 50 miles northwest of Saginaw, 39 east of Reed City, and 148 northwest of Detroit. Harrison, the county seat is 18 miles north. Clare has 2 churches, Congregational and Methodist, a graded public school with 300 pupils, a public hall seating 500, 2 weekly newspapers, the *Clare Press* and the *Clare Democrat*, a bank, 2 elevators, 2 hotels and several saw and shingle mills, a flouring mill, a tannery and a brick yard. Much of the contiguous country is covered with heavy growth of pine and hardwood timber, but it contains some rich agricultural land, specially adapted to the culture of wheat and grass. The shipments are shingles, hoops, staves, flour, wheat and general produce. Population, 1,100. Exp., Am., Tel., W. U. Mail, daily. Money order office. Wm. Giberson, postmaster.

Alger House, V L Brown Propr.
Alward Denis E, propr Clare Press and justice.
Beebe Abyron, grocer.
Beemer Oliver, saloon.
Bicknell Nathan, Dealer in General Merchandise, Hay, Grain and Real Estate; Warehouse on the F. & P. M. R. R.
Boge Theodore, shoes.
Boorn George W, saw mill.
Brown George H, barber.
Brown Vincent L, Propr Alger House.
Bulman Wm, saloon.
Calkins George C, barber.
Carpenter Joseph H, physician.
Chase Seymour, physician.
Chase & Curtiss (Charles S Chase, Wm J Curtiss), meat market.
Clare County Bank (Charles W Perry, Wm Wolsky, Clark H Sutherland).
Clare Democrat, M D Eaton propr.
Clare Press (weekly), D E Alward propr.
Clare Water Works, H O Squires supt.
Davis Malcolm D, physician.

Dawson George E, notions.
De Gez Thomas, harnessmaker.
De Vogt E Henry, photographer.
Doherty Alfred J, insurance and hdware.
Duncan James, justice of peace.
Dunlop John W, druggist.
Dunwoodie James D, blacksmith.
Eaton Marvin D, propr Clare Democrat.
Ehrhardt Christopher, grocer.
Elden Wm H, books and sew machines.
Ervey Albert M, shoemaker.
Exchange Hotel, Henry Orth Prop.
Feighner Bros (Isaiah and Wm A), meats.
Galliver James H, railroad and exp agent.
Giberson Wm, clothing.
Giberson Mrs Wm, milliner.
Goodman W & Co (Wm H and Wm A Goodman), hardware.
Groms Edgar, brick mnfr.
Halstead George W, grocer.
Hampton James, justice of peace.
Haynes Philip, livery.
Hickey Fred, saloon.

Hollinshead Henry E, harnessmaker.
Horning Edward B, grocer and grain.
Horning Josiah, lumber mnfr.
Horning Tobias P, saw mill.
Husted & Mason (John G Husted, Jacob D Mason) saloon.
Keller Warren, livery.
Lambeck Henry F, tailor.
Lange Frederick, baker.
Lawrence George B, saloon.
Leach Lyman W, justice of peace.
Lossing Mrs. D J, dressmaker.
Lossing Monroe J, dentist.
Louch Alfred, blacksmith.
McIntyre Arthur W, justice of peace.
McKinnon Archibald J, blacksmith.
Mason & Dwyer (Mrs M M Mason, Mrs M E Dwyer) milliners.
Maynard Thomas, physician.
Morris James, wagonmaker.
Mussell Robert M, Druggist and Grocer.
Northey Richard, wagonmaker.
Ort & Dixon (Henry Ort, Joseph Dixon), planing mill.
Orth Henry, Propr Exchange Hotel.
Parrish Wm, livery and veterinary surg.
Patient Benjamin, shoemaker.
Perry Charles W, lawyer.

Randall Frank H, Groceries and Provisions, Flour, Feed, Grain, Lime, etc.
Ranft Frederick, cigar mnfr.
Ross Wm, general store.
Schilling Henry, tanner.
Seeley James H, justice of peace.
Shaver Albert A., Furniture and Undertaker.
Smith George W, grocer.
Sterns Caleb W, restaurant.
Struble Jacob D, restaurant.
Sutherland Clark H, cash Clare Co Bank.
Tatmann and Shilling, grocer.
Todd Francis J, physician.
Tooley Morgan, physician.
Trevidick Henry, general store.
Van Brunt & Reist (Albert Van Brunt, John Reist), flour and shingle mill.
Walsh James, saloon.
Webb John A, grocer.
Wheaton Elijah D, probate judge.
White Edward A, jeweler.
Wing Lanson, justice of peace.
Whitney & Holbrook (Charles E Whitney, Henry H Holbrook), painters.
Wolsky Wm, general store.

1891-1892

CLARE. First settled in 1870, is a prosperous incorporated village, located in Grant township near the southern boundry of Clare county. It is a prominent station at the junction of the F. & P. M R. R. and T. A. A. & N. M. Ry, and is also the southern terminus of the Harrison branch of the F. & P. M. R. R., 50 miles northwest of Saginaw, 39 east of Reed City and 148 northwest of Detroit. Harrison the county seat is 18 miles north. Clare has two churches, Congregational and Methodist, Free Methodist, Baptist and United Brethren Societies, a graded public school with 389 pupils, a public hall seating 500, one weekly newspaper, the *Clare Democrat-Press*, a bank, 2 elevators, 2 hotels and several saw and shingle mills, a flouring mill, a tub and pail factory, a tannery and a brick yard. Much of the contiguous country is covered with pine and hardwood timber, but it contains some rich agricultural land, specially adapted to the culture of wheat and grass. The shipments are lumber, shingles, hoops, staves, flour, wheat and general produce. Population 1,200. Exp., Am. Tel., W. U., Money order office. S. C. Kirkbride, postmaster.

Abram Harris A, propr Alger House.
Ackerman Jacob, grocer.
Alger House, H A Abram, propr.
Austin Melvin O, marshal.
Baker Wm, confectioner.
Beemer & Ackey (Oliver Beemer, Alphonso Ackey), saloon.
Bicknell Nathan, General Store, Hay, Grain, Horses and Cattle; Warehouse F & P M R R.
Bigley Mrs Catherine, confectioner.
Bigley Charles I, Clerk of the Village, Justice, Real Estate, Insurance and Collections. (*See ad. opp*)
Bogardus Mrs Martha, Milliner.
Boge Theodore, boots and shoes.
Boorn George W, saw mill.
Brown George H, barber.
Bush Alexander, livery.
Carpenter Joseph H, President of Village; Physician, Druggist and Justice of Peace.
Chase Charles S. meat market.
Clare County Bank (Charles W Perry, Wm Wolsky, Clark H Sutherland)
Clare Democrat-Press, Marvin E Eaton propr.
Clare Water Works, Thomas Seath engineer.
Clare Woodenware Co, Wm Tunnicliffe mngr.
Cooley Wallace S, marble worker.
Corkins George, barber.
Cramm Rev George W (Baptist).
Crouse Daniel, blacksmith.
Cunningham Andrew, saloon.
Davis Dr Malcolm D, druggist.
Dawson George E, saloon.
Defoe Mrs Sarah J, grocer.

De Gez Thomas, harnessmaker.
Derby Otto S, furniture.
De Vogt Eugene H, photographer.
Dibble Mortimer, justice.
Doherty Alfred J, hardware.
Duncan James, justice.
Dunlop John W, druggist.
Dunwoodie & McKinnon (James D Dunwoodie, Archibald J McKinnon), blacksmiths.
Eaton Marvin D, propr Clare Democrat-Press.
Ehrhardt Christopher, grocer.
Elden Wm H, books and farm impts.
Exchange Hotel, Henry Orth Propr.
Feighner & Co (Isaiah and Wm Feighner, Ananias Linsea), meat market.
Fine Samuel L, justice of peace.
Fishley Frederick, justice of peace.
Fox David, carpenter.
Galliver James H, railroad and exp agt.
Garland John D, jeweler.
Giberson Mrs Helen M, milliner.
Giberson John, lawyer.
Giberson Wm, general store.
Goodman W & Co (Wm H and Wm A Goodman), hardware.
Gorr E B, planing mill.
Grathwohl Lawerence, tailor.
Harris & McKay (Issac Harris, Addison McKay), laundry.
Herrick & Harris (Maurice A Herrick, John W Harris), grocer.
Holbrook Henry H, painter.
Horning Adam, justice of the peace.
Hornng Josiah, shingle and saw mill.
Hubbell, flour mill.
Husted John G, saloon.

Kelly Wm J, cigar mnfr.
Kirkbride Samuel C, dry goods.
Knights of Pythias' Band.
Kump Delaware H, barber.
Lackie Archibald, restaurant.
Lamb Randolph, saw mill.
Lange Friedrich, baker.
Lawrence George B, wagonmaker.
Lindloff Rev William (German Luthern).
Lister & Archamboult (Frederick Lister, George A Archamboult), Lumber Mnfrs.
Lossing Mrs D J, dentist.
Lossing Monroe J, dentist.
Louch Alfred, blacksmith.
Louch James, shoemaker.
McFarland Peter, justice of peace.
McIntyre Arthur W, justice of peace
McKay Paulina A grocer.
McPhall David, grocer and meats.
Mack Andrew E, painter.
Mason & Boyd (Jacob Mason, James S Boyd), grocers.
Mason & Dwyer (Mrs Martha Mason, Mrs Margaret E Dwyer), milliners.
Maynard Thomas H, physician.
Mitchell Joseph C, grocer.
Muscott Ralph, chair stock mnfr.
Mussell Robert M, druggist.
National Loan and Investment Company of Detroit, Mich, Officers of Advisory Board at Clare: C S Chase Pres, Gibersen Vice-Pres, C H Sutherland Treas, C I Bigley John Giberson Atty.
Northey Richard, wagonmaker and baker.
Ort & Dixon (Henry Ort, Joseph Dixon), planing mill.
Orth Henry, Propr Exchange Hotel.
Palmer C E, principal school.
Parrish Wm, livery.

Patient Benjamin, shoemaker.
Patterson F D & Co (Frank D Patterson, Thomas Pickard), lumber.
Perry Charles W, lawyer.
Phinisey & Co (John Phinisey, Allen McKinley, confectioners.
Phinisey & Dixon (Theodore W Phinisey, Wm J Dixon), photographer.
Rhoades Andrew S, Shingle Mnfr.
Rhoades A S & Co (Andrew S Rhoades, Frederick Lister, George A Archamboult), Shingle Mnfrs.
Rockafellow John C, insurance.
Rorison John, planing mill.
Rosemann Julius, tanner.
Ross Wm, general store.
Sexsmith John, lumber.
Shearer & Co (Peter M and Elliot Shearer, Wm B Curtis), furniture and undertaking.
Smith Albert, meat market.
Stearns C W, livery.
Stevens Henry C, boarding house.
Sutherland Clark H, cash Clare County Bank.
Sweetman & Waller (John Sweetman, Edward H Waller), saloon.
Tatman & Schilling (James F Tatman, Jared Schilling), grocers.
Thompson Wm A, justice of peace.
Todd Francis J, physician.
Tower Rev L L (Methodist).
Van Brunt Albert, boots and shoes.
Walt Howland P, carpenter.
Wayman George, carpenter.
Welch James L, meat market.
Whitmore Franklin A, Single Mnfr.
Whtney M E, second hand goods.
Wilber Mrs Caroline A, restaurant.
Withman Rev W A (Free Methodist).
Wolskey Wm, general sore.

1893-1894

Clare. First settled in 1870, is a thriving incorporated city, located in Grant township near the southern boundary of Clare county, and at the junction of the Flint & Pere Marquette and Toledo, Ann Arbor & North Michigan railroads. It is also the southern terminus of the Saginaw & Clare County railroad. Geographically Clare is near the center of the lower peninsular of Michigan; 148 miles from Detroit, 50 northwest of Saginaw, 94 from Lansing and 18 south of Harrison, the county seat. Clare has 4 churches, Congregational, Methodist, Free Methodist and Baptist; a graded public school with 490 pupils; a system of waterworks; an opera house, lately built at a cost of $13,000, with a seating capacity of 700 and lighted by electricity; an electric plant, a public hall seating 500; 4 hotels, one of which "The Calkins" has just been opened, equipped with modern improvements such as heating throughout by steam and lighted by electricity. There are also several saw, shingle and planing, 2 flour mills, the Tobacco River Milling & Mnfr. Co having lately completed one which has a capacity of 100 barrels per day, a tub and pail factory employing 50 workmen, 2 machine shops, a tannery, hoop factory, 2 brick yards and a creamery. Much of the contiguous country is covered with pine and hardwood timber, but it contains some fine and well developed agricultural land. Several minor villages and hamlets are within a radius of five or six miles. The shipments are lumber, shingles, handles, flour, wheat, and general produce. Population 2,000. Exp., Am. Tel., W. U. and Postal. Money order office. S. C. Kirkbride, postmaster.

Adams W L, R R lunch room.

Alger Frank, brewers' agent.

Alward D E, Sec and Treas Clare Wooden Ware Co.

Austin Melvin O, apiarist.

Baker Wm, ice cream parlor.

Becker Wm E, saloon.

Beemer Oliver G, saloon.

Bicknell H M & Co (H May and James S Bicknell) General Store, Hay, Grain, Horses, and Cattle.

Bicknell Nathan, Real Estate, Loans and Stock Dealer.

Bigley Mrs Catherine, florist.

Bigley Charles I, real estate and insurance.

Boyd James, city treasurer.

Brown George H, barber.

Brown J A, laundry.

Calkins Hotel, John W Calkins Propr, cor McEwan and 5th.

Calkins John W, Propr Calkins Hotel, cor McEwan and 5th.

Carpenter Joseph H, Physician, Druggist, Justice and Health Officer.

Carter B H & Co (Benjamin P Carter), bazaar.

Central Hotel, Henry Orth propr.

Chase Charles S, grocer.

Clare County Savings Bank (capital, $20,000) Wm Wolsky pres, C W Perry vice-pres, R H Jenney, 2d vice-pres, C H Sutherland cash.

Clare Creamery Co (capital, $5,000).

Clare Democrat-Press (weekly Dem), Martin D Eaton propr.

Clare Electric Light Co, A J Doherty Propr.

Clare K of P Band, H Stickles leader.

Clare Mnfg Co (capital $5,000) S C Kirkbride pres, D E Alward sec and treas, R Muscott mngr, chair stock and handle mnfrs.

Clare Water Works, J C Brown engineer.

Clare Wooden Ware Co (Capital $30,000) C W Perry Pres, J H Galliver Vise-Pres, D E Alward Sec and Treas, R H Jenney Gen Mngr, Mnfrs Tubs and Pails, Union Depot. (*See opp*)

Clark Charles H, chief of fire dept.

Clark Mrs Mary, carpet weaver.

Clute & Terbush (Andrew Clute, Wm Terbush) shingle mnfrs, 3½ miles s.

Cooley Wallace S, marble works.

Coors Rev August H (Methodist).

Crouse Daniel, blacksmith.

Cunningham John, saloon.

Davis Dr Malcolm D, druggist.

Dawson George E, saloon.

Dean Wm A, carpenter.

De Gez Thomas, saddlery.

Derby Otto S, furniture.

De Vogt Eugene H, photographer.

Dibble Mortimer, justice, 6 miles n e.

Doherty Alfred J, Hardware and Saddlery, Propr Doherty Opera House, McEwan and 5th. (*See below.*)

Doherty Opera House, A J Doherty Propr and Mngr, McEwan. (*See below.*)

Dowd Samuel P, meat market.

Duncan James, justice.
Dunlop John W, drugs and jewelry.
Dunwoodie James D, blacksmith.
Dwyer John, saloon.
Dwyer Mrs Margaret E, milliner.
Dwyer Wm J, saloon.
Eaton Marvin D, publr Clare Democrat-Press.
Edwards Charles H, dentist.

Elden & Holbrook (Wm H Elden, Thomas C Holbrook), bazaar.
Field Rev Floyd C (Congregational)
Fishley Frederick, justice 3 miles s.
F & P M R R, J H Galliver genl agt, C F Marshall pass agt.
Forbes Frank, wagonmaker.
Fox David, carpenter.
Galliver James H, genl agt F & P M R R and agt Am Exp.

208

Garland John D, jeweler.

Giberson John, lawyer.

Giberson & Curtis (Wm Giberson, Wm B Curtis), furniture.

Goodman W & Co (Wm H and Wm A Goodman), hardware, lime, etc.

Gordanier Archie C, barber.

Gorr & Arrand (Edwin B Gorr, James M Arrand), planing mill.

Gratwohl Lawrence, tailor.

Gray Robert A, physician.

Halstead George W, grocer.

Harring John, saloon.

Harris Miss Ella J, dressmaker.

Holbrook Henry H, painter.

Holbrook Thomas, mason.

Horning Adam, justice.

Hubbell Wm E, flour mill ½ mile w.

Huffman Julius, machinist.

Husted John G, saloon.

Hutchinson W J, prin public school

Imerman John, clothing.

Irwin Miss Mina, dressmaker.

Johnson James, vet surgeon.

Kelley Peter, gunsmith.

Kelly Wm J, cigar mnfr.

Keyes & Smalley (Calvin B Keyes, Roderick Smalley), brickyards.

Keystone Mnfg Co (Wm H Bowen, V F Conlogue, F D Patterson) threshing machines, 3 miles e.

Kirkbride Samuel C, postmaster and dealer in dry goods, boots and shoes, etc.

Kuffler John, machinist.

Kump Adelbert D, barber.

Lackie Alexander, boarding house.

Lamb Randolph, lumber mnfr and founder.

Lange Friede, baker.

Langworthy Alphonso, justice.

Lee Charles S, barber.

Lee George W, flour and feed.

Levington Samuel G, supt Meredith Div F & P M R R

Lindloff Rev Wm (German Luthern.)

Lister & Archambault (Frederick Lister, George Archambault), saw mill.

Louch Alfred, blacksmith and farm impts.

Louch James, shoemaker.

Lowe Rev J H (Baptist.)

McGuire Peter H, shoemaker.

McIntrye Arthur W, justice of peace.

McPhall David, grocery and meats.

Mack Andrew E, painter.

Mack Mrs A E, dressmaker.

Marshall C F, mngr W U Tel Co.

Martin Robert J, justice.

Mason & Boyd (Jacob Mason, James S Boyd), grocers.

Mason & Storey (Mrs Martha M Mason, Miss Winifred A Storey), milliners.

Mater Bros (Daniel E and George A) planing mill.

Maynard Thomas H, Physician, 5th.

Michigan Hoop Co (of Saginaw), Willis D Perrin mngr.

Murphy Miss Minnie, dressmaker.

Mussell Robert M, Drugs, Books, Stationery, Paints and Oils, McEwan.

National Loan and Investment Company of Detroit, Michigan. Officers of Clare Advisory Board: Charles S Chase Pres, Wm Giberson Vice-Pres, Charles H Sutherland Treas, Charles I Bigley, Sec, John Giberson Atty.

Newgreen Mrs Beata C, boarding house.

Northey Richard, baker and wagonmaker.

O'Donald Charles H, shingle mnfr.

Ort Henry, builders' materials.

Orth Henry, prop Central Hotel.

Palmer Curtis, general store.

Parrish Wm, livery.

Patient Benjamin, shoemaker.
Perry Charles W, lawyer.
Phinisey & Trainor (John B Phinisey, Edward I Trainor), saloon.
Postal Union Tel Co, C H Snyder opr.
Redson Mrs Annie, dressmaker.
Rhoades Andrew S, Shingle Mnfr and Grocer, McEwan (*See [adv]*.)
Rockafellow John C, insurance.
Rogers Jay, ice dealer.
Rogers Rev M D.
Rorison John, city marshall.
Rosemann Julius, tanner.
Ross Wm J, genl store and apiarist.
Sanford Frederick C, physician.
Sexsmith John, Lumber Mnfr and Dealer, Union Depot, (*See [adv]*.)
Smith Albert, meat market.
Snyder Charles H, agt T, A A & N M R R.
Squires Harris O, restaurant.
Sterns Caleb, livery.
Sterns House, Mrs A Sterns propr.
Stevens House, Henry C Stevens propr.
Stickles Harrison, carpenter.
Sutherland Clark H, cash Clare County Savings Bank.

Swanston Wm, restaurant.
Sweetman & Phinisey (John Sweetman, John B Phinisey), saloon.
Tatman & Schilling (James F Tatman, Jared Schlling), grocers.
Thompson Wm A, justice, Sheridan twp.
Tobacco River Milling & Mnfg Co (Capital $30,000: Paid in $12,000) Henry H Varney Pres, George L Holmes (of Detroit) Vice-Pres, A M Varny Sec and Treas, Flour Mill and Power Owners.
Todd Francis J, physician.
Tower Rev Lee L (Methodist).
Unicume Edward, R R contractor.
Van Brunt Albert, groceries and shoes.
Waller Edward H, boots and shoes.
Waller Manly, mason.
Welch James L, grocery and meats.
Western Union Tel Co, C F Marshall mngr.
White Edward A, jewelry.
Whitlock George W, apiarist.
Whitney Edwin, grocer.
Wildman Frank, justice.
Wilson John H, tailor.

1897

Clare. Population 1,800. On the F & P. M. and Ann Arbor R. Rs., in Grant township, Clare county, 18 miles south of Harrison, the county seat, 50 from Saginaw, 94 from Lansing and 148 from Detroit. It is lighted by electricity, has Baptist, Congregational, Free Methodist and Methodist churches, a graded public school, an excellent system of water works, an opera house, seating 700, a public hall, seating 500, a bank and 3 hotels. There are several saw, shingle and planing mills, a tub and pail factory, an electric light plant, machine shop, tannery, hoop factory, foundry, creamery, etc. Three weekly newspapers, Courier, Reporter and Sentinel are published. The shipments are lumber, shingles, hoops, handles, bark, telegraph poles, wheat and general produce. Exp., Am. Tel., Postal and W. U. Money order office. T. H. Maynard, postmaster.

Adams Wm L, lunch room.

American Express Co, J H Galliver agent.

Austin Melvin O, apiarist.
Beemer Oliver G, saloon.
Benner George, beer agt.
Bicknell Bros & Co (James S and Wm H Bicknell, H May Ballinger), General Store, Hay, Grain, Horses and Cattle.
Bicknell Nathan, Real Estate, Loans and Stock Dealer.
Brown George H, barber.
Burrier George W, physician.
Calkins Charles W, hardware.
Calkins John W, hotel.
Canfield & Vandercook (A R Canfield, E A Vandercook), publrs Clare Courier.
Carpenter Dr Joseph H, jewelry and drugs.
Central Hotel, Henry Orth propr.
Choate Rev A H (Baptist).
Clare Band, A E Mulder leader.
Clare County Savings Bank (capital $30,000), C W Perry pres, Wm Wolskey vice-pres, C H Sutherland cash.
Clare Courier The, Canfield and Vandercook publrs.
Clare Creamery Co, J R Heas mngr.
Clare Electric Light Co, A J Doherty mngr, C H Clark sec.
Clare Hardware Co, Charles W Calkins propr.
Clare Publishing Co, A E Harvey mngr, publrs Clare Report.
Clare Reporter (weekly), Clare Publishing Co publrs.
Clare Sentinel The, R G & F A Jefferies proprs.
Clare Water Works, A J Doherty mngr.
Clare Woodenware Co (capital $30,000) C W Perry pres, J S Ross vice-pres, A J Doherty sec and treas.
Clark Charles H, insurance.

Coors Rev August H (Methodist).
Creeper Silas, shoemaker.
Crouse Daniel, blacksmith.
Davis Dr Malcolm D, druggist.
Davy & Co (V R Davy, Fred B Smith, L E Davy), dry goods.
Dawson George E, cigars.
Defoe Sarah J, furniture.
De Gez Thomas, harnessmaker.
Delaney Edward, Foundry.
Derby Oto S, furniture.
Doherty Alfred J, hardware.
Doherty Opera House, A J Doherty propr.
Dorsey Thomas S, marble.
Duncan James, cigars.
Dunlop John W, drugs and jewelry.
Dunwoodie James D, blacksmith.
Dwyer Mrs Margaret E, milliner.
Egbert & Field (James Egbert, C C Field), flour and feed.
Elden Wm H, books, stationery, etc.
Elliston & Stone (Orson A Elliston, Charles J Stone), laundry.
Falk Frank, barber.
Fishley Frederick, justice, 3 miles s.
Foss John E., baker.
Fox David, carpenter.
Galliver James H, railroad, exp and tel agt.
Giberson John, lawyer.
Goodenow Charles N, ice and cartage.
Goodman John R, hardware.
Goodman Mrs K M, millinery.
Gordanier Archie C, barber.
Gorr & Arrand (Edwin B Gorr, James M Arrand), planing mill.
Gratwohl Lawrence, tailor.
Graves Mrs George W, grocer.
Harris A & Son (Alwilda & Clyde), grocers.
Harris Miss Ella J, dressmaker.
Holbrook Thomas, mason.
Holbrook Thomas C, grocer.

Horning Edward, bark dealer.

Huffman Julius, machinist.

Husted John G, saloon.

Imerman John, dry goods.

Jackson John A, meats.

Jacobs W W, railroad and tel agt.

Jefferies R G & F A (Remick G and Frances A), prop Clare Sentinel.

Joiner Horace, saloon.

Kelley Peter, gunsmith.

Keystone Mnfr Co, Wm H Brown mngr, threshing machines, 3 miles e.

Kirkbride Samuel C, dry goods.

Kuffler John, machinist.

Kump Adelbert H, barber.

Lamb Randolph, lumber mnfr.

Lane Benjamin R, Machinist.

Lee George W. feed mill.

Lewis Wm P, cigar mnfr.

Lister & Ort (Frederick Lister, Henry Ort) saw mill.

Long Rev Samuel (Congregational).

Lossing M J, dentist.

Louch Alfred, blacksmith.

Louch James, shoemaker.

Luce Mrs Harriet, carpet weaver.

McIntyre Arthur W, lawyer.

Mack Andrew E, painter.

Mack Mrs A E, dressmaker.

Mason & Boyd (Jacob Mason James S Boyd), grocers.

Mater & Naylor (George Mater, Thomas Naylor), planing mill.

Maynard Dr. Thomas Maynard H, Postmaster.

Michigan Hoop Co. (Saginaw), Willis D Perrin mngr.

Morgan Richard mngr, telegraph poles.

Mulder Allen E, dentist.

Mussell Robert M, drugs.

National Loan and Investment Company of Detroit, Mich, makes Real Estate Loans at low rates, and issues Prepaid Dividend Bearing Stock paying 6 per cent per annum, semi-annually, with accumulated profits at maturity. This stock can be surrendered and principal and 6 per cent withdrawn at any time. John Giberson Agent.

Nix Rev Frank H (Methodist).

O'Donald Charles H, Shingle mnfr.

Orth Henry, propr Central Hotel.

Palmer Mrs E D, music teacher.

Parrish Mrs Mary E, livery.

Parirsh Wm, city marshal.

Perry Charles W, lawyer and pres Clare County Savings Bank.

Postal Telegraph Cable Co, W W Jacobs mngr.

Rassat Mrs Mary, propr Stevens House.

Redson Mrs Annie, dressmaker and milliner.

Rhodes Andrew S, grocer.

Rhodes A S & Co (Andrew S Rhodes, John T Hornning) heading mnfrs.

Ritter & Bogardus (Harvey Ritter, Simon Bogardus), meats.

Rockafellow John C, insurance.

Rockwell Claude C. Confr.

Rorison David, hardware and mayor.

Rosemann Julius, tanner.

Ross Wm J, apiarist.

Sanford Fred C, physician.

Schilling Jared H, grocer.

Sexsmith John, lumber mnfr.

Sherman Rev Washington (Free Methodist)

Smalley Robert, wagonmaker.

Squires Harris O, restaurant.

Stevens House, Mrs Mary Rassat propr.

Sutherland Clark H, cash Clare County Savings Bank.

Sutherland S A, blacksmith.

Tatman James F, grocer, etc.

Telman Erastus D, chief fire department.

Unicume Edward R, contractor.

Van Brunt & Son (Clarence and Albert), grocers.

Vandercook Ernest A, photographer.

Waller Edward H, shoes.

Weir Wallace T, wagonmaker.

Welch James L, grocer and meats.

Western Union Tel Co, J H Galliver agt.

White Edward A, jeweler.

Whittock George W, apiarist, 4 miles n e.

Wilson John H, tailor.

Witherspoon P E W, physician.

Wolskey Wm, dry goods.

1903

Clare. Population, 1,800. Incorporated as a village in 1879 and as a city in 1891. Is located on the P. M. and A.A. Rys, in Clare county, 18 miles south of Harrison, the county seat, 50 from Saginaw, 94 from Lansing, and 157 from Detroit. It is lighted by electricity, has water works, churches of the Baptist, Catholic, Congregational, Free Methodist, German Lutheran, and Methodist denominations, a new public school building costing $35,000, a public hall, an opera house seating 700, first class hotels, a bank, and 2 weekly newspapers – the Courier and the Sentinel. There are several saw, shingle, and planing mills, a stave and heading factory, knitting factory, electric light plant, foundry, 2 machine shops, creamery, etc. The shipments embrace lumber, shingles, hoops, handles, bark, telegraph poles, wheat, cattle, and general produce. Stages daily to Dover and Colonville. Telephone connection. Exp., Am. Tel., Postal and W. U. S. C. Kirkbride, postmaster.

Adams Joseph & Son (Joseph and August), grocers.

Adams Wm L, lunch room.

Allen Herbert, live stock.

Athouse Clarence W, staves and headings.

Axford Bert. r r and tel agt.

Beemer Oliver G, saloon.

Benner George E, insurance.

Bicknell Bros (Wm H and James B), genl store.

Bicknell Nathan, Groceries and Provisions, Glassware, Etc; Real Estate; Loans; Live Stock Dealer; Farm Property a Specialty.

Brown George H, barber.

Buell C Mell, city clerk.

Bump & Mays (Ace Bump, Henry Mays), grocers.

Calkins CharlesW, propr Clare Hardware Co.

Calkins John W, Propr Calkins House.

Calkins House, John W Calkins Propr.

Callam & Cornwell (Wm Callam, Frank Cornwell), flour mill.

Canfield A R, propr Clare Courier.

Carpenter Dr Joseph H, drugs.

Central Hotel, James M Lackie Propr, Special Attention to Commercial Men; Livery in Connection; Rates $1.00 per Day.

Clare County Savings Bank (capital $20,000), C W Perry pres, C H Sutherland cash.

Clare Courier, A R Canfield propr.

Clare Creamery Co, E Switzer mngr.

Clare Electric Light Co, F B Doherty pres, A J Doherty sec.

Clare Hardware Co, Charles W Calkins propr.

Clare Iron Works, Edward Delaney propr.

Clare Sentinel The, Welch & Bennett Publrs; Circulation Larger than the Combined Circulations of All Other Papers in Clare County; Fine Job Printing a Specialty.

Clare Water Works, A J Doherty mngr.

Creeper Silas, shoemaker.

Crouse Daniel, blacksmith.

Davy & Co (V R Davy Fred B Smith, L E Davy), dry goods.

Delaney Edward, propr Clare Iron Works.

Derby Otto S, furniture.

De Vogt Eugene H, photographer.

Doherty A J & Sons (Alfred J, Floyd E and Frank B), hardware.

Doherty Opera House, F E Doherty propr.

Dorsey Thomas E, marble works.

Duncan James, saloon.

Duncan Mrs John, dressmaker.

Dunlop Dr John W, drugs and jeweler.

Dunwoodie James D, farm impts.

Dwyer Mrs Margaret E., milliner.

Elden Wm H, bazaar.

Exchange Hotel, Con Mullen Propr, Located Opposite Depot; Newly Furnished Throughout; Rates $1.00 Per Day.

Falk Frank, barber.

Forbes Frank, wagonmaker.

Fox David, carpenter.

Galliver James H, railroad, exp and tel agt.

Gibson Frances, prin of schools.

Goodman John R, hardware.

Goodman Mrs K M, milliner.

Gordanier A C, agt Standard Oil Co.

Gorr Edward B, planing mill.

Gray R A, physician.

Greaser Paul, tailor.

Haley Wm, live stock.

Halstead George W, grocer.

Harris & Son (Alwida and Clyde), grocers.

Hathaway Rev W J, (Methodist).

Hazeltine Rev J L (Free Methodist).

High John, bazaar.

Holbrook Thomas, mason.

Holbrook Thomas C, department store.

Huffman Julius, machinist.

Jackson John A, meats.

Kirkbride & Co, (S C Kirkbride), flour mill.

Kuffler John, machinist.

Kump Adelpha H, barber.

Kump Wm, barber.

Lackie James H, Propr Central Hotel.

Lacy Arthur, lawyer.

Lamb Gerald E, physician.

Lamb Randolph, lumber mnfr.

Lee George W. flour and feed.

Leusenkamp Bros (Gerritt and Harry) dry goods and clothing.

Lewis Wm P, cigar mnfr.

Louch Alfred, blacksmith.

Louch James, shoemaker.

Loundra Wm, city marshal.

McKinnon A James, blacksmith.

Mack Andrew E, painter.

Mack Mrs A E, dressmaker.

Malone Rev Denns E (Catholic).

Mason Jacob, saloon.

Mater & Lamb (George Mater, Roy Lamb), planing mill.

214

Maynard Albert E, insurance.
Maynard Thomas H, physician.
Mullen Con, propr Exchange Hotel.
Mussell A E, drugs and paints.
Neelands H E, dentist.
Northey Samuel, carriage painter.
O'Connor James, grocer.
Palmer Rev F D (Free Methodist).
Parrish Wm, vet surgeon and livery.
Pelton Fred, drayage.
Perry Charles W, lawyer.
Potter Rev N D (Baptist).
Price Wm, harnessmaker.
Rapson R A, laundry.
Reeder J A, physician.
Rhodes Andrew S, grocer and feed
    mill.
Rhodes A S & Co (Andrew S
    Rhodes, John T Hornung), heading
    mnfrs.
Riggs W D, supt of schools.
Robinson Faith, teacher.
Ross Wm J, apiarist.
Sanford Fred C, physician.
Shaw B C, physician.

Smalley E Roderick, wagonmaker.
Smalley Frederick, painter.
Squires Harris O, restaurant.
Stanley & Harris (Eugene Stanley,
    Isaac Harris), potash mnfrs.
Sutherland C H , cashr Clare Co
    Savings Bank.
Sutherland Mrs Otto, music teacher.
Switzer E, mngr Clare Creamery Co.
Tatman James F, groceries and shoes.
Their Orlando B, feed barn.
Thurston A & Son (A and Charles),
    undertakers.
Van Brunt & Son (Clarence and
    Albert), grocers.
Waller Edward H, shoes.
Welch & Bennett, Publishers The
    Clare Sentinel.
Welling John, shoemaker.
White E A, jeweler.
Whittlock A W, apiarist, 4 miles n e.
Willoughby Robert J, photographer.
Wilson John H, merchant tailor.
Wolsey Wm & Co, knitting works.
Woodlock Rev A E (Congregational).

1907-1908

Clare. Population 1,800. Incorporated as a village in 1879 and as a city in 1891, is located on the P. M. and A. A. R Rs. In Clare county, 18 miles south of Harrison, the county seat, 50 from Saginaw, 94 from Lansing and 157 from Detroit. It is lighted by electricity, has a water works, churches of the Baptist, Catholic, Congregational, Free Methodist, German Lutheran and Methodist denominations, a $25,000 school building, a public hall, and opera house seating 700, first-class hotels, 3 banks, and 2 weekly newspapers, the Courier and the Sentinel. There are several saw, shingle and planing mills, stave and heading factories, knitting factory, electric light plant, foundry, machine shops, creamery, pickle salting station, etc. The chief shipments are lumber, shingles, hoops, handles, staves, heading, bark, telegraph poles, wheat, hay, produce and cattle. Tel., W. U. Exp., Pacific and U. S. Telephone connection. Samuel C Kirkbride, postmaster.

Adams Wm L, lunch room.
Alger Frank, hand broom factory.

Allen Herbert, live stock.
Anderson Elmer A, drugs.

Axford Bert L, agt A A R R and Pacific Express.

Beagle Alfonso P, feed stable.

Beemer Oliver G, saloon.

Benner George E, mayor, cashr Citizens' Bank and ins agt.

Bicknell James S, groceries.

Bicknell Wm H & Co (Wm H and Nathan), dry goods.

Bowers M A, vet surg.

Brown George H, barber.

Burch-Wyman Grain Co (Logan Burch, Jay Wyman) Shippers of Grain, Beans, Hay, Potatoes, Seeds and Wool.

Burch Mrs Cynthia, boarding house.

Calkins Charles W, propr Clare Hardware Co.

Calkins House, John W Calkins Propr, McEwan cor 5th. Both Tels.

Callam & Cornell (Wm Callam, Benjamin F Cornwell), Proprs Clare Electric Roller Mills.

Canfield A R, propr Clare Courier.

Carrow Nelson, treas Clare Percheron Horse Breeders' Assn.

Central Drug Store, Anna E Mussell Propr. Bell Tel 53. (See [ad].)

Central Hotel, James H Lackie Propr, Special Attention to Commercial Men, Livery in Connection, Rate $1 Per Day.

Citizens' Bank The (capital $10,000). Frederick Lister pres, George E Benner cashier.

Clare Board of Pblic Works, L E Davy president.

Clare County Savings Bank (capital $20,000), C W Perry pres, C H Sutherland cashier.

Clare Courier The, A R Canfield Propr, First Paper in the County to Increase in Size to Eight Pages to Meet Growing Demands of Advertisers, Both Tels 34.

Clare Electric Light Co, F B Doherty pres, A J Doherty sec.

Clare Electric Roller Mills (Wm Callam, Benjamin F Cornwell), Buyers of all kinds of Grain.

Clare Furnace Co The (capital $15,000), Charles W Perry pres, L E Davy treas, George B Wells sec, H Byron Wells vice-pres and genl mngr.

Clare Hardware Co, Frank B Doherty pres and sec.

Clare Knitting Mills.

Clare Percheron Horse Breeders' Assn, Frank Gorr pres, E G Welch sec, Nelson Carrow treas.

Clare Sentinel The, Welch & Bennett publishers.

Clare Steam Laundry, Andrew Gibbs & Son proprs.

Clare Water Works, municipal.

Clark David W, drayman.

Clute A J, poultry.

Cloe Laura, teacher.

Cole Wm N, meats.

Cooley Horace S, horse breeder.

Courtland Mrs E R, millinery.

Creeper Silas, shoemaker.

Crouse Daniel, boots and shoes.

Dailey E G Co, Almeron N Smith mngr, pickles.

Davy & Co, (capital $75,000), Vernon R Davy pres, Fred B Smith vice-pres O C Johnson sec, L E Davy treas, dry goods.

Derby Otto S, furniture.

De Vogt Eugene H, photographer.

Doherty Alfred J, ins and mngr Clare Electric Light Co.

Doherty Frank B, hardware.

Doherty John E, undertaker.

Doherty Opera House, F E Doherty propr.

Dorsey Thomas E, marble works.

Duncan James, saloon.

Duncan's Hall, James Duncan propr.
Dunlop Dr J W, drugs.
Dunlop's J W Banking House, bankers.
Dunwoodie James D, mngr Union Telephone Co.
Easler George W, furniture.
Elden Wm H, agrl impts.
Ellis Miron D, Diamonds, Watches and Jewelry.
Falk Frank S, barber.
Farmers' Institute, E W Allen pres, George Pease sec.
Fishley Frederick, justice of peace.
Fishley F & Co, Butter, Eggs, and Poultry.
Forbes Frank, wagonmaker.
Forward Mrs G W, millinery.
Foss John E, restaurant.
Galliver J H, R R, expt and tel agt.
Geek Bros (Philip F and Nicholas F), Lumber, Lath, Shingles and Moldings, Coal and Wood, McEwan nr P M R R, Bell Tel 7.
Gibbs Andrew & Son (Andrew and Mark), propr Clare Steam Laundry.
Giberson Grace, music teacher.
Goodman John R, city treasurer.
Gorr E B, planing mill.
Gorr Frank, pres Clare Percheron Horse Breeders' Assn.
Gray R A & F R (Robert A and Frank R), physicians.
Grieser Paul, tailor.
Grover Frank, thresherman.
Haley Wm, livestock.
High John, bazaar.
Holbrook Thomas, mason.
Holbrook Thomas C, department store.
Hornung John T, staves and heading mnfr.
Jackson J A, meats.
Johnson Arthur D, county surveyor.
Johnson R D & Son, dairy.

Kirkbride Samuel C, postmaster.
Kirkbride & Co (Samuel C Kirkbride), flour mill.
Kirkbride's Orchestra, S C Kirkbride ldr.
Kons Kate, teacher.
Kuffler John, machinist.
Kump Adelpha H, barber.
Lackie J H, propr Central Hotel.
Lacy Arthur J, Attorney-at-Law and Real Estate, McEwan cor 5th. Both Tels 74.
Ladd Mrs J E, millinery.
La Peirre Albert E, baker and confr.
Leahy James F, dry goods.
Lee Charles S, dairy, 2 miles s.
Lee G W, flour and feed.
Le Roy Sarah, principal of school.
Lewis Wm P, cigar mnfr.
Lewis & Patrick (Burton S Lewis, Ulysses H Patrick), hardware.
Lister Frederick, pres Citizen's Bank.
Lloyd Chauncey B, livery and feed stable.
Louch Guy T, Blacksmith, Horseshoer and Carriage and Wagonmaker, McEwan opp 3d.
Louch James, shoemaker.
Louch Louie, teacher.
Lowe Rev John H (Baptist).
McDonald & Lackie (Collins McDonald, Jamie H Lackie), saloon.
McKeever George, shingle mnfr.
McKerracher John, harnessmaker.
McKinnon A J, blacksmith.
McNeill Wm L, blacksmith.
McPhall David, saloon.
Mack Andrew, painter.
Maloney Agnes, teacher.
Martin John H & Son (John H and Wess), threshermen.
Mason Jacob, saloon.
Maxwell Rev George W (M E).
Maynard Albert E, insurance.

Maynard Thomas H, physician.

Michigan Telephone Co, Frank E Bowers mngr.

Midland Produce Co, G W Forward mngr.

Morse Sherman H & Son (Sherman H and Henry), harnessmakers.

Mulder A E, dentist.

Mussell Anna E, Propr Central Drug Store, Bell Tel 53 (see below).

Neeland H E, dentist.

Northey Samuel, cigar mnfr.

O'Callaghan John, feed stable.

O'Connor James, Groceries and Provisions, Hay, Straw and Salt, Bell Tel 19, Union Tel 124.

Parameter Wm, meats.

Parrish Mrs Mamie T, dressmaker.

Parrish Wm L, city marshal.

Pastorino Antonio G, fruits and confr.

Pelton Fred, express and drayage.

Perry Charles W, lawyer and pres Clare County Savings Bank.

Pierce Webster H, carpenter.

Ray Robert, pool room.

Reeder James A, physician.

Rhoades Andrew S, general store.

Rhoades & Shaffer (Andrew S Rhoades, Levi Shaffer), heading mnfr.

Robinson George, vet surgeon.

Rogers & Falk (Atherton L Rogers, Frank Falk), barbers.

Roode J Q, supt of schools.

Ross Giles A, tailor.

Sanford Fred C, physician.

Schaffer Cora, teacher.

Simonson L, cigar mnfr.

Smalley & Son (E Roderick and Frederick E), carriagemakers.

Smith Almeron N, mngr E G Dailey Co.

Smith John E. baker.

Smith Thomas, drayman.

Squires Harris O, restaurant.

Standard Oil Co, Chauncey B Lloyd agt.

Sterling Charles B, vet surgeon.

Sutherland C H, cashr Clare County Saving Bank.

Switzer E, market gardener.

Thurston A & Son (Albert and Charles A) Livery, Undertakers and Licensed Embalmers. Bell Tel 86-2r; res Bell Tel 86-3r.

Union Telephone Co, J D Dunwoodie mngr.

Van Brunt Albert, grocer.

Ward David, hardware.

Weir Wallace T, 2d-hand goods.

Welch E G (Welch & Bennett), school commissioner.

Welch Mrs E G, music teacher.

Welch & Bennett, publrs the Clare
Sentinel.
Wermuth George L, propr Wermuth
House.
Wermuth House, Geo L Wermuth
propr.

Westfall Anna, teacher.
Williams Rev S H (Free Methodist).
Wilson John H, clothing.
Wolsey Wm, knitting mill.
Woodward John, drayman.
Worden Joseph, saloon.

1921-1922

Clare. Population 1,350. Incorporated as a village in 1879, as a city in 1891, is located on the P and A A R Rs, in Clare county, 18 miles south of Harrison, the judicial seat, 50 from Saginaw, 94 form Lansing and 157 from Detroit. It is lighted by electricity, has a water works, churches of the Baptist, Catholic, Congregational, Free Methodist, German Lutheran, and Methodist denominations, a $25,000 school building, a public hall seating 500, first class hotels, 2 banks, and 2 weekly newspapers, the Courier and Sentinel. There are cream and produce stations, grain elevators, grist mills, planing mills, etc. The chief shipments are farm produce, cream, sheep, cattle and hogs. Telegraph and express. A J Doherty mayor. John A Jackson, postmaster.

Acre F E, grocer
Adams Wm L, restaurant
Allen Elton, live stock
Allen Herbert, live stock
Allen John A, grocer
Anderson Elmer, drugs
Andrus Enoch, publisher The Clare
Sentinel.
Barrus Bart, grocer
Bicknell James S, cashr The Citizens
State Bank
Bicknell Wm H & Co, dry goods
Bogardus Simon, grocer
Boone Clarence, feed barn
Borden's Condensed Milk Co, John
Oliver foreman milk station
Bowler Joseph F, lawyer
Brand J Frank, cattle breeder
Brewer M E, farm implts
Butterfield M J, cider mill
Canfield A R & D W, publishers The
Clare Courier
Caple Wm H, real estate and insurance
Carey Edward, feed barn

Central Gas Co, J H Gibbs (Edmore)
pres, N J Brown (Mt Pleasant) sec,
treas and genrl mgr
Central Hotel, J H Lackie propr
Central Michigan Light & Power Co,
C A Wellman mngr
Citizens State Bank The (Capital and
Surplus $40,000), A E Sleeper Pres,
James S Bicknell Cashr, Prompt
Attention Given to all Collections
Clare City Mills, C M Jones propr,
flour and feed
Clare County Savings Bank (capital
$40,000 surplus $40,000), C W
Perry pres, C H Sutherland cashr
Clare Courier The, A R & D W
Canfield Publrs, M D Feighner
Editor and Business Mgr,
Established 1895, Strictly Home
Circulation Over 1,400 Copies
Weekly, Largest and Best Printing
Establishment in Clare County
Clare Elevator Co, George Johnson
mgr, grain and bldrs supplies

Clare Hardware & Implement Co, (Wm Webb, Morton Gallagher)

Clare Hay, Grain & Bean Co, W S Allister mgr

Clare Oil Co, David Ward mgr

Clare Produce Co, I E Feighner mgr

Clare Sentinel The, Enoch Andrus Publisher, Established 1878, The Largest Circulation of any paper in Clare County, "Everybody Reads the Clare Sentinel," Job Printing

Clute Jay, hay presser

Clute Wm F, physician

Crouse Daniel, wagonmaker

Cudney H C, agt American Exp Co

Dawson George E, cigar mfr

Demarest B H, dry goods, shoes and clothing

Derby O A & Co (Olse A Derby), confrs

Dionese John, fruits

Doherty John E, undertaker and plmbr

Dunlop J W Dr, drugs and medicine mfr

Dyer O E, drayage

Easler George W, furn and hdw

Fairman & Graham, garage

Farmers Independent Produce Co, R S Archamboult mgr

Feighner M D, editor and business mgr The Clare Courier

Foss J E, baker

Gould Charles H, undertaker

Grill Charles J, optometrist

Grill & White (C J Grill, George White) jewelers

Haley Wm, live stock

Hampton Gladys, milliner

Hampton Isaac H, garage

HanleyBros (Edward and John), poultry and cream

Harris & Hirt (C C Harris, T B Hirt), hardware

Harrison E M, auto repairer

Harvey C D, auctioneer

Hawes Edward C, dog breeder

Holbrook Thomas C, general store

Home Tavern, C H Jones propr

Hudson Joseph, live stock

Hulbert L Claire, photographer

Hutchinson M J, general store

Jackson John A, postmaster

Jackson L W and Frank, meats

Johnson Arthur D, surveyor

Jones Howard M, tailor

Joslin Fred, electrical contr

Kirkpatrick Floyd, drugs

Kratz H D, auto livery

Lackie J H, feed barn

Lewis Bert S, plumber

McKinnon Roy C, blksmith

McNeill W L, blksmith

McPhall David, restaurant

Mater D E, furniture

Maynard Thomas H, physician

Michigan State Tel Co, E M Cosgrove mgr

Morgan Fred, grocer

Mulder A E, dentist

Newsom Fred, auto accessories

Northern John, poultry breeder

O'Connor James, Wholesale and Retail Groceries and Provisions, Both Phones

Perry Charles W, lawyer

Peterson E S, piano tuner

Powers A E Mrs, grocer

Princess Theater, Harry McKerring mgr

Ramey Eli, billiards and lunch

Ramey & Mance, meats

Reading C A, lawyer

Reeder James A, physician

Roe Joseph B, dentist

Sanford Fred C, physician

Smalley Bros (E Frederick and Elsa), wagonmakers

Sterling Charles, veterinary surgeon

Stevens Ernest A, thresher

Sutherland C H, cashier Clare County Savings Bank

Tatman J F & Son (James F and James A), general store

Terwilliger Grant, harnessmaker

Thompon & Wlkinson (L H Thompson, S A Wilkinson), Dodge Bros Cars, Farm Implements, Buggies, Wagons, Cutters, Cream Separators, Manure Spreaders, Haying and Harvesting Tools, Oils, Fertilizer, Gas Engines, Auto Tires, Tubing and Casing

Thurston A & Son (Charles A Thurston), undertakers and pictures

Tibbils M J, jeweler

Veder Williard, baker

Ward David, auctioneer, feed and bldrs' supplies

Westfield & Fall River Lumber Co, C Kirkpatrick mgr

Whitlock C & N, milliner

Wild Herman, billiards

Wilson – Davy Co (capital $30,000), J H Wilson pres, L E Davy sec and treas, dry goods and clothing

West side of the 500 block of North McEwan looking northwest
Circa 1970
Photograph from the Forrest Meek Collection

Index

A & P Grocery 48, 49
A & P Tea Co. 127, 157
AAA 104
AAA Motor News 167
The Aardvark Store 17, 104
Abram, Harris 204
Ace Hardware 99
Ackerman, Jacob 204
Ackey, Alphonso 204
Acre, F. E. 219
Adams, August 213
Adams, Bill 68
Adams, Charles 40
Adams, Joseph 213
Adams, Joseph & Son 213
Adams, W. L. 206, 210
Adams, Wilbur and Betty 88
Adams, Wm. L. 215, 219, 210, 213
Alexander Shoes 66, 67
Alexander, Marlin and Betty 66
Alger House 142, 161, 162, 198,
   199, 201, 202, 204
Alger, David 199
Alger, Frank 199, 206, 215
All In One Store 49
Allen Agency Insurance 43
Allen and Bells Department Store
   51, 53
Allen and Manee 66
Allen, David 104
Allen, E. W. 217
Allen, Elton 219
Allen, Ethel 43
Allen, H. Rexford 43
Allen, Herbert 213, 215, 219
Allen, J. A. & Co. Grocery 50, 52
Allen, James 43
Allen, Jean 63
Allen, John A. 50, 219
Allen, Nick and Norm 52, 53
Allen, Robert 43
Allister, W. S. 220

Alma City Hall 56
Almost Up North 41
Alward Dennis 61, 160, 165, 168,
   201, 202, 206, 207, 208
American Beauty Shop 118, 119
American Cleaners 26
American Express Co. 208, 210, 220
American Legion 23, 24, 178, 183
American Radiator Company 120
Anderson, Elmer 63, 64, 66, 157,
   215, 219
Anderson, Elmer "Bud" 63
Anderson, Josephine 64
Anderson's Drug Store 63, 64, 154
Andrus, Enoch 36, 169, 219, 220
Anglo-American House 142, 161
Ann Arbor Railroad 210, 213, 215,
   216, 219
Apple Tree Lane 17, 66, 69
Applegreen, Donald 49
Archamboult, George A. 205, 209
Archamboult, R. S. 220
Arrand, James M 209, 211
Artibee, Estelle 43
Artistic Engraving and Marketing 96
Asline, John 127, 130, 180
Athouse, Clarence W. 213
Atkinson, Elmer J. 49
Atwood, Mary 90
Aube's Service 85
Austin, Melvin 204, 206, 211
Autry, Ella 91
Autry, Elvin 91
Axford, Bert 213, 216

Badour, Stephanie 41
Bailey, O. H. & Co. 146, 147
Bailey, Sandra 112
Baker, Wm. 204, 206
Ballard, Harmon 15, 16, 36

Ballinger, Frank   126
Ballinger, H. May   211
Band Box Cleaners   25, 49
Baptist Church   181, 203, 204, 206,
   209-211, 213, 215, 217, 219
Baranski, William & Monica   136
Barb's Infant and Gift Shop   112
The Bargain Shop   39
Barris & Linsea   126
Barrus, Bart   219
Barrus, George   105
Barz, William   124
Bay City Times   167
Beach Tanning & Toning Salon   49
Beagle, Alphonso P.   216
Beagles Café   89
Bebee & Davis   201
Bebee, Abiram   201
Becker, Wm. E.   206
Beeb, A.   142
Beebe, A. Byron   198, 199
Beebe, Abyron   202
Beemer & Ackey   204
Beemer Saloon   87
Beemer, Mrs. A.   36
Beemer, Oliver   87, 202, 204, 206,
   211, 213, 216
Belknap, Ivan F.   49
Bell, Willard   118, 119
Belle, Ruth Beauty Shop   118
Bellnap, George   133
Beltinck, Marion   96, 99
Beltinck, James, Roy J. and Charles
   96, 99
Beltinck, Roy N.   96, 97, 99
Benchley, Tina   104
Benmark, Keith and Doris   66
Benner, George   57, 87, 88, 159,
   211, 213, 216
Bennett, Philip A   36, 169, 214-216,
   218
Berger Manufacturing Company
   187
Berrant, Elizabeth   90
Best Insurance   131

Bicknell Bros. & Co.   211, 213
Bicknell Building   155, 190, 191
Bicknell Department Store   51-53,
   154
Bicknell Dry Goods Store   50
Bicknell H. M. & Co.   206
Bicknell R. A. & Co.   201
Bicknell W. H. & Co.   216, 219
Bicknell, H. May   206
Bicknell, James S.   52, 118, 154,
   155, 159, 201, 206, 211, 213, 216,
   219
Bicknell, John   51, 53
Bicknell, Martha   201
Bicknell, Nathan   50, 52, 53, 154,
   199, 201, 202, 204, 206, 211, 213,
   216
Bicknell, Richard A.   201
Bicknell, Willard   77
Bicknell, William   50-52, 123, 124,
   154, 155, 211, 213, 216
Bicknell's Home Delivery Dairy   144
Big Chicken   37
Bigley, Charles I.   204-206, 209
Bigley, Mrs. Catherine   204, 206
Bill Lewis Market   66
Bill's Tavern   88, 127
Black Bear & Broadcloth   51, 53
Bliek, John and Lynn   53
Blind Tiger Pub & Eatery   127
Bliss and Fisher   118
Bloom, N. A.   159
Blue Moon Hotel   164
Bluebird Café & Deli   115, 116
Bob's Lounge   36
Bogardus Building   113
Bogardus, Eva   113
Bogardus, Mrs. Martha   198, 199,
   201, 204
Bogardus, Simon   113, 126, 212, 219
Bogart   52, 190
Boge, Theo   118, 202, 204
Bogies Tavern   127
Bond Hubbard Company   55, 56
Books R Us   131

Boone, Clarence 219
Boorn, George 198, 202, 204
Borden's Condensed Milk Co. 219
Bovey & Wood 105
Bowdish, Seth 142, 199
Bowen, Wm. H. 209
Bowers, Frank E. 218
Bowers, M. A. 216
Bowler & Bowler 64
Bowler, Joseph 57, 61, 74, 219
Boyd, James S. 205, 206, 209, 212
Brand, J. Frank 219
Bransdorfer, Alfred 34
Bread of Life Coffee Shop 39
Brenda's Hair and Tanning Salon 44
Brewer Implement Store 175
Brewer-Bouchey Monument Co. 79
Brewer, M. E. 219
Brewin' on McEwan 127
Bristol, D. M. Professor 179
Broderick, 38
Broderick, W. F. 118
Brown, E. W. 61
Brown, George H. 204, 206, 213, 211, 216
Brown, J. A. 206
Brown, J. C. 207
Brown, J. T. 38
Brown, Norris J. 127, 219
Brown, Vincent 202
Brown, Wells 127
Brown, Wm. H. 212
Brown's Produce 41
Bryant, Ernie 128
Buckner, E. E. 33
Bud's Furniture 41
Bud's Second Hand Store 41
Buell, C. Mell 213
Bulman, Wm. 202
Bump & Mays 213
Bump Ace 213
Bumpus, Pvt. Admiral 139
Burch & Wyman 172, 173, 216
Burch, Logan 216
Burch, Mrs. Cynthia 216

Burdo, Ben 62
Burdo, Dan and Bill 62
Burdo, Stanley 61, 62
Burrier, George H. 211
Busche Motor Sales 15
Busche, Fred 15
Bush, Alexander 204
Butcher Shop 104
Butterfield, M. J. 219

Cadillac Cream Station 41
Cadillac Produce Co. 41
Calkin's House (Hotel) 77, 163, 164, 206, 213, 216
Calkins, Charles W. 66, 211, 213, 214, 216
Calkins, George C. 202
Calkins, J. W. Hardware Store 142, 175
Calkins, John and Mary 61
Calkins, John W. 140, 159, 163, 164, 198, 199, 201, 206, 211, 213, 216
Callam & Cornwell 213, 216
Callam, Catherine, 57
Callam, Peter 133, 140, 141, 153, 198, 199, 201
Callam, Peter Grocery Store 142
Callam, William 56, 57, 60, 173, 213, 216
Callihan, Sheral M. 34
Calvird, Dr. J. P. 64
Camp Grayling 165
Campbell Printing 47
Campbell, Eugene 47, 167
Campbell, Larry 47, 49
Campbell, Linda Lou 47, 49
Campbell, P. 142
Campbell, Robert 17
Campbell-Morse Realty 131
Canfield & Vandercook 211
Canfield, A. Ray 160, 165, 168, 211, 213, 214, 216, 219

Canfield, D. W. 219
Canton Steel Ceiling Company 187
Caple, William 126-128, 133, 219
Carey, Edward 219
Carlton, William and Carol 127
Carpenter, Dr. Joseph H. 202, 204, 207, 211, 213
Carrow, Nelson 216
Carter, B. H. & Co. 207
Carter, Benjamin P. 207
Cartwright, M. W. 110
Cascarelli, Joe and Julia 133
Catholic Church 181, 213-215, 219
Central Drug Store 216, 218
Central Gas Co. 127, 219
Central Hotel 161, 207, 209, 211-214, 216, 217, 219
Central Michigan Light and Power Co. 219
Central Michigan Music 51
Central Michigan Travel Services 133
Central Travel Agency 133
Central Travel & Cruise Center 133
Chaffee Grocery 123
Chamberlin M. F. & Sterns 199, 200
Chamberlin, Millard F. 199
Chapman, Bob 128
Chapman Business Machines 128
Chase & Curtiss 202
Chase, Charles S. 202, 204, 205, 207, 209
Chase, Roger and Emily 17, 96, 99
Chase, Seymour 202
Chatterton & Son 81, 174
Chemical Bank 159
Chesapeake & Ohio Railroad 82
Chiaoutis, Michael 99
Children's Center 15, 16
Choate, Rev. A. H. 211
Cimmerer Pharmacy 109
Cimmerer, Levi 128
Cimmerer, Minerva 127
Cimmerer, Robert and Gayle 109
Cimmerer, Roy 108, 109, 127, 156

Cities Services Filling Station 85, 86
Citizens State Bank 55, 57-59, 61, 159, 160, 177, 216, 217, 219
Civil Works Administration 23, 182
Clare Auto Parts Co. 98
Clare Band 211
Clare Board of Public Works 216
Clare Business Service 16
Clare Candy Co. 127
Clare Chamber of Commerce 104, 131, 164
Clare, Charles W. 211
Clare City Bakery 121, 186, 187, 190
Clare City Hall 7, 13, 23, 24, 152, 178, 182, 190, 191
Clare City Library 58, 77, 128
Clare County Bank 144, 158, 202-205
Clare County Credit Bureau 62
Clare County News 169
Clare County Press 168, 199, 201
Clare County Review 104
Clare County Savings Bank 73, 74, 84, 85, 100, 102, 103, 145, 150, 151, 158, 159, 177, 183, 184, 188, 207, 210-212, 214-216, 218-220
Clare Courier 160, 168, 169, 210, 211, 214-216, 219, 220
Clare Creamery Co. 88, 207, 211, 214, 215
Clare Democrat 168, 202
Clare Democrat and Press 168, 203, 204, 207, 208
Clare Dramatic Club 179
Clare Drug Co. 127, 157
Clare Electric Company (Business) 112
Clare Electric Company (Utility) 148, 207, 211, 214, 216
Clare Electronics 112
Clare Elevator Company 173, 219
Clare Factory Outlet 16
Clare Family Fitness 49
Clare Furnace Co. 216

Clare Furniture Co.   62
Clare Hardware & Furniture Co.   61, 62
Clare Hardware & Implement Co. 61, 175, 220
Clare Hardware Building   150, 160
Clare Hardware Company   55-58, 60-62, 152, 154, 186, 211, 213, 214, 216
Clare Hay Grain & Bean Co.   81, 174, 220
Clare High School   19
Clare Inn   161
Clare Insurance and Realty Company 133
Clare Iron Works   214
Clare K of P Band   207
Clare Knitting Mills   216
Clare Library Assoc.   178, 179
Clare Loan Company   17
Clare Main Street   64
Clare Masonic Building Assoc.   71
Clare Mini Mall   49
Clare Mnfg Co.   207
Clare Nursing Home   130
Clare Office Supply Co.   16
Clare Oil Co.   220
Clare Party Store   85, 86
Clare Percheron Horse Breeders Assoc.   216, 217
Clare Press   168, 202
Clare Print & Pulp   91
Clare Produce Co.   220
Clare Publishers   34
Clare Publishing Co.   211
Clare Realty Co.   130
Clare Reporter   210
Clare Restaurant   61
Clare Roller (City) Mills   173, 216, 219
Clare Sentinel   34-36, 79, 168, 169, 210-216, 218-220
Clare Sentinel and Democrat-Press 169
Clare Steam Laundry   216, 217

Clare Study Club   178
Clare Telephone Company   149
Clare Water Works   149, 202, 204, 207, 211, 214, 216
Clare Wooden Ware Co.   204, 206-208, 211
Clare-Trading Post   41
Clarified Bakery   71, 75
Clark & Son   120
Clark David W.   216
Clark Drugs   124
Clark, Charles   124
Clark, Charles H.   207, 211
Clark, Mrs. Mary   207
Cleveland, P. J. 201
Cloe, Laura   216
Cloze N-Stuff Womens Apparel   112
Clute & Terbush   207
Clute, Andrew   207, 216
Clute, Jay   220
Clute, Wm. F.   220
Coffee Talk 505   109
Colburn, Frank   179
Cole, William and Mary   31
Cole, Wm. N.   216
Colonial Motion Picture Company 180
Commercial House   161
Congregational Church   13, 18, 19, 143, 181, 182, 198-200, 202, 203, 206, 208, 210, 212, 213, 215, 219
Conlogue, V. F.   209
Connie & Margaret's Hallmark Shop 64
Consolidated Light & Power   126
Consumers Power Company   113
Continetal Home Center   94
Cooley, Horace S.   216
Cooley, Mrs. Wallace S.   201
Cooley, Wallace "Deacon"   142, 198, 199, 204, 207
Coon, Rose and Robert   115
Cooper, W. T.   18, 19, 182
Coors, Rev. August H.   207, 211

Cops & Doughnuts Bakery 26, 119, 121, 124, 186, 191
Corkins, George 204
Corky's Diner 40, 41
Corman Motor Sales 167
Cornwell, Benjamin F. 216
Cornwell, Frank 213
Corporate Title 72
Cosgrove, E. M. 220
Cotton Radio Hospital 130
Courier Printing 110
Courtland, Mrs. E. R. 216
Covet Cut & Color 131
Cowles & Mutscheller 100, 103, 189
Cowles, Clarence 76, 103, 189
Cox, Kenneth and Gertrude 71, 72
Cradit, Neilan 128
Cramm, Rev. George W. 204
Crawford, Robert 142, 189,199
Creeper, Silas 211, 214, 216
Crouse, Daniel 118, 204, 207, 211, 214, 216, 220
Creguer Building 17
Creguer, Peter 15, 17
CSX Transportation 82
Cudney, H. C. 220
Cunningham, Andrew 204
Cunningham, John 207
Currie, W. E. 164
Curtis, Wm. B. 205, 209
Curtiss, Wm. J. 202
Curves Womens Fitness Center 58
Custom Sportswear 99
Custom T-Shirt & Garment Shop 104
Cutler Dickerson 81, 174

D & C Store 72, 75
D & L Bar and Café 90
Dailey E. G. Co. 216, 218
Damoth Agency 130-133
Damoth, Art Real Estate 133

Damoth, Arthur 130-133
Danielson, Anne Marie 109
Davis Block 48
Davis, J. M. 48
Davis, Malcolm D. 198, 199, 201, 202, 204, 207, 211
Davis Poultry & Produce 41
Davy and Co. 105, 106, 153-155, 211, 214, 216
Davy Building 106, 153, 155, 185, 186
Davy, Lew E. 105-108, 150, 155, 156, 211, 214, 216, 221
Davy, Vernal R. 105, 106, 155, 211, 214, 216
Davy/Mussell/Elden Building 111, 149, 153, 155
Dawson Building 97
Dawson Brothers 41
Dawson, George 33, 40, 41, 98, 202, 204, 207, 211, 220
Dawson, George & Sons 41
Dawson, Ora 33, 75
Dawson, Theron 33, 34
De Gez, Thomas 202, 204, 207, 211
Dean, Wm. A. 207
Defoe, Grant 179
DeFoe, Mrs. Sarah 204, 211
Delaney, Edward 211, 214
Demarest Cash Bargain Store 123
Demarest, B. H. 123, 220
Demasi, Vincent and Elaine 62
Demo, Vivian 66
Demo-Sadler, Diane 66
Dennis, John 144
Derby O. A. & Co. 220
Derby, Olse A. 71, 220
Derby, Otto S. 204, 207, 211, 214, 216
Design Spectre 104
Desired Skin 16
Detroit Free Press 167
Detroit Safe Company 74
Deuell, Harvey 198

De Vogt, Eugene Henry   144, 202, 204, 207, 214, 216
Dibble, Mortimer   204, 207
Dionese, John   220
Dionese, John and Virginia   88
Dionese, Paul P.   88
Dixon, Joseph   203, 205
Dixon, Wm. J.   205
Doherty A. J. & Sons   214
Doherty Building (400 Block)   94, 150, 151, 153, 177, 178
Doherty Building (500 Block)   63, 66, 94, 178, 186
Doherty Electric Light Co.   148
Doherty Hardware   74, 144, 148, 207
Doherty Hotel   7, 12, 76-79, 103, 149, 152, 157, 164-167, 176, 177, 179, 189
Doherty Hotel Cabins   166
Doherty J. E. & Son   75
Doherty Opera House   57, 63, 70-72, 74, 85, 148-150, 178-180, 183, 184, 207, 211, 214, 216
Doherty, Alfred J and Alice   133
Doherty, Alfred J.   63, 70, 71, 74, 75, 77, 84, 85, 137, 148-150, 158, 164, 165, 167, 178, 179, 184, 186, 202, 204, 207, 211, 214, 216, 219
Doherty, Alfred J. II (Fred)   66, 71, 75, 77, 109
Doherty, Alfred J. III   75, 78, 109
Doherty, Dean and James   78
Doherty, Floyd E.   74, 126, 167, 179, 214, 216
Doherty, Frank B.   74, 126, 173, 214, 216
Doherty, Helen   66, 71, 109
Doherty, John E.   71, 75, 216, 220
Donahue, Patrick   198
Dorney, Arthur   118
Dorsey, Thomas S.   179, 211, 214, 216
Douglas, Homer   36
Dover School   148
Dowd, Samuel P.   207

Downtown Clare Professional Building   92
Downtown Dani's Restaurant   90
Downtown Development Authority   152
Downtown Drugs   124
Drapery Boutique   41, 112
Duncan Hall   98, 178, 217
Duncan Hines Adventures in Good Eating   167
Duncan, James   98, 99, 202, 204, 208, 211, 214, 216, 217
Duncan, Mrs. John   214
Dunlop Building   26, 122, 125, 151
Dunlop Medical Hall   144, 151, 159, 180
Dunlop, Dr. J. W.   159, 180, 202, 204, 208, 211, 214, 217, 220
Dunlop, William   41
Dunlop's, J. W. Banking House   159, 217
Dunwoodie & McKinnon   204
Dunwoodie Building   126, 179, 180
Dunwoodie, James   126, 202, 204, 208, 211, 214, 216-218
Dwyer, Daniel R.   201
Dwyer, John   208
Dwyer, Mrs. Margaret E.   203, 205, 208, 211, 214
Dwyer, Wm. J.   208
D-X Service Station   85
Dyer, O. E.   220

Early American Room (Doherty Hotel)   77
Easler, George   33, 217, 220
Eaton, Marvin D.   168, 202, 204, 207, 208
Edward Jones   54, 66
Edward, Charles H.   208
Egbert & Field   211
Egbert, James   211
Ehrhardt, Christopher   202, 204

Elaine's Hair & Nail Expressions   43
Elden & Holbrook   208
Elden, Norris   109
Elden, William   34, 107-109, 142,
   150, 156, 198, 199, 202, 204, 208,
   211, 214, 217
Eller Manufacturing Co.   123, 187
Eller, J. H. & Co.   187, 188
Ellis, Miron D.   111, 217
Elliston & Stone   211
Elliston, Orson A.   211
Emerald Room (Doherty Hotel)   77
Emory, Scott W.   144
The Emporium   64
Equity Investment Corporation   72
Ervey, Albert M.   198, 199, 201, 202
Eureka Heating & Ventilation
   Company   56
Evening Post Bar & Grill   36
Evert, Howard   113
Evert, Lawrence   113
Evert's Jewelry   114
Exchange Hotel   161, 162, 202-205,
   214, 215

415 Corporation   92
505 Café   109
515 Gallery   116
F. Marshall   208
Facing Alcohol Concerns through
   Education (F. A. C. E.)   104
Fairbairn, Jacklyn,   106
Falk, Frank   211, 214, 217, 218
Fall, Jennie   21
Family Grill   41
Fantastic Finds Antique Store   51, 64
Fantastique Bridal & Formal Wear
   115
Fairman & Graham   220
Farmers Independent Produce Co.
   220
Farmer's Institute   217
Farwell Register   168

Feighner & Co.   204
Feighner Bros.   202
Feighner, Isaiah   202, 204, 220
Feighner, Malcom D.   34, 36, 169,
   216, 220
Feighner, Wm. A.   202, 204
Fellers Cut Rate Store   36, 39-41
Fellers Department Store   104
Fellers Shoe Store   47
Field, C. C.   211
Field, Rev. Floyd C.   208
Fielder Shoe Store   66
Fielder, Robert   66
Fife, M. C.   66
Fine, Samuel   204
Firestone Store   157, 167
Fishley F. & Co.   217
Fishley, Frederick   204, 208, 211,
   217
Fix-it-Shop   15
Fleming Shoe Store   106, 155
Fleming, F. L.   106
Flint & Pere Marquette Depot   142,
   144, 161
Flint & Pere Marquette Railroad   82,
   83, 139-145, 161, 171, 198-200,
   202-204, 206, 208-210
Folkert, Deirdre   106, 109
Folkert, Glen C.   106, 155
Folkerts Coffee Creations   109
The Food Shop   109
The Food Store   109
Forbes, Frank   208, 214, 217
Ford Times   167
Ford, Elmer   40
Ford, Henry   166
Forest Lawn Cemetery Comfort
   Center (Saginaw)   189
Forward, G. W.   218
Forward, Mrs. G. W.   217
Foss Bakery   120, 154, 186
Foss, Earl   98
Foss, Earl and Ernest   120, 121
Foss, Mr. and Mrs. Ernest   121
Foss, J. E. and Jennie   120, 121

Foss, John E. 211, 217, 220
Four Fifteen North McEwan Co. 92
Four Leaf Brewing 49
Fox, D. J. 68, 204, 208, 211, 214
Fox, L. G. 61
Fraternal Order of Masons 64, 71, 72, 74, 178, 180
Free Methodist Church 203, 205, 206, 210, 212-215, 219
Freeman Oil Co. 25, 160, 176
Friends & Coffee 127
Friz Undertaking Co. 128
Friz, Andrew 128
Fullerton, G. O. & Son 175
Fuson, Dani 90

G & G investments 34
G. I. S. S. U. S. A. East Corp. 54
G. L. S. Investments 54
Gadberry, Debra 115
Gallagher, Mortimer B. 61, 71, 175, 219
Galliver, James H. 202, 204, 207, 208, 210, 211, 213, 214, 217
Galloway, Lon M 71
Gambles Store 95, 96, 99, 112, 157
Grandma's House 31
Gardener, John 175
Gardner Elevator Co. 107
Gardner, J. 126
Garfield Memorial Library 55, 58
Garfield, Sam 58, 177
Garland, John D. 204, 209
Gas Corporation of Michigan 112
Gates Computer and Gaming 134
Gateway Realty 131
Gay & Brezner 182
Gay, Florence (White) 183
Gay, James, Evelyn and Richard 72
Gay, R. V. 23, 129, 182, 183, 190
Gay's 5 & 10 Store 71
Geek Brothers 122, 217
Geek, Nicholas F. 217

Geek, Philip F. 217
George's Tavern 88
German Lutheran Church 181, 205, 209, 213, 215, 219
Gibbs, Andrew 217
Gibbs, Andrew & Sons 216, 217
Gibbs, J. H. 219
Gibbs, Mark 217
Giberson & Curtis 209
Giberson, Grace 217
Giberson, John 204, 205, 209, 211, 212
Giberson, Mrs. Helen 204
Giberson, Mrs. Wm. 202
Giberson, Wm. 202, 204, 209
Gibraltar Insulation Company 25, 160
Gibson, Frances 214
Gibson, John & Delphine 31
Glory Be 118
Gollish, Steven and Kristi 133, 134
Goodenough, Alvardo F. 168, 199
Goodenow, Charles N 201, 211
Goodman House 30, 183
Goodman W. & Co. 202, 204, 209
Goodman, John R. 57, 211, 214, 217
Goodman, Kittie 31
Goodman, Mrs. K. M. 211, 214
Goodman, William 31, 133
Goodman, Wm. A. 202, 204, 209
Goodman, Wm. H. 202, 204, 209
Gordanier, Archie C. 209, 211, 214
Gorr & Arrand 209, 211
Gorr, Edward B. 63, 122, 126, 187, 204, 209, 211, 214, 217
Gorr, Frank 216, 217
Gould Undertaking Co. 128
Gould, Charles H. 128, 220
Graham, Allen 103
Graham, David & Virgil 94
Graham, George and Betty 94
Grand Army of the Republic (GAR) 178-180
Grandma's House 31, 32
Grathwohl, Lawrence 204, 209, 211

Graves, Mrs. George 211
Grawey, James 115
Gray Frank R. 217
Gray, Robert A. 209, 214, 217
Greaser, Paul 214
Great Lakes Central Railroad 11, 82
Green Maxine 69
Green, Jay J. 68, 69
Green, Jay Jr. 69
Green's Bargain Center 104
Green's Clothing and Shoes 69, 154
Green's Clothing Store 68, 69
Greer, Bert 52
Greiser, Paul 57
Grieser, Paul 217
Grill & White 220
Grill, Charles J. 220
Grinnell Brothers 41
Groms, Edgar 202
Grove Brothers Five & Ten Store
   92-94
Grover, Frank 217
Groves, Arlene 94
Groves, James 94
Groves, Thomas 38
Gulf Oil Co. 173
Gulick, Rev. J. 201
Gushon, Dr. E. J. 21

Haines, Dr. James 22
Haley, William 159, 214, 217, 220
Hall, Frances, Ellen and John 109
Halstead, George W. 142, 198, 201,
   202, 209, 214
Halsted, George W. 199, 201
Halsted, Herschel 57
Hamburger Hill 158
Hammerberg, Dr. Kuno 79, 80
Hampton, Emerson and Eileen 96,
   99
Hampton, Gladys 220
Hampton, Issac (Ike) 47-49, 133,
   167, 220

Hampton, James 202
Hampton, Nellie 49
Hanley Brothers 220
Hanley, Edward 220
Hanley, John 220
Hardy, Edward 124
Hardy, Llewellyn 198, 199, 201
Hardy, Mrs. Theresa 198
Harper, Wiliam 18, 19
Harrell, Benjamin and Joan 136
Harring, John 209
Harris & Herrick 145, 204
Harris & Hirt 66, 220
Harris & McKay 204
Harris A. & Son 211, 214
Harris, Alwilda, 211, 214
Harris, C. C. 220
Harris, Clyde 69, 211, 214
Harris, Issac 204, 215
Harris, John W. 204
Harris, Julia 179
Harris, Miss Ella J. 209, 211
Harrison, E. M. 220
Harrison, Travis 54
Harrison & Newman 34, 54
Harshman, Brenda 115
Hartzler, Virgina 88
Harvey, A. E. 211
Harvey, C. D. 220
Hathaway, Rev. W. J. 214
Haug & Scheurman 55, 56
Haug, Charles H. 56
Hawes, Edward 220
Haynes, Philip 202
Hays, Clyde M. 52
Hazeltine, Rev. J. L. 214
Hearnes, Curtis and Dolores 135
Heart of Michigan Café 109
Heas, J. R. 211
Heather, Ralph and Helen 21
Hebner, Mike 131
The Helium Connection 118
Helping Hands Shop 39, 41
Hendrie Brothers Market 66, 67
Hendrie, Kenneth and Jay 66

232

Her Place 125, 151
Herrick House 31
Herrick, Maurice A. 204
Hickey, Fred 202
Hicks Jewelers 114
Hicks, Rodger 114
Higelmire & Assoc. 25, 160
High, John 214, 217
Hirt, T. B. 220
Hirzel, Mrs. Jeanette 200
Holbrook, Cora 118
Holbrook, Donald Jr. 25, 26, 133
Holbrook, Donald Sr. 25, 26, 160
Holbrook, Henry H. 203, 204, 209
Holbrook, Thomas 133, 135, 208,
    209, 211, 214, 217
Holbrook, Thomas C. 109, 118, 208,
    211, 214, 217, 220
Holbrook, William 122
Holbrook/Mair Building 25, 160,
    177
Holcomb, Iva 41
Hollinshead, Henry E. 203
Hollister, Fred 70, 73, 184
Holmes, George L. 210
Holmes, Warren S. Company 182,
    183
Holridge House 20
Holridge, Henry 21
Home Tavern 220
Hometown Variety 119
Horning & Schaffer 171, 200
Horning, Adam 204, 209
Horning, Edward B. 203, 212
Horning, John T. 173, 198, 200,
    208, 212, 215, 217
Horning, Josiah 203, 204
Horning T. P. & Reist 171
Horning, Tobias P. 198, 201, 203
Hoskins, James 127
Houghton Drug Store 124
Houghton, Murl 124, 127, 157
House, Oles and Bailey 18
Household Appliance Company 109
Hubbell, Wm. E. 204 209

Hubel, Harry 39
Hubel, W. E. 171
Hudson, Joseph 220
Huffman, Julius 209, 212, 214
Hughes, Harold 75
Hughes & Trucks 75
Hulbert, L. Claire 110, 220
Humphrey, Bradley and Brittney 99
Hustead, Berton 198
Husted & Mason 203
Husted Opera House 144, 145, 179
Husted, John G. 203, 204, 209, 211
Husted, Julius B. 201
Hutchinson, M. J. 220
Hutchinson, W. J. 209

I. B. T. Title-Clare County 44
I. G. A. Store 157
Ideal Theater 127, 129, 130, 180,
    190, 191
Image Quest Active Wear 16, 49
Imerman, John 209, 212
Independent Order of Odd Fellows (I.
    O. O. F.) 154, 178
Industrial School for Boys 184
Irwin, Miss Mina 209
Isabella Bank 72
Isabella Bank & Trust 72, 73, 75
Isabella Bank Investment & Trust
    Services 72
Isabella County Indian Reservation
    139
Isabella-Houghton Lake Indian Trail
    139, 140
Isabella-Tobacco River State Road
    140

Jablonski, Antoinette 121
Jackson Meat Market 151
Jackson, John A. 212, 214, 217, 219,
    220

Jackson, L. W. and Frank   220
Jacobs, W. W.   212
Jan-Dor Fashion   66
Jean's Dress Shop   118
Jefferies, Frances A.   211, 212
Jefferies, George W.   198, 200
Jefferies, M. R.   201
Jefferies, Mrs. George W.   198
Jefferies Meat Market   142
Jefferies, Remick G.   168, 169, 179,
   211, 212
Jenkins, O. W. Co.   76, 77
Jenks, Denise   136
Jenks, Jay   201
Jenney, Burt   66
Jenney, R. H.   207, 208
Jerry's Bar   127
Jewett, Herschel   66
Jim's Recreation   127
John Q. Look No. 404 Lodge of the
   Masons   63
Johnson, O. C.   216
Johnson Electric Shop   112
Johnson, Arthur D.   217, 220
Johnson, George   219
Johnson, James   209
Johnson, R. D. & Son   217
Johnston Elevator   81, 174, 175
Johnston Hay Grain & Bean Co.   81,
   174
Johnston, Ed G.   81, 174, 175
Johnston, Joe   81, 174
Joiner, Horace   212
Jones & Ross   57
Jones Floor Covering   118
Jones, C. H.   220
Jones, C. M.   219
Jones, Donald and Octavia   118
Jones, Howard M.   220
Jones, John Paul   36, 169
Jones, Jonathan   118
Jones, Kenneth and Patricia   112
Jones, Patricia   16
Joslin, Fred   220
Joslin, Roy   34, 75, 89

Joslin, Roy Lunchroom   75
Just Kidding   99

Kane, Floyd   133
Kane, Miss Barbara   64
Kap's Koins   134
Karen's Bridal Gallery & Boutique
   118
Karr, Leslie   16
Keiser, Sherry   39
Keiser, Warren   35, 36, 39, 41
Keller, Warren   203
Kelley, Peter   201, 209, 212
Kelly, Wm.   205, 209
Kevin's Carpet   124
Keyes & Smalley,   209
Keyes, Calvin B.   209
Keyes, Dr.   36
Keystone Mnfg. Co.   209, 212
Kinsey, Vere   36
Kirkbride & Co.   171, 172, 214, 217
Kirkbride Orchestra   179, 217
Kirkbride, Samuel C.   71, 149, 204-
   207, 209, 212-215, 217
Kirkpatrick, C.   221
Kirkpatrick, Floyd   108, 220
Kleiner, Walter   25
Kleinhardt, Thomas and Kim   64, 92,
   115, 116
Knights of Pythias   178, 205
Koch, Mark   54
Koch, Michelle   125
Koch, Ruby   125
Koch, Susan   104
Koch, Tom   130
Koch, Willard   125, 130
Kons, Kate   217
Kosciuszko, Edward   133
Kratz, H. D.   220
Kreiner, Nick   41
Krell, Barb and Robert   112
Kroger Grocery Store   71, 103, 157
Kuffler, John   209, 212, 214, 217

Kuhlman Dolores 136
Kump, Adelbert D. 209, 212
Kump, Adelpha 36, 214, 217
Kump, Delaware H. 205
Kump, Wm. 214
Kunse, Ronald and Barbara 104,
  127

La Peirre, Albert E. 217
Lacey, Arthur J. 74, 214, 217
Lackie House 161
Lackie, Alexander 209
Lackie, Archibold 161, 205
Lackie, James H. 213, 214, 216, 217,
  219, 220
Lackie, Jamie 217
Ladd, Mrs. J. E. 217
Lamb & Son 198
Lamb, David W. 198
Lamb, Gerald 214
Lamb, Roy 214
Lamb, Rudolph W. 198, 200, 205,
  209, 212, 214
Lamback, Henry 144, 203
Lane, Benjamin 212
Lange, Fred 142, 200, 201, 203,
  205, 209
Lange, William 118
Langworthy, Alphonso 209
Lawrence, George B. 203, 205
Le Roy, Sarah 217
Leach, Lyman W. 203
Leahy, James F. 217
Lee, Charles S. 209, 217
Lee, George W. 142, 172, 173, 198,
  200, 201, 209, 212, 214, 217
Lee's Carpet 49
Leebove, Isaiah 103, 177
Lemm, Victor and Patty 119
Lenny's Hair Styling 75
Leprechaun Shop 133, 134
Leprechaun's Gift & Gadget Store
  104

Leusenkamp Bros. 214
Leusenkamp, Gerritt 214
Leusenkamp, Harry 214
Levington, Samuel G. 209
Lewis & Patrick 217
Lewis, Alphia 69
Lewis, Burton S. 217, 220
Lewis, Chris 112
Lewis, William 66
Lewis, William P. 68, 69, 212, 214,
  217
Liberty Professional Building 56
Lighthouse Book & Gift Shoppe 49
Lindloff, Rev. William 205, 209
Linsea, Ananias 204
Lister & Archamboult 205, 209
Lister & Ort 212
Lister, Fred 57, 159, 205, 209, 212,
  216, 217
Little Miss & Master Shoppe 109
Live and Let Live Livery 141
Livingston, Carl (Jack) 177
Lloyd, Chauncey 217, 218
Loar-Perras, Pamela 96
Loar, Pamela Wilson 96
Lockwood, Mabel 133, 134
Loeffler, Miss Louise 127
The Lofts 92
Lone Pine Cabins 166
Long, Alberta 179
Long, Rev. Samuel 212
Lossing Building 117
Lossing, Dorothy J. 118, 201, 203,
  205
Lossing, Monroe J. 201, 203, 205,
  212
Lotis, Albert 141
Louch, Alfred 141, 198, 200, 201,
  203, 205, 209, 212, 214
Louch, Frank 179
Louch, Guy T. 217
Louch, James 205, 209, 212, 214,
  217
Louch, Louie 217
Louise's Flower & Gift Shop 127

Loundra, Wm. 214
Lowe, Rev. John H. 209, 217
Luce, Mrs. Harriet 212
Lumberman's House 201
Lund, Aaron 119
Lund, Mary Faith 115
Lynch, Thomas 118
Lynn's, Deborah Department Store
 104

Mack, Andrew 205, 209, 212, 214,
 217
Mack, Mrs. A. E. 209, 212, 214
Mackinac Island 149
Mackenzie, Kenneth 121
Made with Loving Hands Art & Craft
 Consignment Shop 109
Mahon, Norell and Barbara 26
Mair, David 25
Mair, Jackson 118
Mair, Robert 25
Makin, Jean 118
Malcolm, Sarah 179
Malone, Rev. Dennis E. 214
Maloney, Agnes 217
Mammoth Oil Company 58, 160
Mammoth Petroleum Company 177
Mammoth Producing & Refining
 Company 58, 103, 177
Mammoth Producing Corporation
 115
Mandy's Discount Fabric 109
Manny's Bar 36
Manor Inn Rooms & Cabins 166
Manpower 104
Marchiando & Rau 55
Marion's Record Shop 130
The Market City 175
Markley George Boarding House
 141, 161
Marshall, C. F. 209, 210
Martin, Brad 104
Martin, John H. 217

Martin, John H. & Son 217
Martin, Robert J. 209
Martin, Wess 217
Mason & Boyd 205, 209, 212
Mason & Dwyer 203, 205
Mason & Storey 209
Mason, Jacob 198, 200, 203, 205,
 209, 212, 214, 217
Mason, Martha M 118, 201, 203,
 205, 209
Mater & Lamb 214
Mater & Naylor 212
Mater Brothers 209
Mater, Daniel E. 61, 209, 220
Mater, George A. 209, 212, 214
Maurice Studios 58
Maxwell & Bryant 145
Maxwell, Dave and Donna 127
Maxwell Flowers 69, 127
Maxwell, Rev. George W. 217
Maxwell, William and Dorothy 127
Maynard, Albert 215, 217
Maynard, Dr. Thomas H. 198, 200,
 203, 205, 209, 210, 212, 215, 218,
 220
Mays, Henry 213
McCambly Building 33
McCambly John 33
McCarthy, Diane R. (Flinn) 41
McClure, Neil 200
McCready's Produce 41
McDonald & Lackie 217
McDonald, Collins 217
McEwan Professional Building 54,
 151
McEwan Street Real Estate 99
McEwan, John 181
McEwan, William 139-141, 143,
 181
McFarland, Peter 205
McGuire & Campbell Firestone
 Home & Auto Supply 47
McGuire Brothers Firestone 47
McGuire, Clarence 47, 167
McGuire, Floyd 47, 167

McGuire, Peter H. 209
McGuire, Warren 47
McIntyre, Arthur W. 84, 198, 200, 203, 205, 209, 212
McKay Gas Field 176
McKay, Addison 204
McKay, Pauline 205
McKeever, George 61, 217
McKerracher, John 175, 217
McKerring, Harry 220
McKinley, Allen 205
McKinley, Rev. J. F. 198
McKinnon Blacksmith Shop 42
McKinnon Building 65
McKinnon, Archie 42, 65, 66, 203, 204, 214, 217
McKinnon, James 36, 214
McKinnon John Boarding House 141, 161
McKinnon, Kyle 66
McKinnon, Margaret 66
McKinnon, Martha 66
McKinnon, Roy 42, 43, 220
McKinnon's, Roy Tourist Cabins 166
McKnight, Dr. Frank 110, 112, 160
McKnight, Margaret 112
McLaren, J. D. 174
McLaughlin, Emery 99
McNeill, Wm. L. 217
McPhall, David 205, 209, 217, 220
Meek, Forrest 131
Meeting Place 16
Melick, Neal 27
Menthen, Ray 89
Menthen's Café 89
Mercer, Ben 61
Mercer, Guy 41
Mercer, Stephanie 39, 41
Merillat, John 81
Merrell Auto Electric Service 41
Merritt Oil Co. 85, 177
Mester, James 66
Mester, John Robert 42

Methodist Church 198-200, 202, 203, 205-207, 210-215, 219
Methodist Episcopal Church 143, 181, 201, 217
Michigan Bell Telephone Company 104
Michigan Consolidated Gas Co. 115
Michigan Creamery Co. 84, 85
Michigan Hoop Co. 209, 212
Michigan School for the Deaf 184
Michigan Soldiers Home 184
Michigan State Fair 148
Michigan State Univesity Board of Trustees 149
Michigan Telephone Co. 218, 220
Michigan's Democratic Party 160
Michigan's Republican Party 61, 160
Midland Produce Co. 218
Midland, High School 183
Mid-Michigan Big Brothers/Big Sisters 17
Mill End Store 106, 109, 155
Miller, Christopher 66
Millies Downtown Gift Store 64
Millis, E. D. 85
Mitchell, Joseph C. 205
Mitchell, Mitzi 121
Modern Food Market 124
Modern Woodman of America 25
Mogg, Glen and Stephanie 31
Moline, Harold 48
Montgomery Ward 96
Montini, Louis 91
Montini, Peter 91
Mood Makers 64
Moody's, Russ Tavern & Restaurant 127
Morgan Grocery 109
Morgan, Fred 220
Morgan, Mary 109
Morgan, Richard 212
Morgan, Robert 109
Morris, James 201, 203
Morris, William J. Co. 76, 77, 100

Morse, Henry 218
Morse, Sherman. H. & Son Harness
  Shop 57, 218
Morse, Sherman H. 218
Mosler Safe Company 56
Mott, Sanford 18, 93
Mount Pleasant Agency 133
Mowbray Insurance Agency 58
Mowbray, Mr. and Mrs. Gordon 58
Moyer's Store 128
Mulberry Café 31
Mulder, Dr. Allen E. 58, 118, 159,
  160, 211, 212, 218, 220
Mullen, Con 214, 215
Mummon, Cyrus 112
Murphy, Carolyn 16, 54, 127
Murphy, Mr. and Mrs. Joe 89
Murphy, John and Martha 66
Murphy, Miss Minnie 209
Murphy's Café 89
Muscott, Ralph 205, 207
Mussell Drug Store 154, 156
Mussell, Anna 108, 109, 156, 159,
  179, 215, 216, 218
Mussell, Robert 107, 108, 144, 150,
  156, 203, 205, 209, 212
Mussell/Elden Building 107, 118,
  160
Mutscheller, George 103, 189
Mutz, James 200

National Grocery Co. 61
National Loan & Investment Co. of
  Detroit 205, 209, 212
Naumes, Joseph K. 64
Naylor, Thomas 212
Neeland, Dr. Hugh E. 110, 160, 215,
  218
Neff, Dr. C. B. 21
Neff, Dr. Thomas and Gail 21
Nelson House (Mount Pleasant) 199
New Horizon Travel 54, 104

New Yorker Children's Clothing
  Store 16
Newgreen, Mrs. Beata C. 209
News-Argus 168
Newsom, Fred 220
Nicholls Hotel 143, 144, 161, 162,
  198
Nicholls, John 198
Nichols, Lambert 201
Nivison, Ruth 85
Nivison, Richard 75
Nix, Rev. Frank H. 212
Norris, Rev. Austin Hull 181, 198
North Ten L. L. C. 58
Northern Communication 34
Northern Michigan Tuberculosis
  Sanitarium 182
Northern, John 220
Northern Realty 131
Northey, Richard 203, 205, 209
Northey, Samuel 215, 218
Northland Hardware 49
Northquist, Fred 180
Northwestern University Medical
  School 79
Norwood Building 15
Norwood, James 15

Oberloier Smith Properties Inc. 96,
  99
O'Callaghan Building 45, 46
O'Callaghan John 47, 200, 201, 218
O'Callaghan's Grocery 142
O'Connor, James 215, 218, 220
O'Donald, Charles and Ann 31
O'Donald, Charles H. 57, 159, 179,
  209, 212
O'Donald-Kidder Ann 31
Oden, Hazel 31
Office of Supervising Architect of the
  Treasury 27, 183
Ohio Dairy Co. 38
Oil & Drum Co. 66

Olds, L. T. Dairy 144
Oliver, John 219
Olson, Anne Irene 133
Olson, James 130
Olson, W. James 133
Oriental Theatre 180
Ort & Dixon 203, 205
Ort, Henry 198, 200, 203, 205, 209, 212,
Orth, Henry 161, 202-205, 207, 209, 211, 212
Osborn & Randall Roller Mills 144
Osborn, D. W. 23
O'Toole, Patrick 84

P. T. Billings Service 34
Palace Theater 38, 180
Palmer, C. E. 205
Palmer, Curtis 209
Palmer, Erastus 36, 168, 169
Palmer, Eugene 198
Palmer, Mrs. E. D. 212
Palmer, Rev. F. D. 215
Palshan, Charles and Maxine 121
Panda Chinese Restaurant 119
Parameter, Wm. 218
Parish, Benjamin 36, 169
Parish, Florence 34, 36, 169
Parrish Brothers 141
Parrish, Mrs. Mamie T. 218
Parrish, Mrs. Mary 212
Parrish, Wm L. 203, 205, 209, 212, 215, 218
Pastorino, Antonio, G. 218
Patient, Benjamin 203, 205, 210
Patrick, Ulysses H. 217
Patterson, F. D. & Co. 205
Patterson, Frank D. 205, 209
Patty Ann's Quilts 34
Pearson Dress Shoppe 15, 16
Pearson Genevieve 15
Pease, George 217
Pelton, Fred 215, 218

Pere Market 110
Pere Marquette Railroad 82, 213, 215, 217, 219
Perras, Joe 96
Perrin, Willis D. 209, 212
Perry, Charles W. 74, 85, 158, 200-205, 207, 208, 210-212, 214-216, 218-220
Peterson, E. S. 220
Petit, Walter 38
Pettibone, Nathan Boarding House 141, 161
Phinisey & Co. 205
Phinisey & Dixon 205
Phinisey & Trainor 210
Phinisey, Elizabeth 133
Phinisey, John 205, 210
Phinisey, Ova 133
Phinisey, Theodore W. 205
Photographic Reverie 17, 96, 99
Pickard, Thomas 205
Pisces Beauty Salon 39
Pierce, H. W. & Sons 35, 45, 60
Pierce, Webster H. 218
Plonski, Kenneth 115
Pollasky Block (Alma) 56
Post J. & F. L. 200
Post, Floyd L. 200
Post, John 200
Postal Telegraph Cable Co. 212
Postal Union Tel. Co. 210
Potter, Rev. N. D. 215
Powers, Mrs. A. E. 220
Pratt & Co. 142
Presbyterian Society 181
Price, Wm. 215
Prichkaitis, Edward, Ramona and Linda 39, 41, 112
Princess Photo Co. 180
Princess Theater 126, 127, 130, 180, 220
Pugaley, Harold 41
Pullman Railroad Car Co. 149
Punches, George and Margaret 64
Purple Gang 177

R. Chain Grocery 61
R. P. Y. C. Investments 88, 90
Radio Shack 112
Rainbow Grill 99
Rainbow Video II 49
Ramey & Mance 220
Ramey 5¢ to $5.00 Store 128
Ramey Building 89, 90
Ramey, Earnest 89
Ramey, Eli 220
Ramey, Mrs. Tom 128
Rand, Sgt. William 139
Randall, Frank H. 203
Randall, Herb 23
Randolph, Lewis 141
Ranft, Frederick 203
Rapson, R. A. 215
Rassat, Mrs. Mary 212
Ray, Robert 218
Raymond James Financial Services 72
Ray's Bike Shop 95, 96, 99
Razek, H. 71
Reading, C. A. 220
Reardon, William 128
Re-Claimed Wood 58
Red Front Cash & Carry Store 109
Red Hook Properties 96
Redick, Richard 49
Redman Agency 131
Redson, Mrs. Annie 210, 212
Reeder, James A. 215, 218, 220
Reist, Jacob 201
Reist, John 203
Render, Thomas 200
Renew Health Family Chiropractic 54
Rengert, Michael and Michele 17
Revive Coffee Shop 109
Rexall Drug Store 157
Rhoades & Shaffer 218
Rhoades A. S. & Co. 205, 212, 215
Rhoades Block 122, 124, 186-188
Rhoades Grocery Store 171

Rhoades, Andrew 123, 171, 174, 205, 208, 210, 212, 215, 218
Rider, Ebenezer 198
Riggs, W. D. 215
Ringelberg, Jon 26
Ritter & Bogardus 212
Ritter, Harvey 212
Riverview Leasing 47, 49
Roberts, Frank 15
Robinson, Faith 215
Robinson, George 218
Rock Road Express 99
Rockafellow, J. C. 142, 198-201, 205, 210, 212
Rockwell, Claude C. 212
Roe, Joseph B. 220
Rogers & Falk 218
Rogers, Atherton L. 57, 218
Rogers, Jay 210
Rogers, Rev. M. D. 210
Roode, J. Q. 218
Rorison, David 212
Rorison, John 205, 210
Rosemann, Julius 205, 210, 212
Rosier, Mr. and Mrs. Floyd 118
Ross, Amanda 21
Ross, Giles A. 218
Ross, J. S. 211
Ross, William 21, 142, 200, 203, 205
Ross, Wm J. 210, 212, 215
Roth, Filbert 170
Roy's Economy Drug Store 109, 110
Ruby, Robert 36
Ruckles Pier Bar & Grill 88, 90
Ruckles, Gary and Cheryl 88, 90
Russ's Paint Shop 130
Russ's Record Shop 115, 116, 130
Rustic Creations 115
Ryan, William 126

Sadler, Diane   69
Sadler-Demo, Diane   17
Sailsbury, Wm.   201
Salon 518   64
Samborn, Everett   39, 41
Sam's Brothers   66
Sanford, Dr. Burton J.   89, 133
Sanford, Dr.   110, 160
Sanford, Dr. Frederick C.   133, 210,
    212, 215, 218, 220
Sarah's Law Firm   58
Saxton Stage Coach   141
Schaffer & Reist   201
Schaffer, Cora   218
Schaffer, Julius   200, 201
Scheer, George   16
Scheurman, Fred T.   56
Schilling, Henry   203
Schilling, Jared   205, 210, 212
Schlieder Building (Owosso)   56
Schmitt, Carl   128
Schultz, Mr. and Mrs. Roy   135
Schumacher Insurance Agency   44
Scott, Dr. Alan   128
Seath, Thomas   204
Second Hand Treasures   69
Seeley, James H.   203
Seibt, Gabe and Jonathan   81
Seibt, John   118, 119
Seibt, John and Jane   51, 53
Seiter Brothers   76
Seven R's Co.   26
Seventh Day Adventist Building   178
Sexsmith, John   205, 208, 210, 212
Shaffer, Levi   218
Shamrock Lake Dam   171
Shamrock Real Estate   131
Shaver & McIntyre   198, 200
Shaver, Albert A.   73, 142, 198, 200,
    201, 203
Shaw, B. C.   215
Shear Envy   44
Shearer & Co.   205
Shearer, Elliot   205
Shearer, Peter M.   205

Sherman, Rev. Washington   212
Sherry's Gift World   39
Shoup, Floyd   88
Shumway & Rogers   68
Shumway, Forest   58, 108
Shurlow, Dr. E. C.   130
Shurlow, Dr. Elmer and Mary Ann
    31
Sian, Denis and Kathy   62
Siberneck, Dr. Richard   58
Siegel, Lewis   49
Simon, Louis A.   27
Simonson, L.   218
Sirrine, Mr. and Mrs. Oakley   41
Skeets, Arthur   16
Slater Joseph Boarding House   141,
    161
Slattery, John B.   198, 200, 201
Sleeper, Albert E.   159, 219
Slocum & Mason   198
Slocum, James A.   198, 200
Smalley & Son   218
Smalley Brothers   220
Smalley, E.   141
Smalley, Elsa   220
Smalley, Frederick E.   218, 220
Smalley, Robert   212
Smalley, Roderick   209, 215, 218
Smith, Albert   205, 210
Smith, Almeron   216, 218
Smith, Fred B.   155, 211, 214-216
Smith, George   203
Smith, Jay   40
Smith, John E.   218
Smith, Lyle   124
Smith, Mark   54, 66
Smith, Thomas   218
Smith's Appliance Shop   42
Snyder, Charles H.   210
Solutions Psychotherapy   54
Spence Brothers   27
Spenny, Mr. and Mrs. Wayne   118
Spider Submissions Gymnasium
    109
The Sports Shop   128

Spring, Edwards J. 198
Squires, E. L. 145
Squires, Harris O. 145, 202, 210, 212, 215, 218
St. Mary's Catholic Cathedral (Saginaw) 189
Standard Oil Co. 214, 218
Stanley & Harris 215
Stanley, Eugene 215
Star Theatre 180
State Board of Agriculture 148
State Farm Insurance 104
Steffke, Amanda Photography 110
Stephenson Funeral Home 130
Stephenson, Carl 130
Stephenson, W. J. 40
Sterling, Charles B. 218, 220
Sterns House 142, 161, 162, 198-201, 210
Sterns, Caleb 161, 198-201, 203, 205, 210
Sterns, Mrs. A. 210
Stevens House 161, 163, 210, 212
Stevens, Ernest 220
Stevens, Henry C. 205, 210
Stevens, Kevin 124
Stevens, Ralph 75
Stevins, Leo 16
Stickles, H. 207
Stickles, Harrison 210
Stitches for Britches 39, 41
Stone Soup 72opera
Stone, Charles J. 211
Storey, Miss Winifred A. 209
Strange Oil & Gas Co. 176
Struble, Jacob D. 203
Stuckert, Charles and Martha 96, 99
Stuckert's Home Decorating Center 96
Subway 44, 151
Superior Ttile & Settlement Agency 104
Sutherland, Clark H. 74, 85, 158, 202-205, 207, 209-212, 214-216, 218, 220

Sutherland, Mrs. Otto 215
Sutherland, O. M. 42, 60, 65, 68, 186
Sutton, Manuel 36, 39
Sutherland, S. A. 212
Sutton, Violet 39
Suzanne James Flowers 104
Swanston, Wm. 210
Sweetman & Phinisey 210
Sweetman & Waller 205
Sweetman, John 205, 210
Switzer, E. 214, 215, 218
Sykora, James 133

T. I. Investment 99
T. S. R. Development 44
Tatman & McKeever 61
Tatman & Shilling 203, 205, 210
Tatman Building 60, 160, 186
Tatman, J. F. & Son 221
Tatman, James A. 221
Tatman, James F. 57, 60-62, 205, 210, 212, 215, 221
Teeter, William S. 58, 177
Telman, Erastus D. 212
Temple Theatre 180
Terbush, Wm. 207
Terwilliger, Grant 30, 31, 33, 57, 221
Terwilliger, Loretta 31
Their, Orlando B. 215
Theodoris, Peter 99
Theron, Ora 33
Thomas, Allan 28, 29, 183
Thompson & Wilkinson 167, 221
Thompson Hotel 163
Thompson, Francis 31
Thompson, Lewis, H. 31, 41, 175, 221
Thompson, Wm. A. 205, 210
Thorpe, A. W. 98
Thurston Funeral Home 154
Thurston Undertaking 110, 128

Thurston, A. & Son 215, 218, 221
Thurston, Albert 21, 160, 215, 218
Thurston, Charles 20, 21, 126, 215,
  218, 221
Thurston, Nellie 21
Thurston, Russell 21
Tibbils, M. J. 221
Tibbils, N. L. and Hilda 113
Timeout Tavern 128
Tobacco River Milling & Mnfg Co.
  206, 210
Todd, Francis J. 203, 205, 210
Toledo & Ann Arbor Railroad 82
Toledo, Ann Arbor & Northern
  Michigan Railroad 144, 145, 161,
  206, 210
Tooley, Morgan 203
Tower Finance 17
Tower, Rev. L. L. 205, 210
Track Side Market 85
Trainor, Edward I. 210
Travis, J. J. 201
Trevidick, Henry 141, 153, 198,
  200, 203
Trombley, Thomas 189
Tucker, Clarence 39, 41
Tucker, Mrs. Hattie 201
Tunnicliffe, Wm. 204
Tuscola & Saginaw Bay Railroad
  82, 85
Tyler, Patricia 115

Ulrich, Arthur 47, 167
Uncle Tom's Recreation 127
Unicume, Edward H. 210, 213
Union Depot 144, 161, 207, 210
Union School 179
Union Telephone Co. 217, 218
United Agency 133
United Brethren Church 203
United States Post Office 71, 141,
  142, 149, 183

United States Post Office Building
  (5th Street) 7, 13, 27, 29, 152, 182,
  183
The Upper Rooms 110

Valley Restaurant 38
Valley, George 38
Van Brunt & Reist 203
Van Brunt & Son 213, 215
Van Brunt, Albert 85, 203, 205, 210,
  213, 215, 218
Van Brunt, Clarence 213, 215
Vandercook, E. A. 211, 213
Vanderwark's Grocery 127
Varney, Henry H. 201
Varney, Mr. 171
Varny, A. M. 210
Vaudette 180
Veder, Williard 221
Venue at 501 106
Vernon Hill 161
The Village Pub 88
Virginia's Drapery Shop 130
Vintage Type Antiques 51
Virtue, W. H. 159
Vogue Shop 57, 75, 118, 119

Walgreens 157
Waller, Edward 118, 205, 210, 213,
  215
Waller, Manly 210
Walsh & Gordon 167
Walsh, James 203
Walt, Howland 205
Ward, David 218, 220, 221
Warner, Roy 49
Warren, Jon and Vicki 85
Warren, Rev. Leroy 181
Wayman, George 205
Webb, John A. 203
Webb, W. B. 61, 175, 219

Wee Pets 'N Things 118
Wedgewood Room (Doherty Hotel) 112
Weible, Mr. and Mrs. Joe W. 16
Weir, Wallace 38, 40, 213, 218
Weisman, Louis 158
Welch & Bennett 169, 214-216, 219
Welch, Edgar G. 36, 169, 215, 216, 218
Welch, James L. 205, 210, 213
Welch, Mrs. E. G. 218
Welling, John 215
Wellman, C. A. 219
Wells Fargo Investors 104
Wells, George B. 216
Wells, H. Byron 216
Wermuth House 219
Wermuth, George L. 219
Western Auto Store 49, 91, 104, 157
Western Union Tel. Co. 163, 209, 210, 213
Westfall, Anna 219
Westfield & Fall River Lumber Co. 221
Wheaton & Perry 158, 200
Wheaton, Elijah D. 158, 198, 200, 203
White & Son 112
White Jewelry Store 111
White, Carl 111
White, Dr. John 128
White, Edward 36, 37, 71, 108, 111, 112, 118, 203, 210, 213, 215
White, George 220
White Law Office 54
Whitehouse Restaurant 135, 154
Whiteside, G. O. 41
Whitley & Co. 198
Whitley, Grace 142, 198, 200
Whitlock, C & N 221
Whitlock, George 210, 212
Whitmore, Franklin A. 205
Whitney & Holbrook 203
Whitney & Sutton 180
Whitney, Charles E. 203

Whitney, E. N. 180, 210
Whitney, Edwin 210
Whitney, Melanthon E. 38, 39, 205
Whitney, R. J. 132
Whittlock, A. W. 215
Wilber, Mrs. Caroline A. 205
Wild Bill's Pub 127
Wild, Herman 221
Wildman, Frank 210
Wilkinson, S. A. 221
Williams, Rev. S. H. 219
Willoughby, Robert J. 215
Willow Classic Women's Apparel Store 53
Wilson & Davy Co. 106, 221
Wilson Decorating Center 96
Wilson, John H. 106, 210, 213, 215, 219, 221
Wilson, William and Pamela 96
Wilson-Sutherland Building 149, 151, 178
Wing, Lanson 203
Winter, Russell Insurance Agency 44, 54
Witbeck I.G. A. 103, 104
Witbeck, Lawrence and Linda 112
Witbeck, Marvin 103
Witherspoon, P. E. 213
Withey, Dr. C. A. 52
Withman, Rev. W. A. 205
Wobig, Roeske 129
Wolsey Building 155
Wolsey, William 98, 219
Wolsey, Wm. & Co. 215
Wolsky, William 74, 85, 149, 158, 200-205, 207, 211, 213
Women's Relief Corp. 178
Wong, Meng Mei and Ling Li 119
Wood, C. B. Building 115
Wood, Cornelius 103, 104, 115
Wood, Cornelius Jr. 104
Wood, James 109
Wood, Winston and Neil 115
Woodcock & Walters
Woodlock, Rev.

Other Clare History Books by Kenneth Lingaur

Where They Lived

Historic Clare Michigan Homes
and the
People Who Lived in Them

Kenneth Lingaur

Clare, Michigan may seem like your ordinary Midwest town, but some of the people that lived here were far from usual. In these pages you will read about a man who was ship wrecked in the middle of the Atlantic Ocean, a couple who missed their trip to America on the Titanic, a man who came to Clare with nothing and became her most famous citizen, and what story about Clare would be complete without gangsters.

Where They Lived chronicles the lives of the people who lived in fifty-one historic Clare homes. After reading this book you will see these houses in a new light, and hopefully appreciate the history behind them.

Sacred Buildings

Historic Clare Michigan Churches

Kenneth Lingaur

From simple wood frame buildings to a church listed on the National Register of Historic Places, the church buildings in Clare, Michigan are varied.

Spanning from the founding of Clare to the present *Sacred Buildings: Historic Clare Michigan Churches* tells the story of seventeen different church buildings from thirteen congregations.

This is the story of the places that the people of Clare built to share their common faith and worship their God.

Sacred Buildings: Historic Clare Michigan Churches is full of photographs and descriptions which take you inside many of these buildings.

These books are available at Amazon.com and
local Clare, Michigan retailers

About the Author

Kenneth Lingaur is a native of Lake Leelanau, Michigan, and has lived in Clare since 2003. He earned his Master's Degree in Historic Preservation from Eastern Michigan University in 2014, and the following year founded Lingaur Preservation LLC. Lingaur Preservation LLC is dedicated to preserving history in a wide variety of areas.

He started researching the history of Clare while writing the National Register of Historic Places nomination for Clare's downtown in 2009. The downtown district was listed on the National Register in 2016. He has since written two books related the history of Clare: *Where They Lived: Historic Clare Michigan Homes and the People Who Lived in them* (2017) and *Sacred Buildings: Historic Clare Michigan Churches* (2018).

Ken Lingaur has been married since 1995, and along with his wife Sherrie have four boys.

For more information on Lingaur Preservation LLC, and to see other books written by him, visit his website at www.lingaurpreservation.com.

Woodruff, Roy   165
Woodward Auto Sales   167
Woodward, John   219
Worden, Joseph   219
Worldtronic   104
Wright, Ammi W.   139
Wright, E. H.   108, 156
Wright, James A.   198
Wylie, A. E.   61, 160
Wyman, Bernard   133
Wyman, Jay   84, 216
Wyman-Damoth Agency   133

The Yarn Mart   75, 128
Young, Barbara   92
Your Putting Us On   104
Your R Grocer   109

Zemmer Motors   167
Zemon-Sable Store   144